ABBEY'S ROAD

ABBEY'S ROAD

BY EDWARD ABBEY

TAKE THE
OTHER

E.P. DUTTON *New York*

Illustration of tree Copyright © 1979 by Jean Pruchnik

Grateful acknowledgment is also made to the publishers of the
following periodicals and books for permission to reprint portions
of *Abbey's Road*, which appeared originally, in somewhat different
form, in their pages: *Audubon Magazine Harper's, Mountain
Gazette, Outside Magazine, Penthouse, Playboy, Pioneer
Conservationists of America.*

For information contact:
E.P. Dutton
2 Park Avenue,
New York, N.Y. 10016

Library of Congress Cataloging in Publication Data

Abbey, Edward
    Abbey's road.

    I. Title.
AC8.A115   1979   081   78-27165
ISBN:0-525-05006-X (cloth)
    0-525-03001-8 (paperback)

Published simultaneously in Canada
by Clarke, Irwin & Company
Limited, Toronto and Vancouver

10 9 8 7 6 5 4 3 2 1

First Edition

For Renée

Topsman to your Tarpela! This thing,
Mister Abby [*sic*], is nefand.
                    —Joyce, *Finnegans Wake*

Never apologize, never explain.
                    —British Foreign Office

CONTENTS

Introduction: Confessions of a
Literary Hobo   *xiii*

Travel
1. The Reef   *3*
2. Anna Creek   *16*
3. The Outback   *33*
4. Back of Beyond   *46*
5. A Desert Isle   *69*
6. Sierra Madre   *81*
7. On the River Again   *98*
8. A Walk in the Park   *107*
9. Down There in the Rocks   *117*

Polemics and Sermons
10. Science with a Human Face   *123*

11. The Right to Arms   *130*
12. The Conscience of the Conqueror
    133
13. Merry Christmas, Pigs!   *138*
14. The Winnebago Tribe   *142*

Personal History
15. My Life as a P.I.G., or the True Adventures of
    Smokey the Cop   *147*
16. In Defense of the Redneck   *158*
17. Death Valley Junk   *170*
18. Fire Lookout   *176*
19. The Sorrows of Travel   *181*
    Coda: Cape Solitude   *191*

INTRODUCTION: CONFESSIONS OF A LITERARY HOBO

Day after day, the letters trickle in from strangers all across this broad and handsome nation of ours. Like this from a lady in Waukegan, Illinois:

> Dear Abbey:
>
> Do you realize how funny you are? Funny in a sick way, I mean . . .

Letters we never finished reading. Or the one I got the other day, addressed to a Mr. Edward Albee, Wolf Hole, Arizona:

> Dear Mr. Albee:
>
> Though a great admirer of your early work (*Zoo Story, Who's Afraid of Virginia Woolf?,* etc.), I must confess to a feeling of disappointment, even disgust, upon complet-

ing your most recent novel, *The Monkey Wrench Gang.* It seems to me . . .

A few arrive from strange, exotic places like Toronto, Canada, and São Paulo, Brazil.

> Dear Senhor Abbey,
>
> I have reading your new article in the *Readers Digest* about the desert, the Arizona, the Gila monsters and other real estate people and wish to say I admire very much all about American cowboy. As your foreign friend may I do you one big favor?
> Please send two pair blue jeans (cowboy style) low rise cut narrow in legs size small please? Sir I thank you.
>
> > Your friend and "pen pal",
> > Mario Roderigo Rodriguez-Silva
>
> PS: Call me Rod

Letters, letters. Letters from college sophomores asking me, in effect, to write their term papers for them. Letters from discontented shoe clerks asking me to find them jobs as forest rangers. Letters from lonely homosexuals in North Dakota (all of which I refer to my wife) suggesting an assignation:

> Dear Ed Abbey, if you're half the man you pretend to be you'll have the guts to try something different, man . . .

They trickle in, day by day. Most of the letters, I must say, are not like those quoted above. The majority are kind, intelligent, touching me with a sense of my own unworthiness. Are people still capable of being affected, that much, by the written word? Heartening, if so. And how can they imagine that the author, hiding behind his typewriter, shielded by publishers, agents, and facetious addresses from direct contact with his readers, could possibly measure up to the glorified image of himself he hopes to project through his books?

The writer puts the best of himself, not the whole, into the work; the author as seen in the pages of his own book is largely a fictional creation. Often the author's best creation. The "Edward Abbey" of my own books, for example, bears only the dimmest resemblance to the shy, timid, reclusive, rather dapper little gentleman who, always correctly attired for his labors in coat and tie and starched detachable cuffs, sits down each night for precisely four hours to type out the further adventures of that arrogant blustering macho fraud who counterfeits his name. You can bet on it: No writer is ever willing—even if able —to portray himself as seen by others or as he really is. Writers are shameless liars. In fact, we pride ourselves on the subtlety and grandeur of our lies. Salome had only seven veils; the author has a thousand.

But the letters. Back to the letters. They drop in every week, missives from total strangers—sweet, kind, and generous letters that should be all the encouragement a writer could need. Those we want most to hear from, however—old friends, old school chums, other novelists, poets, essayists—almost never write.

Nor do old girl friends often write. "Once a woman leaves a man, she never returns," said Tennessee Williams, somewhere. I quote from memory. Is he correct? Not always. But they certainly don't write letters. Even former wives—women I was legally and solemnly married to—never write directly, keeping in touch with me only through their attorneys and the occasional sheriff's deputy bearing important documents.

But those gentle strangers, scattered but loyal readers, continue to address me. Compulsively, I always answer. I complained once to my present (and final) wife that I seemed to be spending more time answering letters than writing books. She visited a printer and had him make up a batch of formal cards. Each card says,

> Edward Abbey finds it impossible to answer all the kind letters he receives from his readers. He extends his warmest thanks to the many friends and strangers who send him their good wishes, gifts, and comments.

Neat and elegant. But I've never had the heart or lack of heart to use the cards in replying to fan mail. I use them only when responding to job seekers, hostile magazine editors, anti-fans, summoners, and bill collectors. And, of course, in maintaining correspondence with relatives, friends, and relative friends.

I've sent my own share of letters, including fan letters, which never got answered. Long ago, returning a friendly greeting from the poet Gary Snyder, I wrote: "Dear Gary, I admire your work too, except for all that Zen and Hindu bullshit." One potentially lengthy correspondence craftily nipped in the bud.

My letter to *Ms.* magazine, though not printed, was answered. Perhaps both letter and reply may be of sufficient interest to bear repeating in full. I wrote as follows, from Winkelman (pop. 225 incl. dogs), Arizona:

> Editors
> Mizz Magazine
> New York
>
> Dear Sirs:
>
> Some us menfolks here in Winkelman aint too happy with this here new magazine of yourn. Are old wimmin is trouble enuf to manage as is without you goldam New Yorkers sneaking a lot of downright *sub-versive* ideas into their hard heads. Out here a womin's place is in the kitchen, the barnyard and the bedroom in that exackt order and we dont need no changes. We got a place for men and we got a place for wimmin and there aint no call to get them mixed up. Like my neighbor Marvin Bundy says, he says "I seen men, I seen wimmin, I haint *never* seen one of them there *persons*. Least not in Pinal County." Thems my sentiments too. You ladies best stick to tatting doilies. Much obliged for your kind consideration, I am
>
> Yrs truly,
> Cactus Ed

The reply arrived promptly:

Dear Cactus,

Many thanks for your amusing and thorough expression of sentiments concerning *MS.* and the Women's Movement. I'm pleased to learn that some Winkelman women are reading the magazine and becoming hard to manage as a result. Seems like it must be kind of boring out there with everybody in his or her place, especially if it's in your kitchens, barnyards or bedrooms. But then again, someone capable of making a remark like Marvin's must add a bit of excitement to the town. Zzzzzzzzzzz . . .

> Truly yourn,
> G. Steinem

And P.S. I ain't never tatted a doily in my life.

Crushed. Sometimes the correspondence gets downright nasty. Irritated by something Tom Wolfe had published in *Harper's* (I mean Tom Wolfe the journalist—not Tom Wolfe the distinguished writer, author of *Look Homeward, Angel* and other novels), I wrote this to the magazine.

Tom Wolfe's fabulous fables of American life complement nicely the current rash of full page and double page ads (tax deductible, no doubt) by corporate executives exhorting us to support tax "reform" laws that will enable the rich to become still richer. As a sycophant to the wealthy and powerful, Tom Wolfe has no peer but William Buckley.

I wonder though about this Happiness Explosion he's been writing about for the past decade. I live in the same country Tom Wolfe says he does and what I've noticed is not an explosion but a thunderous muffled implosion, a deep withdrawal into private inner space. Happy smiling faces, rosy cheeks galore, yes, but in the eyes what Korean war veterans used to call "the 40-mile stare."

An M.D. friend explained the whole thing to me the other night. Tom Wolfe's Happiness Explosion began in this country concurrently with the widespread use of Valium, those little capsules of jellied bliss now manufactured by the billions each year. For the 150 million Americans for whom alcohol, marijuana, heroin, methadone, angel dust,

Percodan, cocaine etc. is not enough, it is Valium and Librium—not exploding—which helps them make it through the night.

The letter was printed. Tom Wolfe rose to the bait, biting back—but mildly, feebly, I thought—by pointing out the non sequitur in my first paragraph and dismissing the remainder by urging my physician friend and me to come out of our "caves" and "see what life in America is really like."

The war of words. Why are writers such soreheads, such hard losers, so jealous and envious of one another? How did I get into this writing business anyway? Or "typing," as my wife calls it. "Oh, Ed's in his cave typing again," she explains to visitors. Why don't I stick to poker, a game at which I am fairly competent, that satisfies the soul? (There's something about winning at poker that restores my faith in the innate goodness of my fellow men.) Any why, with five published novels and three volumes, including this one, of personal history to my credit—or discredit if you prefer—why am I classified by librarians and tagged by reviewers as a "nature writer"?

What is a nature writer? I'm not sure. How was I driven into that particular literary corral? Well, as to that, I remember all too clearly.

A publisher's editor once had the gall, the brass, the temerity to return a novel to me with a letter of rejection that said: "This alleged novel, Mr. Abbey, has no form, no content, no style, no point, no meaning. It's not even obscene—has no redeeming social value whatsoever. I advise you to burn it before it multiplies."

He was right, of course, and that book never will be published. But my policy was, Always reject rejections. Apply unremitting pressure until the editors crack and yield. I replied by return mail.

"Dear Sir: In simple justice I must inform you that I am saving your letter for the laughter and ridicule of posterity. You have committed the greatest literary blunder since Simon and Schuster rejected the New Testament. Balzac's early work, too, was scorned by the academic critics of his day. . . ."

The editor invited me to lunch. (I was living at the time in

New York's sixth borough, Hoboken, just across the river from Manhattan.) I put on my galoshes and slogged across the Hudson toward those awful monuments, those solemn towers that crowd and overcrowd the Isle of the Living Dead. We met in Sardi's, ate a meal served in the colors of Italy: red sauce, white cheese, green meat. Write about something you know, the editor suggested; write about Hoboken, for example. Write us a book about the Wasteland.

The wasteland. I went back to my condemned tenement in Hoboken and typed up, out of nostalgia, an account of a couple of summers I had frittered away, playing the flute and reading Dreiser, in the Utah desert. *Desert Solecism,* I called the book —a title later corrupted to *Solitaire* by the publishers.

A very good New York author once told me that whereas he was a small frog in a big puddle I was a big frog in a small puddle. How characteristic of the New Yorker to think of grim little Manhattan as the big puddle, of the American West as a small puddle. In any case, are we not all, these days, anxious frogs struggling for survival in the same eutrophic little pond?

But he was right, my friend back in that vertical village, about one thing: No book about the American West is ever taken seriously by the New York critics, who still command, anachronistically, the control centers of literary opinion making. Most other regions of our nation—New England, the South, the Midwest—have been recognized as legitimate locales for our national literature. Even California, thanks to the work of writers who could not be ignored, like Jack London, Robinson Jeffers, John Steinbeck, Wallace Stegner, has been admitted to the scene. But California is not part of the West. California is the West *Coast*—something else, a department unto itself.

But the West. The real West. The great American *West,* that one third of a nation which lies between the West Coast and the central plains, from Canada to Mexico, remains little more, in the literary world, than an old joke. A vast, grand but empty stage whereon cavort, from time to time, the caricatures of myth and legend, noble cowboys and ecological Indians, sentimental gunfighters and whores with vaginas of pure gold. Hollywood on location. Whores, bores, and melodrama. Who can overcome such a curse? Should we even try? Only a few have dared. Walter Van Tilburg Clark. Wright Morris. William Eastlake. Larry McMurtry. Perhaps a couple of others whom I'll regret having failed to remember at this moment in my typing. A. B. Guthrie? Paul Horgan? Tom Lea? Frederick Manfred?

It may turn out in the long run that the best writers on the West were the scientists and explorers, men like John Wesley Powell and Clarence Dutton. As our finest graphic art was that inscribed and painted on remote canyon walls by the anonymous warrior-hunters who roamed this region a thousand years ago.

Enough of regionalism. Back to nature writing, which is or should be a broader and happier field. Sons and daughters of Thoreau abound in contemporary American writing, if we can believe the reviewers. Edward Hoagland, the Thoreau of Central Park and also Vermont. Krutch and Abbey, Thoreaus of Arizona. Wendell Berry, Thoreau of Kentucky, and Annie Dillard, the Thoreau of Virginia and now, I guess, of Puget Sound. John McPhee, the Thoreau of New Jersey, Alaska, Scotland, and anything else he may choose to investigate. Ann Zwinger, the Thoreau of the Rockies. Peter Matthiessen, the Thoreau of Africa, South America, the Himalayas, and the wide wild sea. And others too numerous to mention. Like vacuum cleaner salesmen, we scramble for exclusive territory on this oversold, swarming, shriveling planet.

Of them all only Annie Dillard, it seems to me, is the true heir of the Master. Only she has earned the right to wear the Master's pants, and this for the good reason that she alone has been able to compose, successfully, in Thoreau's extravagant and transcendentalist manner. My one objection to her otherwise strong, radiant book *(A Pilgrim at Tinker Creek)* is the constant name dropping. Always of one name. People who go around muttering about God make me nervous. It seems to me that the word "mystery," not capitalized, should suffice.

Joseph Wood Krutch I admired because he was so gentle, rational, learned, and wise a man. He abhorred the empty spaces of windy rhetoric and never indulged.

Hoagland is a master of the personal essay. I like him most when he is writing about women, himself, the streets of New York, writers and writing, the courage of turtles, the circus, tugboats, dogs, Cairo, the hills and woods of New England.

I also envy Wendell Berry and Peter Matthiessen. The former

is not only a good novelist and poet, but a brilliant essayist, able to combine clear thinking, strong language, and comprehensive ideas in a sure, graceful, wholly unified style. See *The Unsettling of America* or *The Long-Legged House* for powerful examples of what I mean. On top of that, Berry has been successful in teaching, in farming, and most difficult of all, in marriage; he actually lives what he preaches. Which seems grossly unfair to the rest of us; how can we forgive him his happiness?

As for Matthiessen, I cannot forgive him for writing *The Snow Leopard, Far Tortuga,* and *At Play in the Fields of the Lord,* that strange, green, haunting, and lovely novel.

Why so many want to read about the world out-of-doors, when it's more interesting simply to go for a walk into the heart of it, I don't fully understand. I suppose it is because the natural world, as we call it, has already become remote, out of reach, mysterious, in the minds of urban and suburban Americans. They see the wilderness disappearing, slipping away, receding into an inaccessible past. But they are mistaken. That world can still be rescued. That is one reason why I myself am still willing to write about it. That is my main excuse for this book.

Among journalists I have but one hero, and that is Dr. Hunter S. Thompson. I honor him because he reports the simple facts, in plain language, of what he sees around him. His style is mistaken for fantastic, drug-crazed exaggeration, but that was to be expected. As always in this country, they only laugh at you when you tell the truth. Dr. Thompson's problem is how to equal, without merely imitating, the scholarly precision of *Fear and Loathing in Las Vegas.* He is really much more than a journalist. Not a journalist at all, but one who sees—a seer.

I too have been mistaken for a member of that squalid profession—journalism. Answering questions after a lecture at some country campus in Virginia I was reprimanded by a student because—dressed in tie, shirt, shoes, etc.—I failed to fulfill his image of what "Edward Abbey" should look like. "You don't look right," he said.

"What? Don't *look* right?"

"Well," he said, "you're supposed to be a, I mean, you know, a wilderness writer. An environmental writer."

"You mean a journalist?"

"Well," he said, "yeah, you know, a kind of journalist."

"I am an artist, sir," I explained, "a creator of fictions." Suppressing with difficulty my sense of outrage, I continued, "I am not and never will be a goddamned two-bit sycophantic *journalist* for Christ's sake!"

Henry Miller said it good: "The newspaper lies, the radio lies, the TV lies, the streets howl with truth."

Yes, the streets. And the schoolyards. And the bedrooms and the junkyards, the kitchens and gas stations and warehouses of America. Out in the countryside the fields of corn speak the truth, though not with a howl but a murmur. Far off by the sea, up in the mountains, out in the forest, down in the silent places of the desert, we can hear—if we listen carefully—the longest, oldest, deepest dialogues of all. If we listen.

This crooked chronicle. These melancholy memoirs. These banal confessions of a literary bum. Why write, why write at all? What is the point of this tedious scratching, this laborious typing, this endless monologue written on the wind? How justify the manufacture of yet another book?

When Gibbon presented a complimentary copy of the third volume of his *Decline and Fall* to the Prince of Wales, the prince said, "Another book, eh, Mr. Gibbon? Scribble, scribble, scribble, eh, Mr. Gibbon?" Flaubert's mother wrote to Flaubert: "The love of phrases, Gustave, has dried up your heart." When Tolstoy was writing *War and Peace,* shipping it by installments to his publisher (up the river by barge express; remember the sad chant of the Volga boatmen?), the publisher wrote back, "For God's sake, Leo, stop scribbling!" Was the publisher entirely wrong? Was Madame Flaubert wrong? Or the prince? How justify this wearisome job? Will there be no end to the making of books?

Speaking for myself, I write mainly for the money. Only a blockhead would write for anything else. I sometimes think that I am the only writer in America who has to work for a living. I have no inheritance enabling me to live off the labor of others, no trust fund, no Government pension, no sinecure at the University, no bonds or stocks, no retirement plan, no royalties worth attaching, nothing much of anything but this hackwork typewriter and my fire lookout job on the mountain. So with two wives and three children, two horses, a dog and a cat to support, I write for the pay. Out of need. Under duress, working in desperate convulsions of effort to meet some publisher's insane, irrational, impossible deadline. Then resting for a day, a week, a couple of years.

There are, of course, the other traditional inducements. One thinks of the best-seller, the *big* money, motorcycles, fast cars, fast women. Gustav Mahler and Waylon Jennings on the quadraphonic sound system, booming over the terrace by the beach. Wild Turkey in the fist. Fame and glory, the easy life, alcoholism, and an early death. All of them adequate, if not good, reasons for writing another book.

But maybe there's something a little better. We write in order to share, for one thing—to share ideas, discoveries, emotions. Alone, we are close to nothing. In prolonged solitude, as I've discovered, we come very close to nothingness. Too close for comfort. Through the art of language, most inevitable of the arts—for what is more basic to our humanity than language?—we communicate to others what would be intolerable to bear alone.

We write as well in order to record the truth, to unfold the folded lie, to bear witness to the future of what we have known in the present, to keep the record straight.

We write, most importantly, to defend the diversity and freedom of humankind from those forces in our modern techno-industrial culture that would reduce us all, if we let them, to the status of things, objects, raw material, personnel; to the rank of subjects.

One other truism. Writers write for the pleasure of it. For the sheer ecstasy of the creative moment, the creative act. For that blazing revelation when we think, if only in delusion, that we have finally succeeded in grasping, if only for an hour, the thing that has no name. It is this transient moment of bliss which is for the artist, as it is for other lovers, the one ultimate, indescribable, perfectly sufficient justification for the sweat and pain and misery and humiliation and doubt that lead, if lucky, to the consummation we desire. That is the reason men and women write books, and of it—the mystery—there is no more to be said. Until we achieve that end, we cannot rest. Until the work is finished, we can only pray, as Brother Job prayed,

Oh that my words were now written!
Oh that they were inscribed in a book!
That with an iron pen and lead
They were graven in the rock forever!

TRAVEL

1. THE REEF

For me, the journey to Australia began with an abstract seige of time and space in a QANTAS (Queensland and Northern Territory Air Service) 707. It was more a process than a flight. We started in the dark at San Francisco's International Airport in the midst of an oppressive metallic uproar—jets like wounded dinosaurs bellowing around us—then lunged upward into deeper darkness where we hung, not moving at all for all I knew, for about three and a half hours until we descended into the clammy balm of Honolulu. A pause. After the stop, the processing was resumed through the longest night anyone ever paid good money to endure. We sat or lounged or lay huddled in this darkened aluminum cigar-shaped capsule while the space transformers whined steadily beyond the insulated walls. From Honolulu's vernal eve across the equatorial circle into the night of the Southern Hemisphere, we submitted, my fellow passengers and I, like docile patients in an intensive-treatment ward, to the ministrations of the machine. Not a journey, not a flight, but simply the transference of human bodies from one

3

point to another by geometrical theorem, or what Ortega y Gasset called "the annihilation of distance." By which process some small but maybe critical element of the human spirit is also annihilated (how annihilate distance without damaging time?), day and night extinguished by our crossing of the international date line. There is no sensation of significant movement in such a mode of transportation; therefore, no sense of travel.

What we have accomplished through jet-engine aircraft is the abolition of the journey. Next time I'll go by sea—or not go at all. Why I've seen more of the world in a subway train from Hoboken to Brooklyn than I saw in that aerial shuttle through the Pacific night.

At dawn we landed in Brisbane. Nothing had changed. I could have sworn I was still in the States, in some familiar town the name of which I had, for the moment, forgotten. The people looked the same. The buildings looked the same, except for some of the older homes and hotels, tropical-style bungalows perched on stilts above the ground, many with wrought-iron balconies that recalled New Orleans. Even the money came in dollars and cents, though the bills were bright with color, not so serious as ours. The heavy motor traffic, under the nostalgic pall of smog, looked the same. Only the language was different; when my taxi driver opened his mouth and began to talk to me in the dialect known as Strine, I realized for the first time that I was in a country full of foreigners.

My hosts, Stan and Kay Breeden, however, whom I met later on that first day, made me feel at home, as did Ed Hegerl, to whom they referred me for the latest information concerning the Great Barrier Reef. (First I would inspect the reef—then the interior.) The Breedens, writers and photographers, have produced several books on the flora, fauna, and geography of Australia, but think of themselves primarily as "inlanders." Ed Hegerl, on the other hand, is a specialist in marine biology, a transplanted American whose early interest in the coral beds of his native Florida has become a passionate enthusiasm for what he believes are the even greater wonders of Australia's barrier reef. It was the reef, in fact, which had attracted him to the University of Queensland in the first place, and he has since spent so much time and effort in the struggle to save the reef from its many enemies that he has not yet completed his academic studies. Only twenty-four years old, he is one of the founders of the Queensland Littoral Society, preeminent among defenders of the Queensland coastal area.

We talked of the dangers to the barrier reef: the crown of thorns starfish *(Acanthaster planci),* which has multiplied to plague proportions in recent years and is devouring the living coral polyps of the reef; the threat of oil drilling by a consortium of British, Japanese, and American oil companies; proposals to mine the limestone from parts of the reef; pollution from coastal cities, industry, and agriculture; an excessive development of commercial tourism on the islands of the reef; oil spillage, both deliberate and accidental, from seagoing tankers in the area; commercial and amateur shell collectors; dredging and filling operations along the coast; even proposals to blast (with nuclear power) deeper channels through parts of the reef.

"What about whales?" I asked. The barrier reef was once famous as a nursery for the migrant humpback whale.

"No problem," said Ed. "Hardly any whales left. The industry took care of them years ago."

To me it sounded like a familiar story. I asked young Hegerl what he thought would be the optimum population for a country like Australia.

"Three hundred thousand aborigines," he replied.

We shook hands on that. At the far end of the Pacific, in the dim illumination of a Brisbane (pronounced *Bris-*bun) bar, across a generation gap of twenty years, two fanatics had found each other.

The next morning I rented a car and drove north along the coast to observe a bit of the reef with my own antennae. I was lucky to get out of Brisbane. Not only was the steering wheel mounted on the wrong side of the car, but all the motorists except myself, as I quickly discovered, were driving on the wrong side of the road. I caused a traffic jam in the center of the city when I confronted, head-on, a massive wall of opposing traffic, but soon got the knack of the thing and escaped the city without killing anybody or catching the notice of a policeman.

Finding the main highway leading north was not easy. Brisbane has no freeway system, I am happy to report, but the good inhabitants are eager to advise a stranger on how to find his way. I learned first that the road I was seeking had several names—Bruce Highway, Gympie Road, Pacific Coast Highway, Route 1, etc.—and that in beginning from the center of the city there is a mathematically infinite number of different routes by which to reach it, so that opinions on the *best* way naturally differed. One man advised me to "follow the main traffic north until you come to this big gum tree in the middle of the street, go around it and turn right at the first Ampol petrol station you see, follow that till you come to the railway, go over the bridge, turn left at the chemist's shop, keep on that street till you find the Shell station, stop there, and get more directions."

He was right. Soon enough I found myself out of the city and deep in rural Queensland, which resembles, in a general way, the America of forty years ago: narrow winding roads, scattered villages, isolate farms, open fields, unfenced cattle range, woods and forest everywhere. The hills were dry now, in Australia's early autumn; the land had a lovely golden glow upon it. I saw many birds, mostly strange to me: cockatoos and kookaburras and flocks of what looked like crows but sounded like magpies. When I lay down in the eucalyptus woods that first night, some-where 200 miles north of Brisbane, and drew the hood of my mummy bag over my head—for the clear air became quite cold after sundown—I heard the raucous squabble of more exotic birds fighting for roosts in the trees nearby. I looked at the stars and saw only one familiar constellation—mighty Orion, upside down, far in the north.

I'm in Australia, I told myself. I didn't quite believe it. The differences between the world I saw here and the America I remembered from childhood were too dreamlike to be real. Australia seemed to me not so much another country as my own country in another time.

But that perception was only half-true. The forces that are fouling up America are hard at work in Australia too. I dreamed that night of a planetary starfish enclosing our earth in its thorny, mindless, hungry embrace. Seventeen arms. Lop one off and a new one grows in its place. Give it an inch and it spawns between 12 million and 24 million eggs. Each year. Every year.

Next day I reached the town of Gladstone and took the

launch to Heron Island, seventy miles offshore. Heron Island is the southern anchor of the Great Barrier Reef and also, according to my friend Hegerl, the best surviving example of a typical reef island.

The sky was bright and sunny, the sea a deep dark blue. Dolphins escorted the boat for a mile or two, once we'd left Gladstone Harbor behind. There seem to be plenty of them left, the boat captain told me, but not so many as before. Dolphins have a tendency, he explained, to get trapped in the shark nets that have been set up around popular beaches; once trapped, they drown. Another problem is that dolphins are thought to chase away big-game fish such as black marlin and tarpon. So fishermen shoot them on sight. Had he seen any whales? Not for several years, he answered. And the crocodiles? They're up north around Cape York, he said, but becoming rare. And the sea cow or dugong, a mammal much like Florida's manatee? They too are getting into trouble with man and his works.

These shallow reef waters are also the home of the giant clam, a 500-pound bivalve reputed to have the ability to close on an unwary diver's foot and drown him. This belief was put to empirical test by a fisheries researcher. Deliberately, he put his foot into a giant clam. The clam snapped shut, holding the researcher fast by one ankle. After fifty seconds, he reported, the clam's muscle relaxed for a moment, allowing him to withdraw his foot—by acting quickly. The tide was out at the time, so the experimenter had been able to keep his head above water. What did the test prove? That the giant clam might drown a man? Yes. But only by raising an equally interesting question: Who could be stupid enough or so inattentive as to step into the brilliantly mantled mouth of a giant clam?

Heron Island appeared on the horizon. A true coral island, or cay, it lay flat against the sky, green with pisonia trees, coconut palms, pandanus palms, surrounded by the pale aquamarine waters of the reef. From this point the reef extends some 1,250 miles north at varying distances off the coast of Queensland—from the Tropic of Capricorn to Cape York and beyond to the southern shore of Papua, near the Equator, where, as my Queensland map says, "Kennedy [an early explorer] speared by blacks hereabout, 1848."

The launch entered a narrow channel leading to the island's

sole landing place, a rough coral beach. The channel was marked on one side by buoys, on the other by the hulk of an iron ship, rich with rust, crusty with barnacles, half-sunken, condemned, its crew a flock of seagulls perched on the sagging rails.

On the beach was a circular concrete pad for helicopters. A plan to construct a modern landing field for fixed-wing aircraft had been averted a year before. The strip, if constructed, would clear a wide swath through the center of Heron Island for most of the island's length. Heron is a small island. About half of it is a national park. It is also the site of a scientific research station, winter home of the shearwater—a bird that migrates annually from here to Siberia and back—and a rookery for the noddy tern. Here too comes the great green turtle, *Chelonia mydas,* a 300-pound reptile in a shell, to lay its eggs in the warm sands of Australia's February summer.

As with so much else concerning the reef, there is a lot still unknown about this giant turtle. An herbivorous animal, it spends most of each year a thousand miles to the north in the warm tropical waters of the Coral Sea, where the feeding grounds are more to its liking, but comes south once every four years to bury its eggs in the sandy beaches of Heron Island. Why the journey? And how does the turtle find its way back to the same tiny island in the vast Pacific? The answer is hypothetical: The northern coastline and island are largely enclosed by tangled mangrove swamps, unsuitable for egg hatcheries; therefore, the green turtle comes south. And what guides it? A combination, perhaps, of solar-compass capacity and the ability to smell (in the ocean currents) traces of material from the target island.

The female green turtle swims onto the reef, waits for nightfall, then comes ashore. In the water she is a swift and agile creature, but on land slow, clumsy, vulnerable. Nevertheless, she has no option: The eggs must be deposited in a sandy beach if they are to hatch. Obeying this instinctive command, she digs a pit in the sand well above the high-water line, lays her eggs —usually about a hundred in a clutch—covers them, lumbers back to sea. In earlier times she might never have made it to the water, but would have been caught by man, killed, turned into turtle soup. Now the green turtle is protected by the state of Queensland and has a fair chance of survival. In other parts of the world, as in the South Atlantic and Caribbean Sea, the green turtle is close to extinction.

The laying of the eggs is only the first part of the green turtle drama. After hatching, the two-inch-long baby turtles begin at once a return to the sea, attracted and guided apparently by the radiance of the surf. From each nest a hundred or more hatchlings come scrambling and start a hasty crawl toward the waves. They have good reason for haste: There are enemies along the way. The young turtles are attacked by gulls or scooped up by the big spiderlike ghost crabs and dragged off to the crabs' burrows, there to be vivisected and devoured. The survivors reaching the water become the prey of fish, sharks, stingrays. From each clutch of turtle hatchlings it is estimated that only two or three will live to maturity.

Time for a firsthand look at the reef itself. So far, I had seen it only when the tide was in, the water high enough to cover the coral boulders and the open sandy spaces between. Now, as the tide retreated, I armed myself with a fossicking pole, put on a pair of canvas shoes, and walked out onto the open reef. By keeping to the sand, it was possible to avoid walking directly on the living coral. The purpose of the pole is to test your footing and to turn over the small "boulders" or clusters of coral to see what's living and going on underneath. Fossicking etiquette requires that you return the coral to its original position; otherwise, the living organisms exposed to the air would die. So, in this way, I was privileged to see such things as the bêche-de-mer, a wormlike creature six to ten inches long; diminutive hermit crabs peering at me out of purloined seashells; small clams embedded hinge downward that closed with a smart snap when I touched them, squirting seawater at me; and occasional small fish suspended in the clear water, gliding away when I came near. Something like a shadow drifted before me, slowly moving its broad wings—a stingray.

Approaching the edge of the reef, where the coral cliffs and valleys and canyons begin, I put on flippers, goggles, and snorkel and drifted out over the deeper waters. Here was the true coral wonderland, a complex array of varied forms and subtle, pastel colors. It looked at first glance like some fantastic garden, but here the flowers are living animals—anemones swaying back and forth with the slow surge of the sea, each waving strand having the ability to capture and kill appropriate prey; the amazing variety of coral, some like lacy fronds, others like antlers or like cholla cactus; still others resembling huge disembodied lavender brains four or five feet in diameter.

Each of these objects, whatever its size and color, is a colony, many individual polyps bound together by calcareous secretions to a common base. Transforming calcium from the seawater into limestone, the coral colonies shape themselves outward and upward, each generation forming the base of the next. There are said to be hundreds of varieties of coral here; each one has a distinctive shape and color. Taken all together, over a period of a million years, they have created the largest animal-made structure on earth—the Great Barrier Reef.

Some might say the reef is the most beautiful nature-made structure on earth. Gazing down at the half-tame, gorgeously banded schools of fish drifting over and within the coral caverns, I felt what someone—was it Cousteau?—has called "the euphoria of the deep." The fish themselves seemed to share such a feeling. We hear of the struggle for survival; we see it every day in the streets and cells of a human city. But among these brilliantly enameled fish, swaying in unison with the currents of the water, drifting soundlessly among the fans and veils and candelabra of the coral, that struggle seemed to have been forgotten. They moved past one another, little fish and big fish, like creatures in a trance, in a state of solemn enchantment, indifferent to me floating above as well as to one another. Surely an illusion. Surely, when my eyes were turned elsewhere, something was rending something.

I looked for starfish and saw a few of the small, ordinary, five-armed kind. But not the famous crown of thorns. Later, on another day, I paid a visit to the research station on Heron Island and learned more about the starfish question.

The crown of thorns starfish has attacked the barrier reef from the north, spreading and multiplying southward. When I was on the reef the plague had been observed as far south as Townsville, half the distance from Cape York to Heron Island. It seemed to be continuing in a southerly direction, although the rate of advance was not known.

The starfish invasion was first noticed in the middle 1960s. Later, it was discovered that the crown of thorns was destroying coral reefs in other parts of the Pacific—Guam, Fiji, Borneo, and Majuro. Some marine biologists believe that the starfish swarm is a cyclical event; others, that it follows from human interference with the ecology of the coral reef.

One of the leading proponents of the latter theory is Dr. Robert Endean, professor of zoology at the University of Queensland and chairman of the Great Barrier Reef Committee, an international organization of scientists interested in the welfare of the reef. Dr. Endean proposes that the starfish is multiplying because one of its natural enemies, the shellfish called giant triton *(Charonia tritonis)*, has been drastically reduced in number as a result of commercial and amateur shell collecting. Among collectors and souvenir hunters, the ornate, trumpet-shaped, large (as long as eighteen inches) shell of the triton is considered a prize. Following the advent of mass tourism in the sixties this shell and the snaillike mollusk that creates and inhabits it began to become rare. Although the triton seems to attack and kill no more than one crown of thorns starfish per week, this may be sufficient to make the difference between a stable population of starfish and an exponentially expanding one.

Attempts to verify the triton hypothesis have so far failed. The tritons are hard to find, hard to keep track of in their underwater environment; skilled divers are needed to do the work, and the money to pay them is not available. The starfish themselves are difficult to follow because they cannot be tagged, dyed, or "earmarked." If tagged, the starfish soon rids itself of wire or metal by shedding its own tissue; if dyed, the dye fades away too soon to be of any use; if spines or arms are cut off, the starfish regenerates them, making identification doubtful. All that is known with certainty is that the triton will destroy starfish—but not often.

How does the starfish destroy the coral? By embracing and digesting the individual coral animal. Attacked, the coral polyp —itself a carnivorous little beast—withdraws into the cup of limestone that is its self-secreted home. Not good enough. The starfish extrudes its stomach through its own mouth into the polyp's cavern, surrounds the living tissue with stomach lining, and reduces the polyp to a mucous soup by the action of digestive juices. When the starfish descend upon the coral colonies by the hundreds of thousands, as they were now doing, they cover portions of a reef with a tangle of thorny arms, spiny backs, industrious stomachs. When the coral life is wiped out, the starfish move on to another reef, leaving behind the bare skeletons of their prey. Lifeless, the coral reef begins to break up and dissolve under the pounding of the waves. Meanwhile, the crown of thorns starfish, once a year, lift their arms and release through gonadal ducts clouds of eggs, eggs by the million, which are thoroughly circulated among the reefs and islands by the movement of water currents.

The triton is not the only enemy of the starfish. The giant clams, legendary menace to divers, consume large amounts of plankton—plankton that contains, among other organisms, the larvae and fertilized eggs of the starfish. But like most large, conspicuous inhabitants of the barrier reef ecosystem, the giant clams are themselves being subjected to intensive predation by humans. The clams are considered a delicacy by Asiatics, and clam hunters in powerboats are raiding the reef from places as far away as China.

One of the checks on growth of the *A. planci* starfish population is, or was, the same animal that is now its prey—the coral. Among the many species of microfauna that the polyp captures and stings and ingests are the larvae of the crown of thorns starfish.

Now, in a turnabout, the adult and juvenile starfish are destroying a former enemy. How did this happen? One among the many hypotheses is that another variety of human interference —dredging of ship channels, seismic blasting in oil exploration —by destroying the reef filter feeders, including coral, has opened the way to the expansion of the starfish population. Pollution, too, in its many forms, from city sewage to residual pesticides and herbicides washed down the coastal rivers from agriculture areas, has probably contributed to the disturbance of the barrier reef.

The theory that the plague is a natural episodic event, from which the coral in the course of time will make a natural recovery, has, like the others, one serious flaw: absence of conclusive supporting evidence. It also has one serious advantage: If true, no corrective action is needed. This theory appeals to Australian citizens and politicians reluctant to spend the enormous amounts of money necessary for further research or remedial action.

Until further knowledge establishes the exact cause of the starfish plague, the only remedy is the crude but simple one of employing an army of skin divers to go into the water after the crown of thorns one by one, destroying them *in situ* with injections of formalin or removing them from the coral, bringing them to the surface, loading them in boats, and dumping them on shore to die by exposure. Either method would be expensive; estimated costs run into millions of dollars. Confused by contradictory reports from various investigators, neither the State of Queensland nor the Commonwealth of Australia has appropriated the funds for a war against *Acanthaster planci.*

Maybe the starfish menace will go away, with or without man's intervention. But other dangers to the integrity and life diversity of the Great Barrier Reef remain: excessive tourism, pollution from coastal sources, mining of limestone and mineral-bearing sands, extermination of endangered species by uncontrolled big game hunting and fishing, the seashell business, and other forms of industrial development on the Queensland coast, especially oil.

Extensive oil prospecting has already been carried out on the reef. The identification of commercially profitable petroleum deposits is said to be "promising." At present all drilling has been halted by a state moratorium until a royal commission of scientists, government officials, and laymen appointed jointly by the Australian Commonwealth and the State of Queensland, completes an inquiry.

The debate on oil drilling follows familiar lines. Supported by the Queensland state government, whose premier, Johannes Bjelke-Petersen, is alleged to hold a $700,000 interest in the oil consortium called Japex (Japan and Texas—a logical pair), the backers of the oil companies argue that oil discoveries will provide a great shot in the arm to the Queensland economy, now suffering (as usual) from a recession. Many Australian scientists, especially geologists and mining engineers, support the position that controlled exploitation of the barrier reef's mineral resources can be carried on without "seriously" damaging the reef "as a whole." This is, in fact, the position taken by the Great Barrier Reef Committee. And if this is so, developers contend, it is economic folly not to utilize the mineral wealth available in the reef and surrounding waters of the continental shelf.

Opponents of oil and other mineral development take the line that any amount of oil drilling presents risks to the reef that outweigh the immediate financial benefits. The conservationists do not agree that parts of the reef can be drilled, blasted, dredged, and mined without harm to the remainder. They believe that the web of life in the region is so intricate, specialized, and diversified that harm to any part will harm the whole.

Defenders of the reef invoke the specter of thousands of drilling rigs in operation, as off the coast of Louisiana. Blowouts and oil spills mean certain death to much of the bird life and marine life of the reef, more vulnerable to such contaminants than a place like the Santa Barbara Channel. There are 1,150 different species of fish in the waters off Heron Island alone. There are hundreds of species of coral in the barrier reef; the Caribbean has only about 40.

What are the effects of oil spills? The effect on bird life is well known. Of the 7,800 birds rescued and treated after the wreck of the tanker *Torrey Canyon* off the coast of England, only 443 survived. The wreck of the *Tampico Maru* off Baja California destroyed for a time all life in the tidal pools except one species of anemone and one of periwinkle.

The harm done by oil goes below the surface. The soluble constituents of oil, such as benzene, toluene, and other hydrocarbons, which may escape cleaning-up operations, are highly toxic to fish. Bacterial life too is destroyed by these compounds, except for certain aerobic species that have the capacity to digest oil. Being aerobic, they reduce the oxygen content of the water, endangering the fish population.

In view of these dangers, the Queensland Littoral Society has advocated that the entire barrier reef area be set aside as a national reserve, that oil and gas drilling operations be deferred until the technology of the industry is so advanced that complete safety for the life community of the reef can be assured. This would mean, in all likelihood, no drilling in the near future. Maybe never.

It was an immense pleasure to forget for a while the troubles of the Great Barrier Reef, to walk the coral shore of Heron

Island and swim in that dazzling Pacific sea. Out there above the coral gardens where the fish drift back and forth in their amazing grace and unforeseeable color, I found it possible to think that all was yet well in this enchanted chamber of human-kind's ancestral home. The crown of thorns was 800 miles to the north, the sharks out of sight, the stingray and fatal stonefish nowhere to be seen. Through crystal water I gazed at open polyps below, like red and yellow daisies, filtering their supper from the rich sea that sustains them.

2. ANNA CREEK

Deep in South Australia, west of Lake Eyre and 700 miles north of Adelaide, lies the Anna Creek cattle station. Big is the word: 11,000 square miles. Running 20,000 cattle, give or take a few thousand, and 700 horses, half of them wild, the mustangs or brumbies of the Australian bush. Plus sixteen domesticated camels, broken to harness, and nobody knows how many wild ones still roaming the open ranges around Lake Eyre.

At the center of this uncaged menagerie stands Dick Nunn, presiding. He is the manager, the boss, the chief among many mates. If I'd thought I'd meet him in an office, dressed like some kind of overseer, I was headed for a surprise. I found him in the main courtyard of the ranch headquarters making beef sausages. Under the bright outback sun of early May, he and old Norm Wood, his chief assistant, stood at the tailgate of a Toyota pickup truck mixing ground beef, ground meal, spices, and preservatives with their hands. In a tub. Flies swarmed over the raw feast. Dick Nunn's handshake was a bit on the greasy side, under the circumstances, but firm.

"Well, Yoink," he said, meaning me, "welcome to Anna Creek. Where the bloody hell've you been?" (I'd written to him from the States months before. He'd invited me to visit.) I tried to explain the delay. Passports and visas. This awkward body of water between San Francisco and Brisbane. The side trip to the barrier reef. Trying to get my bedroll through Australian Customs five minutes before our plane took off for Adelaide.

"Never mind all that," he says. "Give me a hand with this tub."

We carried it into a nearby shed, a kind of butcher shop a century old. Ten thousand flies followed us in random formation. The huge chopping block inside was black with ancient blood, rounded and eroded with years of use. Another man, Bob the Meatax, as he's called, stood at the sausage-packing machine. Bob is from Trieste. Or was, many years ago. Now he works as Anna Creek's chief butcher, almost a full-time job, and sometimes as Dick Nunn's agent in the nearby opal-mining town of Coober Pedy—only 100 miles to the west over a one-lane track of red sand and auburn dust. Out here, that's "nearby." I'm from the American Southwest; I can share the perspective these Aussies have on distance.

I watched Bob the Meatax fit one end of a limp, slimy, translucent casing to the nozzle of his machine. He switched the machine on; it pumped the meat into the empty entrail, filling it and extending it like a long, constricted balloon. When the casing was full, Bob shut off the machine and knotted the eight-foot sausage into manageable, natural-looking six-inch links. He hung these chains of pale pink flesh on spikes in the wall and without pausing dumped our tub of sausage meat into the maw of his machine and went on to the next. We talked for a little while of Trieste, of Italy. I'd been there myself once, decades ago, after a certain war. Did he ever get homesick? *"Nunca,"* he said, *"nunca, nunca."* Never! He had a wife and children right here at Anna Creek. Did he ever go back to Italy? About once every two years. When he could afford it. Seeing my smile, he added that his kids would grow up genuine 100 percent bona fide dinkum Aussies.

I returned to my host, Dick Nunn, back at his sausage mixing. The manager of this multi-million-acre, multi-million-dollar cattle operation was wearing nothing but Hong Kong thongs on his feet, faded shorts around the middle, and something that vaguely resembled a cowboy hat on his head—one of the most decayed, grease-stained, sweat-soaked, salt-rimmed, degenerate bonnets I've ever seen, anywhere, including the Flagstaff, Arizona, city jail. "It's the salt holds it together," he explained later. "Till it rains." I thought of the red desert and the huge blazing salt pans—dry lakes—I'd seen when I'd flown from Adelaide to Coober Pedy. When did he expect the next rain?

"Couldn't say," he answered. "Only been here twenty-three years."

And then he offered me a chilled can of Southwark's Bitter Beer, the most popular beer and apparently the only beer anyone drinks between Adelaide and Alice Springs. He opened another for himself. I couldn't help but notice that Nunn carried low over his shorts a formidable belly; like most professional beer drinkers in Australia—and in Australia most of the men are professional beer drinkers; theirs is the national religion—he was proud of his big gut. And what the hell, why not? It was big, but it looked hard. He'd earned it. Dick Nunn is fifty-one years old now, but I wouldn't want to tangle with him. He has blue eyes, a round ruddy face with the inevitable red-veined nose, a wide and easy smile, the unselfconscious assurance of a man who knows what he is doing and knows that he is good at it.

Dick Nunn has been resident manager of the Anna Creek station since 1953. The ranch was founded over a century ago, has passed through several ownerships, and now is the property of the Strangways Peake Syndicate, a corporation of one hundred or so stockholders, with offices in Adelaide. Nunn came here from northern Queensland, where he had worked many years—for most of his life—as a stockman and stock drover. A stockman is a cowboy. A drover is one who helps drive a herd of cattle from home range to shipping point. In most of Australia, before the recent improvement and extension of roads made trucking available, it was often necessary to drive cattle on foot for hundreds of miles, in some places a thousand miles (as on the Canning Track in Western Australia) in order to reach a railroad. These great trail drives would take months to complete, for the cattle had to forage off the land as the drive moved slowly forward from day to day.

Nunn was reluctant to talk about himself; but as I would learn later from others, he had been one of the best of the trail bosses, acquiring a reputation that eventually brought him the managership of the largest cattle station in South Australia and one of the half dozen largest in the entire nation. Dick is paid a salary and occasional bonuses, but no share of the net proceeds. "We ain't had any net proceeds anyway for several years," he said. "The cattle business is null and void these days." Australia has not escaped the worldwide recession of the last four years, that peculiar combination of unemployment and inflation that so baffles the economists. The beef-growing industry has been harder hit than most.

"The frustrating thing," Nunn went on to say, "is that we've had heavy rains the past three years. Even Lake Eyre is full of water now. Our range is in better shape than it's ever been before." He glanced around at the rolling plains, covered with tawny native grasses, that surrounded the homestead. "We could raise five times the cattle we've got on it now. But there's no market for them."

I was curious about various aspects of cattle growing in this part of Australia, which so much resembled my own Southwest and yet was oddly different. "That grass out there looks short and dried up," Nunn said, "but it's good sweet feed for stock, the best there is. Up around Alice Springs you'll see the grass growing up to your waist, but it's sour. Cattle don't do well on it."

What about water? I'd seen a few tanks and windmills around the place, but Anna Creek itself was bone dry, a broad sandy wash lined with gum trees. "We have 150 dams and 120 bores on this station," Nunn said. Bores: drilled wells. Most of the bores were artesian, he explained, producing water under natural pressure from the great artesian basin that underlies much of South Australia. Only fifteen of the wells required windmills to pump the water to the surface. "But some of that bore water is very hard," he said, "salty. Stock will drink it, they can get by on it, but to thrive they need fresh water. That's what the dams are for. They hold the rainwater."

Dams—in the Southwest we'd call them stock ponds or tanks. I'd seen many of them from the air as I was flying toward Adelaide: small rectangles of water flashing under the sunlight, caught by the earthen dams built across drainage channels, scattered out at regular intervals across what otherwise looked, from 5,000 feet above, like an empty wasteland of red and brown. How did they manage before bulldozers were invented?

"Not very well," Nunn admitted. "We used to try to get by with only the bores and the natural springs. And the spring water is usually worse than the bores. It was a chancy business in them days, growing cattle." He grinned at me. "Still is. Gets chancier all the time."

And was there enough rainfall to keep those man-made ponds filled? I knew the precipitation in this area of Australia was said to average two to four inches a year. Not much better than Death Valley. Drier than the canyonlands of southern Utah and northern Arizona. "If the rain comes every year," Nunn replied, "and at the right time of year, we can make it. This station is 100 miles wide and 110 miles long: When it don't rain in one part, it rains in another. We hope. Some years we never get any rain at all. Then we get too much, all at once. Right now there's so much water in Lake Eyre that it's overflowing back down some of the creeks. And that's salt water."

Lake Eyre lies fifty feet below sea level, covering 3,000 square miles. Bigger than our own Great Salt Lake. Ordinarily Lake Eyre is so dry, hard, and smooth that its glittering salt flats are used as a racecourse for land vehicles, like the Bonneville Salt Flats of western Utah.

There was one more thing I had to know about the cattle operation here: Did he raise hay? "Don't need it," Nunn said. "We run our stock on the range all year round. You see, mate, we don't have any real winter here."

How true that statement was, I soon came to realize. May in Australia is Australia's late autumn. And though I'd wake up many a morning with frost on my sleeping bag, the days were always bright, sunny, warm. Thus the ever-present flies. Thus the flocks and swarms and squadrons of always-yammering birds.

I've never seen so many birds in what is supposed to be a desert region. As Dick Nunn and I talked, the kite hawks soared fifty feet above us, scavengers waiting for leftovers. Flocks of crows flapped about from the trees to the rooftops and back again. They looked like American crows and they squawked like American crows, never stopping, but their cries had a way of falling off at the end. There was something maddening about that incessant yawping and groaning. If I ever came to live in central Australia, I'd keep an automatic shotgun handy and about a carload of twelve-gauge shells.

Nobody else seemed to mind the crows. What the people at Anna Creek did complain about were the cockatoos and their games with the telephone line. I soon saw what the complaint was about. Walking south of the station headquarters one day, I observed parrotlike birds swinging from the telephone line that connected Anna Creek to the exchange at William Creek and points beyond. Taking off, landing again, in well-drilled multitudes, hanging upside down from the wire and swinging back and forth, sometimes flipping clear around, the cockatoos were slowly but surely pulling the line to the ground.

"Goes on all the time," Dick Nunn told me. "God knows how much time we spend restringing that line for them bloody birds to play on."

In the evenings we drive the corrugated dirt road to William Creek. The road is ribbed like corduroy and six inches deep in a reddish flour the outbackers call bulldust. We raise a rooster-tail of the stuff, a mile-long golden plume that hangs above the road, waiting for a breeze to disperse it, a trace of wind that may or may not come. Penny Tweedie, Sydney photographer, with her cameras and meters and filters and lights, and I with my can of bitter beer, are driving to William Creek, population seven. William Creek is the social center and cultural heart of the world of Anna Creek. Dick Nunn may be the boss of Anna Creek, but William Creek belongs to Connie Nunn. His wife. She runs the William Creek store, post office, petrol station, airport, and hotel.

Penny and I buzz along in our little rented Suzuki, which has a four-cylinder two-stroke engine and sounds like a lawn mower. Like a hornet in a tin can, according to Geoffrey the Road Grader, a man whom we shall soon be seeing again. Must have a few words with him about this traffic artery. We hang a right at the junction with the road to Oodnadatta, drifting around the corner through the soft dust in true Mario Andretti style. Well done, I tell myself. I am driving on the wrong side of the road, of course, but that's the custom here in Australia; they all do it.

A mile ahead in the clear light of evening appears William Creek. It looks like showdown town out of some classic Hollywood western. *High Noon.* A couple of trees. Windmill and water tank. A couple of buildings. One is a depot of the Central Australian Railway, where five of the seven William Creekers live. They work for the railroad. The other building, a single-story structure with tin roof and rambling white wings, is the William Creek Hotel with its pub, the only beer joint and watering hole within 100 miles, in any direction.

This tiny outlier of what is called the modern world sits alone at the center of an enormous flat, red, empty circle of sand, dust, meandering dry washes (like that which gives William Creek its name), and open space. No hills, no woods, no chimneys, no towers of any kind break the line of the clean, bleak horizon.

We cross the railroad tracks. There's the gasoline pump with the cardboard sign dangling from its neck: No Petrol Today. Across the way, beyond a pair of giant athel trees (product of North Africa), are two diesel-powered road graders, a flatbed lorry loaded with fuel drums and other gear, and a small primitive house trailer—what the Aussies call a "caravan." When not working the highway, Geoffrey Leinart and his mate Butch do some of their living—cooking, sleeping—in that little wheeled box. Not much. I always find them in Connie's pub.

We enter. Geoffrey and Butch are sitting there as usual, on stools at the bar, drinking the bitter beer. Brawny, red-faced blokes. Solid. No one else in sight at the moment. "By God," I say, "good to see some fresh faces in here for a change." They smile, patiently.

"It's the bloody Yoink again," says Butch.

Connie appears, a friendly face behind the bar. Penny orders a Scotch and soda. Connie looks at me.

"I want to buy a beer for every man in the house," I say. "If any."

For just a moment, for the finest split hair of an instant, Geoffrey's smile freezes. I give him my all-American grin to make it clear I'm only kidding. He relaxes. "I mean," I say, "if any beer."

"He's a card, this Yoink," Geoffrey says.

Butch echoes the sentiment. "Yeah, he's a card."

Connie produces three cans of Southwark's finest. We salute one another and drink. There's going to be a party here tonight, a barbecue. Through the ceiling of the pub I can see thin slices of the evening sky. A notice behind the bar: Spirits 60¢ a Nip. On the end wall is a big drawing, caricatures of Dick Nunn and Norm Wood standing at either end of Connie's bar, with Connie behind it. In lieu of a jukebox, the radio—which outback Aussies still call "the wireless"—is playing American country-western songs, broadcast from Adelaide. The nearest city, 700 miles to the south.

Connie and Dick Nunn have been separated, more or less, for ten years and by the ten miles of dirt road that lie between the Anna Creek homestead and William Creek. But they are still good friends. "Better friends now," Connie would say, "than ever we was when we was bunked down in the same humpy." Hard to doubt: Connie strikes me as being every bit as shrewd, tough, and independent as the boss himself. Independent as a hog on ice. The sparks must fly when these two cross each other. I tried to imagine Gloria Steinem explaining women's rights to Connie Nunn. Connie would laugh her all the way to Adelaide. Connie was born liberated.

Now it's Geoffrey's turn, his "shout." He buys me a beer. He asks me about Ronald Reagan: I tell him what I think, and ask him about Gough Whitlam, the recently deposed Labour Party prime minister. He tells me what he thinks. I see we're not going very far together in politics and change the subject to horses. I had just missed by a couple of weeks the race meeting at William Creek, which was why Dick Nunn had chided me for arriving late. But we're all going up to Oodnadatta this weekend for the next round of outback horse racing. Geoffrey speaks with mixed pride and affected scorn of his son Phillip, "that wiry little runt," who wants to become a professional rider. A small, fierce, handsome boy of seventeen, Phillip works now as one of Nunn's stockmen or "ringers." Everybody calls him Jockey. He'll be here tonight, along with most of the other young Anna Creek cowboys, all coming in from four weeks on the open range. Most of them not even old enough to buy a legal beer at Connie's pub.

Did I say cowboys? Strictly speaking—Aussiewise, in the Strine lingo—there is only one "cowboy" at Anna Creek. He is the old man named Burt Langley whose principal tasks are tending the garden and milking the cow back at station head-quarters. He seldom gets on a horse anymore.

I slip outside to inspect the brief outback sunset and the railway installations. The sunset is a red glow on the northwest horizon under a huge aquamarine sky untouched by the hint or whisper of a cloud. Three empty boxcars stand at rest on the siding. Farther up the line is a spur with a string of cattle cars parked on it. Dick Nunn will be loading them tonight—after the barbecue. I climb through the open doors of one of the boxcars and discover a hobo jungle beyond.

A dozen aborigines, men and women, squat on the ground under an athel tree, making tea in a blackened billycan that rests on the coals of a very smoky wood fire. All seem to be talking at once, loudly and rapidly, with many shrieks of laugh-ter from the women and a constant gesturing of thin black arms. They see me and fall silent.

One man wears a condemned sport coat that looks exactly like the one a girl friend of mine stuffed in a garbage can back in Tucson fifteen years ago; the one she called my "wino jacket." The whole mob, men and women both, are dressed in skid row castoffs. They are waiting for the next freight train to Oodnadatta. Like the rest of us, they are going to the races. From Port Augusta up to Alice Springs, *tout le monde,* anybody who is anybody is bound for Oodnadatta.

They stare at me; I stare at them. No one speaks. Their dark faces with the luminous eyes, with the cast of features made from a genetic mold more ancient than that of any other race on earth, seem to withdraw before me as I look at them, reced-ing into the twilight and darkness under the tree. They are a people hard to perceive, even in the sunlight. The losers in one more among a thousand routine historical tragedies. They are the unwanted guests, the uninvited in their own country. They look at me across a gulf of 10,000 years. I turn away, start back to the pub. As I go I hear their voices begin again, the laughter resume.

"Dole bludgers," one Aussie would tell me later. Welfare parasites. "They won't work. Or they'll work for a month and then go walkabout for six months. The only thing those blacks really want to do is sit under a tree and tell stories. That's about all they *ever* did." Really? Come to think about it, that's what I would like to do. Sit under a coolibah tree, drinking wine with friends and telling funny stories, sad stories, old stories, all the day long. And into the night.

When I returned to the pub, it was full. Dick Nunn fills any room the moment he enters. And I don't mean with his girth. Much of his family was there, too: his subteen daughters Anna, Jane, and Margaret; his sons Stewart, Eddie, and Richard; his niece Sue, the homestead cook.

Most of the young stockmen also are here now, a crowd of teenage cowboys, and among them is Richard, Nunn's youngest boy. Though only sixteen, he works as trail boss of the range crews. He has been out "on camp" for a month, hunting, mustering and branding cattle, breaking horses, sleeping on the ground. He seems a friendly, though cocky, lad, with bright eyes, freckles, an easy grin. He looks something like Huckleberry Finn, but more like Billy the Kid. He wears high-heeled boots with spurs, dusty jeans, an old faded flannel shirt, and on his head a wide-brimmed, filthy slouch hat ornamented with silvery studs and a tooled leather band. What the Aussies call a "forty-liter" (ten-gallon) (think metric) sombrero. Like most of the other stockmen, all of whom look like the wildest of desperadoes, Richard is drinking a Coke.

I construct myself a "chuppity-bread" sandwich from the lavish display of makings on the bar—bread, salad, sausages, hamburgers, spareribs, mutton chops, grilled steaks—procure two cold beers and get into talk with one of the few ringers who is old enough to share them with me legally.

His name is Phil, he's twenty-one, and like so many young Australians, he has chosen the life of a drifter. He appears well seasoned: red beard, gap in his front teeth, a rough hulking fellow in black leather jacket with the stars of a brigadier general on the shoulder straps. His cowboy hat looks as weathered as the Kid's: The anchor brand of Anna Creek has been burned into and partly through the front of the brim. Though he resembles a refugee from a motorcycle gang, he turns out to be sociable, if slightly shy. How long's he been working for Dick Nunn? (My guess is maybe four or five years.)

"Two months," he says.

Two months! Then he's done this kind of work before? Phil grins his gap-toothed grin: "Never was on a bloody horse before I came here." So he's learning? "I'm trying." What does the syndicate pay him? "Fifty a week and keep," he says. Since he sleeps on the sand in his own swag, "keep" means he gets all the stewed beef and hamper bread he can eat and all the boiled tea and burnt coffee he can drink. How much time off? "Oh several days every month." Does he like the job? "Reckon I do," he says.

The crowd grows thicker in Connie's pub; the babble of contending voices becomes a steady roar. There must be at least a hundred people in here now—men, women, adolescents, kids, black-skinned and white and various shades in between, sober, half-sober, nonsober, and rotten with the grog. It reminds me of a Saturday night at Eddie Apodaca's Cantina Contenta in Frijoles, New Mexico. Only the hooded Indians are missing, but their place is more than filled by aborigine stockmen with eyeballs turning red under Neanderthal brows.

I meet a few of the black men, Brian Marks for one, a big cowboy with round and jovial face. Once each year, at the annual William Creek Race Meet and Gymkhana, he spends his entire year's wages at the races, buying at the mock auction for one-day ownership one of Nunn's prize thoroughbreds. (All proceeds from the affair go to the flying doctor service.) What does Brian Marks get out of it? He gets the thrill of sometimes sponsoring a winner, trophy cups, the prestige that goes to a generous man.

Whites and blacks and mixed breeds drink and jabber together in apparent confraternity. Most of them have been working together all year out on the range. Only one discord appears. An aborigine named George, one of the best of Nunn's stockmen, keeps badgering Connie and her brother Bill for whisky. He is so drunk he can barely stand: His watery, bloodshot eyes are red as gidgee coals. They refuse to sell him whisky. He persists. They sell him a carton of beer (twenty-four cans), and Bill guides him to the door. In a few minutes George is back, angry now, demanding whisky. Fed up, Dick Nunn grabs him by the collar and the seat of the pants and half-carries, half-throws him out the door, across the road, and into the brush by the railway. This time George does not return.

At some time late in the evening, well after dark, the word is passed around to muster all hands at the siding. Time to load the cattle. I follow the crowd. Geoffrey and Butch, each with a carton of beer under an arm, appoint themselves as guides to the bewildered American tourist. "For Godsake," I want to know, "why load the cattle now? We're having a party. And in the dark? Madness."

Geoffrey tries to explain. Train's coming early in the morning; won't be time to do it then. "But half these men are drunk," I say, "ripped out of their minds, and the other half are children who should have been in bed hours ago."

"Now, mate," says Geoffrey, "don't worry your silly Yoink head about it; these boys know what they're doing. These boys are men. Have another beer. Am I right, Butch?"

"That's the bleedin' bloody flippin' truth," Butch says.

They are right. While Geoff and Butch start a blaze with tumbleweeds and railway ties, adding warmth and firelight to the moonlit scene, the Coke-swilling teenagers in their bandit costumes have already begun to move the cattle. The cattle had been assembled earlier that day in the main siding corral, called a "bronc yard" down here. Now the boys drive them into a series of holding pens, breaking the herd up into manageable bunches. The pens lead to a steel chute and ramp and this to the concrete loading dock.

The boys in the yard are pushing the cattle forward from pen to pen. Butch and Geoffrey throw another wooden sleeper on the fire and open more beers. Their big bellies glow in the ruddy light; no true Aussie would allow himself to be seen, after the age of thirty, without a proper beer gut. Dick Nunn leans against his Toyota truck, sipping beer, conferring with Norm Wood, watching everything. The terrified cattle groan, grunt, bellow, pressed hard against one another inside their bars of planking and iron. The chute is full again. I see one cow with its head caught and twisted between the hind legs of another, unable to extricate itself. Two more cars are loaded. The loading goes on by moonlight, by truck headlights, by the calamitous, sinister, wavering flare of the burning railways ties. The clamor of cattle, men, boys, tractor engine, the clang of steel gates, the rattle of the cattle cars, goes on and on in a confused, violent uproar. Inevitably I think of the use of cattle cars in Nazi Germany, in Stalinist Russia.

"This is a brutal business," I mutter in Penny's ear. "Enough to make a man a bloody vegetarian." She agrees. But sentimental hypocrites both, we know full well that come tomorrow we'll be sinking our fangs in beef again. Pouring the gravy on our potatoes. Pulling on our cowhide boots. Everywhere the smell of blood. Everywhere the brutality and the horror. Nor is it all man-made. Hadn't we seen, only a few days earlier, that cow out on the range, fully alive, with the deformed horn that had curled and grown, somehow, into the cow's right eye?

The loading goes on for half the night. On the last car, door not properly barred, a frenzied bullock kicks it open; four escape, galloping away into the dark.

On another day, a week before the party, we stopped to visit an aborigine camp near Anna Creek. It looked like a dump. The huts, or "humpies," were made of sheets of corrugated iron propped on sticks. Garbage everywhere: paper, beer cans, wine bottles, plastic junk, gnawed bones, disemboweled mattresses, worn-out shoes, broken glass, puddles of grease, ashes, rags, ropes, dung. A few hungry-looking curs snarled at us as we approached. Smoke rose from smoldering wood fires. The camp appeared deserted.

Then three old women scrambled out of their kennels on hands and knees. They looked like the three witches of *Macbeth*. One was blind. One had, instead of a nose, a wrinkled cavity in the center of her face. The third, though structurally intact, was deaf as a stone and gnarled with arthritis. All looked a century old. They wore long, ragged dresses never washed, nothing else. Their feet were bare, crusty with calluses. They waved their claws, their sticklike arms at us, and chattered like birds. I decided all three were insane, crazy as cockatoos, but Penny, who had met them before, said they were simply glad to see us, eager to talk.

Penny introduced them to me as she squinted through her viewfinder: "This is Jean, the blind one; this is Sheila, missing a nose; this is Lily Billy." Sprawled in the dust and ashes, the witch-ladies gaped at me, including the one without eyes, and jabbered away. They were the most physically hideous human creatures I had ever seen—shrunken, mutilated, gray with filth, pot-bellied, spindle-limbed, crawling with flies to which they appeared supremely indifferent—all of them obviously syphilitic and mad as kookaburras. "My God," I asked Penny, "what keeps them alive?" And Penny, snapping pictures, talking to the three old women as well as to me, said, "Why, the welfare helps. They get about thirty dollars a week. Their old men are off spending it right now, I suppose, down at Connie's pub. But it's not only the welfare. These old girls are still alive, still kicking. They're happy, can't you see?"

I stared at Penny, then again at Jean and Sheila and Lily Billy. The warm autumn sunlight lay on their bodies and faces. The air was clear and fresh. They had nothing important to do and nothing at all to fret over. When the situation is hopeless, there is nothing to worry about. I watched their lively hands, their active searching faces, and saw something like gaiety in those irrepressible gestures. Why quit, they were saying. Why quit?

Many miles east of William Creek and Anna Creek we came upon the range crew. Far in advance was the Dogger Man, an old outbacker named Arthur. He drove a Toyota pickup, the front bumper festooned with the scalps and tails of dingoes. This is Arthur's life work, killing the wild dogs. He shoots, traps, poisons them—any way he can get them. The state government pays him a bounty of four dollars for each trophy. He complained that because of the heavy rains there were too many rabbits. Too many rabbits meant that the dingoes were ignoring his traps and poisoned baits.

We drove on, came to a dry lake bed, and stopped. Coming toward us was a herd of horses, fifty or sixty of them, each with a pair of leather hobbles dangling from its neck. Driving the horses were young Richard Nunn, Jockey Leinart and Phil the Drifter. I pulled the Suzuki off the dirt road. We watched them pass. Penny took pictures. We waited. Presently a dog appeared, followed by two pairs of dromedaries harnessed to a rubber-tired wagon. The "bung cart." The camels wore padded collars like horse collars but larger. A small, very dark abo boy drove the camel team, cracking a whip across the rumps of the near pair from time to time. Huddled under his big hat, within the upturned collars of his coat, his face was nearly invisible. His name was Henry. The bung cart carried the camp's food and cooking gear, bedrolls, two fifty-gallon drums for drinking water, tools, spare ropes, and saddles. What we would call a chuck wagon. Later, when I asked Henry why it was called a bung cart, he grinned shyly and said, "I dunno. 'Cause everything in it gets bunged around, I reckon."

The camels paced steadily across the flat red lake bed, pulling their wagon. Heads high, they managed to look at the same time both dignified and ridiculous. A fifth camel followed—the spare.

Another gap in the outback caravan, then finally the cattle came in sight. Obscure figures rode back and forth in the dust at the rear of the herd—George the Drunkard, sober now, in charge, and two other aborigine stockmen.

Penny and I drove south along the railroad and that evening camped with a different crew mustering cattle in a different paddock. On the Anna Creek station, a "paddock" may be twenty by thirty miles wide and long. The "muster" is the roundup, and at Anna Creek these musterings are taking place, somewhere, all year around.

The camp was made near a clump of finish, or finnis, trees, a type of slow-growing desert scrub. Like the mesquite of the American Southwest, the finish makes excellent firewood. On a fire of this fuel the boys were stewing their beef in a pot and heating water for tea. They used the lowered tailgate of their bung cart for a counter, cutting up chunks of salted beef, slicing their camp-baked "hamper" bread. I ate some. Enclosing a slab of stewed beef, it made a substantial sandwich.

A young man named Darrell was the head stockman here. With him were Rodney, and Willie (the son of Norm Wood and his aborigine wife Jean), and a boy called Froggie (about sixteen), and a little aborigine boy named Jonesy. Jonesy looked like a child, hardly big enough to climb onto a horse; I would have guessed he was ten years old, but he insisted he was a full-grown fifteen, and the others backed him up. As I would see the next day, Jonesy did a man's work. They all had been out on the range for five weeks.

Willie, at twenty-one, was the oldest. He was also, among other duties, the camp cook. I asked him what he fed the crew. He pointed to the pot on the fire. "Stewed beef." To the wagon gate. "Hamper and jam. Coffee and tea."

"Right," I said, "that's dinner, and what about breakfast?"
"Same thing."
"And lunch?"
"Same thing."
Two more abo boys came into the firelight, carrying their
saddles. They had been hobbling the horses. There was much
talk of horses around the fire as the crew ate dinner. Some of
the boys asked me questions about America, especially about
cowboys, Indians, the Wild West. I told them a little of ranch
life in the Southwest, explained the differences in technical
terminology. They seemed pleased to hear that our West was
no longer quite so wild as the Red Centre of Australia. As we
talked the battery radio on the wagon played country-western
music, most of it manufactured in a city called Nashville. Every
hour on the hour came the five-minute news bulletin, exactly
as trivial and superficial as the best of NBC, CBS, and ABC.

We were awakened at four-thirty the next morning by that
same radio, playing the same music. Fire blazing, water boiling.
The aborigine boys—the best trackers—were out in the dark
hunting the horses. When the first faint glow of dawn appeared,
the dingoes began to howl, far off in the bush. Arthur the Dogger Man had not got them all. Like coyotes in America, the
dingoes seem to thrive under persecution, breeding smarter all
the time.

I borrowed a horse and rode out to where the camels were
browsing, hull-down on the skyline. Where the land is so flat the
horizon, as at sea, must be generally no more than twelve miles
away from the viewpoint of a man on the ground. The camels
were not nearly so far away as that, of course. I found them
behind a sand ridge, munching on the clumps of short tough
grass.

Hobbled by the forelegs, they made only a half-hearted attempt to escape my approach. I rode close. This was the first
time I'd ever seen camels outside a zoo. They raised their heads
to stare at me, the loose jaws moving with a sideways, rotary
motion as they chewed their feed. Strange beasts out here in
central Australia. "You fellas are a long way from home," I said.
They blinked, nodded, lowered their heads again. Anna Creek
is a long way from Afghanistan, their ancestral stomping
grounds. But the camels have *been* here a long time, too, nearly

a century and a half. Their breed has adapted well to the unbelievable emptiness of Australia. As have, come to think of it, a number of other exotic creatures. Rabbits, for example. Donkeys, horses, sheep, cattle. Pigeons and house cats. Englishmen.

Englishmen? Exotics? I stood up in the stirrups and gazed around. A mile east a cloud of dust rose from the bronco yard, where dark figures moved back and forth. Somewhere beyond was the Central Australian Railway, invisible among the sand dunes. In all directions extended the rolling savannahs of the world of Anna Creek—red earth, scattered green trees, golden grass. Far to the northwest, in a cloudless sky, hung the autumn sun. There wasn't an Englishman in sight.

I thought of Dick Nunn and his proud belly, ruddy face, stubborn and independent mind. He is no more an Englishman than I am. I'm a bloody Yoink. He's a bleeding Aussie barstid. I thought of Connie Nunn, every bit as tough and generous as her old man, and of their sons—Stewart, master mechanic, tamer of wild camels; Eddie the horseman; and Billy the Kid. They had come a long way from that little green and sceptered isle anchored in the North Sea on the other side of the globe. And never would return. Dick Nunn and his wife and his boys had created an island of their own out here in the great sea of the desert. They could, if they ever felt like it, tell the whole world to go to hell. And probably get away with it. I am all for them. If I ever have to, I thought, I could live here myself. It's my kind of bloody country.

But I was pledged to another. The camels lifted their heads again as I turned my horse. Come to think of it, I was a long way from home myself.

3. THE OUTBACK

Oodnadatta, central Australia.

The name of the town, so I am told, comes from an aborigine word meaning "no water." One can easily believe it; everyone here drinks from fliptop tin cans—the children soda pop, the adults Southwark's Bitter Beer. A vile brew with the color of horse piss and the flavor of detergent, but strong, twice as strong as any commercial American beer. The barmaid draws mine from a tap and slides the head off with the side of a table knife. I am reminded of the home brew a neighbor of mine once made back in New Mexico. One quart of that massive potion would rattle the brain cells of a bull. But these outback Aussies are a hardy—as well as hearty—lot.

We're in the bar of the Transcontinental Hotel, Oodnadatta's only pub. Oodnadatta's only hotel. The place is jammed with Aussie stockmen on one side, aborigines on the other. The babble of voices speaking Anglo-Australian, or Strine, blends with the excited, high-pitched gabble of the aborigines to form a continuous, clamorous uproar. A jukebox rumbles in the background: Johnny Cash singing "Ring of Fire." (A big hit in America five years ago.) The decibel level is so high that men lean into one another, foreheads nearly touching, to converse. Though "to converse" is not the right infinitive; "to wrangle opinions" would be more nearly correct.

A few years ago this scene, this uneasy commingling of the races, white and black and interbred, would have been impossible. Liberated by recent federal and state advances in civil rights, the abos are as free as anyone else to bloat their guts and corrode their livers with beer and alcohol in public places. They have taken advantage of their new privileges with gusto. Every country town in Australia now has a bar or pub that has been largely taken over by the blacks. Where voluntary segregation is not possible, as in Oodnadatta with its solitary pub, the races must share. The aborigines, both men and women, are violently attracted to alcohol and, as the whites are always pointing out, "they can't hold their liquor." Whether this is really any more true of the blacks than of the whites is a tricky question. It is certainly true, however, that drunkenness among the abos is much more *visible*. When a white man begins to sag at the bar, his friends lug him out, roll him into a car, and pack him home. The drunken abo, however, most likely has no home, at least not in town; his home is his "swag"—a pile of filthy blankets under a gum tree down by the riverbank in a migrants' camp, a hobo jungle. The drunken abo, therefore, usually ends up sick on the sidewalk, stretched out in alleyways with his mates, male and female. The scene is not unlike that of downtown Flagstaff, Arizona, or Gallup, New Mexico, on a Saturday night—comatose bodies everywhere. But the American Indians are old hands at this game; the Australian aborigines are just getting started.

"We ruined the barstids when we give them equal rights," said one middle-aged Aussie to me, well into his third or fourth bitter beer. His face was flushed, his blue eyes slightly out of focus, but the expression and tone of voice were perfectly straight; I could detect no hint of irony. "We should've killed them all when it was still ly-gel." Peering into my face, he must have seen there something like shocked disbelief. He gave me a ponderous wink. But he probably really meant it. At any rate down in some secret recess of his simple, honest Aussie heart he really meant it. And why not? How many of us are absolutely free of any taint of racism? Who among us has not at one time or another entertained the furtive thought that our social problems would be much simpler if that other race—*them*—would only conveniently cease to exist? A famous American writer has been quoted as saying that he is "bored with the Negroes and their problems." *Their* problems. Ah yes, I know exactly what he means.

I didn't come to Australia to argue with Australians about their racial difficulties. (Trivial compared with ours.) Hardly. But I was now into my second cannister of Southwark's detergent and could not suppress one innocent observation. "They must be a clever people," I said, "to have survived for so long —with so little."

My ad hoc drinking partner gave the statement full consideration. He said, "They *are* bloody good trackers." But quickly amended his concession. "Or they was till they all got on the welfare."

This was an ordinary complaint. I heard it often in the outback towns. The aborigines won't work because they're all on the dole; usually accompanied by the not quite logical corollary that "they'll work for a few months then go walkabout for six months and not come back till they're broke and hungry." Well, I don't know. That attitude makes sense to me; I work best under duress myself. In fact, I work only under duress. And it did seem odd to hear it from Aussies, who are noted for their easygoing approach to hard work. When the Australians have some big project in their minds, they usually import an American firm to do the job. An admirable quality, it seems to me, so long as they take care not to let the Americans—and the Japanese—buy up their country. Most of the Aussies I met seemed more interested in enjoying life than in working their way through it to ulcerdom, cancer, and an early grave.

For instance. Even the humblest Australian working bloke— a janitor, a shop clerk, a stenographer—gets at least a four-week vacation his or her first year on the job. With longer vacations later. The American custom of chaining working people to their jobs for fifty weeks out of every year seems to Australians barbarous, even cruel. As indeed it is.

Another instance. There are no paved highways through the

Australian interior. The only road from the city of Adelaide in the south through Alice Springs in the center to the city of Darwin in the north is an abominable, dusty, corrugated dirt highway that was constructed—by the insane Americans, of course—during World War II. Ever since V-J Day the Australians have been talking about surfacing that road with asphalt, making it a genuine highway in the American sense of the word. By 1976 they had paved the road from Darwin down to Alice Springs and a little beyond, and from Adelaide up to Port Augusta. A 1,000-mile gap of washboard remains in the middle. East by west through central Australia there is not even the pretense of a highway; merely a few meandering tracks of the type that in the western U.S. we call primitive roads or jeep trails. Unlike America, Australia is still a young, healthy country; its maps are free of that tangle of red lines, symbol of varicose decay, characteristic of an overdeveloped, hypertensive economy, which we call the interstate highway system.

What's the hurry? say the Aussies.

What am I doing in Oodnadatta? I don't belong here. I'm on my way elsewhere—to Alice Springs—by railway. Maybe. It's taken me about forty hours to get here, by rail, from Adelaide, which is 800 miles to the south. Twenty miles per hour—not bad. I've stopped in Oodnadatta to replenish my food and drink supplies—neither available on the train. My train is a "slow mixed goods." That is, a freight ("goods") train with one ancient, derelict, condemned passenger car hitched to the rear. Thus "mixed." And "slow" because it's slow—shunted off to a siding for every other train that passes.

I think of my train with emotions that are also mixed. Pleasure in my slow progress across the red heartland of Australia; exasperation at the many and mysterious delays.

The ants, for example. We were making one of our many inexplicable halts in the middle of nowhere—and in central Australia everywhere looks like nowhere—with nothing visible in any direction but the flat and largely treeless plain. The landscape looked something like that of eastern New Mexico. There was nothing human in sight, no town, no siding, not even a corral or windmill. Reading a book, I'd been vaguely aware of the train's coming to a slow, shuddering stop, followed by repeated efforts at forward motion. Much clatter of couplings, the crash of passengers' baggage tumbling from a rack. Then another stop, hesitation, further strain and groan of mechanical effort, and what appeared to be a final stop. Heavy silence. An hour or two passed in the calm autumnal sunshine of May. As usual during these meaningless halts, the train crew seemed to have disappeared. The engine was a half mile ahead, out of sight on a slight upgrade. I could barely hear the sound of its distant panting. A few passengers leaned out the open windows; most were sleeping. Perhaps the crew was doing the same thing, taking a siesta, or maybe off in the bush hunting rabbits, dingoes, lizards.

Another hour of stillness. Finally a brakeman came in view, trudging down the roadbed, bucket in hand. He looked bored and weary. One of the passengers with his head out a window asked about the delay. The brakeman said, "Ants," and walked on by us. He climbed into the crew's car (not a caboose) at the tail of the train. Shortly afterward we heard, coming toward us, the rumble of couplings under stress, one after another in swift succession. I braced myself; there was a clang of iron. The passenger car lurched forward with a violent jerk. Bags fell again. The train began to roll; beneath us the wooden sleepers rose and sank under the weight of the advancing wheels. The sleepers were laid on sand. They creaked and groaned. Looking back, I could see the rails recede toward the southern horizon. They lacked geometric precision; the perspective was that of an informal, cartoonlike sinuosity, the rails rising and dipping in congruence to the rolling profile of the desert. I thought natu rally of the Toonerville Trolley; I thought of the Little Engine That Could.

Ours could not. Not always. Later, we would come to another grade that was too much for the most heroic efforts of our little engine. Here the train was divided in two. The engine hauled the forward half ten miles up the line, parked it on a siding, and came back for the rest of us. That operation helped pass the time, some four or five hours. Nobody, least of all the crew, seemed concerned about schedules.

When Oodnadatta finally appeared on the horizon, we were glad to disembark for a while. The station master (we had no conductor) said there would be an indefinite delay. We knew what that meant. Catching him alone for a moment, I inquired about the ants. He stared at me. "The ants," I explained, "they stopped our train." Were we likely to run into more ants on the way to Alice Springs? He stared at me a moment longer. "I think me phone is ringing," he said, and disappeared into a back office. I didn't hear any phone.

No matter. We had arrived in Oodnadatta, stopping point for many a weary traveler on the epic journey from Adelaide to the Centre (as they call it here). What is there to say about Oodnadatta? Not much, and of that little, nothing good. A bleak town, with a permanent population of some 60 whites and anywhere from 150 to 500 blacks, depending on what, if anything, is happening on a given weekend. When I arrived, the streets were swarming with aborigines—men, women, and children—hundreds of them, all come to town for the annual race meet. The Transcontinental Bar was the focus of prerace activity, and the talk centered on horses and horse racing. Radiating outward from the jammed entrance to the pub were clusters of the black fellows with their wives and progeny, most squatting in the dust in the meager shade of a few mulga trees. Even as I watched, a battered half-ton Toyota pickup truck pulled in, stopped, and unloaded (I counted carefully) seven adult abos from the cab and about five times that number from the open bed in back. They piled into the lefthand entrance to the pub, trying with vigor to force their way in. Bottles of sweet wine and cartons of bitter beer passed out over the heads of the crowd, carried along by willing hands. Taking a closer look at the individuals on the outside, I discovered that most were on the way toward a smashing weekend. Beer cans, pop cans, empty wine bottles everywhere.

The main street of Oodnadatta is broad and unpaved. Each passing motor vehicle stirred up lingering clouds of fine, floury, auburn-colored soil—the bulldust. On one side of the main street is the railway station and yards; on the other, the hotel and pub, a general store and petrol station, the town hall, a church-supported medical clinic, and a row of bungalows. The houses are built mostly of corrugated steel or sheet iron, lumber being a scarce commodity in these arid parts. Most of the houses have screened-in verandahs running along two, sometimes all four, sides. Many stand off the ground on blocks or low piers for easier cooling. Although Oodnadatta has its own power plant,

there is no air conditioning, nor did I notice any of the evapora-
tive "swamp coolers" common in the American Southwest. The
people here rely on cross ventilation and ceiling fans for relief
from the heat.

Except for windmills and water tanks looming against the
sky, Oodnadatta does not much resemble what we think of as
a Western town. What it does look like is a shantytown, one of
those squalid settlements typical of back road areas in our own
Deep South. The flies of Alabama would be at home here.

Did I say something about flies? Have I mentioned the Australian national bird? The subject is unavoidable. The flies are
a fact of life here, at all seasons, a basic datum. Outbackers joke
about the Australian salute: the right hand brushed repeatedly
across the face. In summertime white residents wear fly veils or
a row of corks dangling by threads from the brim of the hat.
These outback flies are persistent, sticky, maddening; they cling
to your skin. Only the aborigines are indifferent to them.

A strange people, these abos, supposedly the most primitive
on earth. Scarcely human, according to some Aussies I met. Yet
they have, or had, as is now well known, a culture more complex
and to me more interesting than anything the white Australians
have so far been able to invent on their own. The traditional
aborigines wandered this continent nearly naked, following the
game and the weather up and down the transient watercourses,
from lake to ephemeral lake. They carried nothing but weapons
like the boomerang and the spear, and a leverlike instrument,
the *woomera,* with which to hurl the spear with great velocity
and accuracy. They had fire sticks, water skins, and stone tools
to grub in the earth with. Nothing more, not even the bow and
arrow. No domestic animals but the dog—and the woman. All
they possessed in worldly goods they carried in their hands.
Their culture was not material and technological, but intellectual, spiritual, esthetic. They carried the world in their minds,
with an elaborate mythology as subtle in its way as our own. Our
mythology we call history and science—knowledge; so did the
aborigines. They could explain to their children everything in
the world as well as we can explain our world to ourselves. Each
rock, tree, hill, and stream, each living thing had its history,
function, meaning. They invented languages—many languages.
They invented their own painting, sculpture, music, dance, rit-

ual, religion, the psychology of dreams, literature. They studied and memorized their land, its climate and weathers, the finest details of the flora and fauna. Without knowledge, there could be no survival. The wisest among them, the old men and old women, knew not only where to find water and game even in the hardest years, but also the whole story of the creation of the human race—the Dream Time.

Few of us would be willing to exchange our place in European industrial culture for a place in that ancient and primitive society. We feel our world is more open, vast, and free than that of primitive man. Perhaps it is. But what we have gained in depth and breadth we may have lost in immediacy and intensity. For the savage hunter, every day and every night must have been an adventure on the edge of exaltation or despair. We don't know. How can we know? We do know what life has become most of the time for most Europeans-Aussies-Americans. It has become soap opera. Tragic but tedious.

But the aborigine world was destroyed long ago. Except for remnant bands rumored still to be wandering the western deserts, the abos of today are a sick and sorry lot. They hang about the white man's towns surviving on federal charity. They buy their suits and dresses at the Good Will store. They drink too much and breed too much—every tribe is stricken with alcoholism, poverty, syphilis, multiplying hordes of unwanted children. Their lands taken away, their mythic culture lost, they exist in the limbo between a vanished past and a new world in which there is no place for them. "Poor fellow, my country," says the black man.

A group of them sat in the dust under a tree, drinking wine, telling stories. As I shuffled past, one of the men called to me, inviting me to have a drink. I paused. The bloodshot eyes in the black faces stared at me. I stared at them.

Some of the men had faces like Socrates, others like Tolstoy. Prognathous jaws, wide mouths, broad flat noses, the eyes sunk deep beneath Neanderthal brows. The skin not so much black or brown as gray, the color of dust and wood ashes. Some of the children had blond, curly hair, characteristic of certain tribes. The old men had white hair, white beards, a certain dignity and beauty. But the women were poor misshapen creatures with no waists, swollen abdomens, limbs like sticks—like a child's drawing of a human. Caricatures. Their voices, as they cackled at one another, sounded like the cawing of crows. The flies crawled unheeded over their syphilitic, ravaged faces. One of these scarecrows squawked at me, lifting her skirts to show me the filthiest pair of knickers I'd ever seen south of Soho. The other ladies shrieked with laughter. I blew the old girl a kiss, but squatted down with the men.

The youngest, a middle-aged chap in a cowboy hat, offered me the wine jug, almost empty. I sensed a trap closing, but took a swallow anyhow and passed it on. "Where you from?" he asked. I told him. "Amedica," he said, "Amedica." The accent Oxonian. No doubt he'd had an immigrant teacher. "There are many black fellows in Amedica?" he asked. "About 15 million," I said. "At last count. Plus the one who lives in Tuba City, Arizona." He whistled in surprise, then translated my words for our circle of listeners. The old men nodded solemnly. The man in the cowboy hat said, "I am going to Amedica. I am going to marry a blonde Amedican gel and live in Hollywood, New York. But she must be rich. She must have . . ." He made the appropriate gesture with both hands and spoke a few words to his mates. The old men laughed and nodded. "You will introduce me to the rich blonde Amedican gel?"

Of course; I pulled out my notebook and scribbled the names, addresses, and telephone numbers of some lady friends in New York; tore off the sheet; and gave it to him. He studied it, folded it with care, and stuck it in his shirt pocket.

The old men watched us eagerly. The one who looked like Leo Tolstoy handed me the wine jug, upside down, tapping on it and smiling. He said something. My friend in the cowboy hat translated. "He says the bottle is empty."

I nodded, and waited for further explanation. The old man spoke again; all the old men stared at me, smiling. "He says there is a grog shop across the street?" I turned my head and read the sign above the doorway of a sheet-iron bungalow: Transcontinental Hotel. My friend in the hat winked, grinning at me. The circle of old men grinned at me. I counted eight grins and twelve teeth. Trapped. I bought the wine.

Our train was scheduled to depart at two in the afternoon, but when I checked in at the station I found departure time adjusted to six-thirty. I spent the afternoon at the races. I won four dollars on a long-legged filly named Morning Star and lost eight on a camel named Stormy Red. Oh they said it was a horse, but it rather resembled a camel, especially when it went down on its knees in the back stretch. Nobody hurt, not even the horse, I regret to say. I bought a huge beefsteak sandwich for fifty cents. Beef is the one thing in Australia that's still cheap.

Back at the station at six, I learned that departure time was now postponed till ten. Apparently the ants were winning. With four more hours to wait I went off to see the walk-in movie. The swift autumn night had already settled in. The walk-in movie was a vacant lot with screen, projector, a few benches, and space for a row of cars at the rear. Most of the patrons brought their own chairs or sat on the ground. The film was an Italian Western starring a Mr. C. Eastwood. Once the moviegoers were hooked on the action, the projectionist walked through the crowd collecting a dollar per head. I left.

Strolling down the unlighted street, I discovered preparations for a dance under way in the one-room town hall. The front door was open, lights on, bunting on the walls; clusters of balloons, filled with gas, clung to the high ceiling. The one-man orchestra, a man in cowboy costume who looked remarkably like America's own beloved Buck Owens, was already warming up with his electric guitar and what he called a rhythm box, an amplifying machine that filled the hall with booming vibrations.

Those aborigines who could not afford a dollar for the movie were gathering around the doorway, peering in. Folding chairs lined the walls; the wooden floor glistened with a fresh wax job. I took a seat near the musician, out of line of the direct blast from the twin speakers. The musician called himself Dusty Slim. When he paused for a beer, I asked him if he knew any Kristofferson or Willie Nelson. Never heard of them, he said, but he knew the entire repertoire of Johnny Cash, Charlie Pride, and John Denver.

The hall quickly filled, with most of the girls on one side, boys on the other. Chatting nervously among themselves, each sex stole furtive glances at the other. All were white's, scrubbed, brushed and rosy, blond and beautiful, dressed for Oodnadatta's big annual Saturday night; many of the girls wore floor-length party dresses, the boys clean cowboy shirts, jackets, pressed jeans. Dusty Slim played a few numbers and gradually the dancing began, led by a handsome couple who turned out later to be Americans, schoolteachers on vacation.

The abos crowded outside the door were filtering in, one by one, first little barefoot kids with wide eyes, staring awestruck at the dancers; then some shoeless teenage girls with bulging pregnant bellies, wearing miniskirts. One of these black girls started to sing along with Dusty Slim in a harsh voice that carried well, despite the mighty rhythm box. The abo men remained outside, drinking. Two witches crept in, dark shriveled little ladies with wild woolly electric hair, claws, broomstick legs, splayed and dusty feet. They wore Mother Hubbards that hadn't been washed since the Year One, so greasy that— as an Aussie would say—your eyes slid off 'em. The first witch crouched in a corner, among the black children. The second staggered onto the dance floor, drunk as a wallaby, and tottered round and round in dreamy parody of the dancers, eyes shut, arms making rotary motions.

A big red-haired girl dropped into the chair beside me. "Hi," she says. "Hi yourself," I says. "Where you from?" she says. "Winnebago, Wisconsin; how about you?" "I'm from Homer City, Pennsylvania." After a moment she added, "This is the funniest dance I ever saw in my life."

Funny? I thought it the most tragic dance I had ever seen in my life. La Danse Macabre, that's what I thought it was. The aborigine lady with the nest of vipers in her hair had now attached herself to one particular couple, mimicking each movement. They whirled, she whirled. They bumped, she bumped, though her timing was off, and some kind of torn gray rag had fallen to her left ankle.

The young man, red-cheeked and blond, fresh as an apple, pretended to ignore the shadow at his side, but his girl friend was exasperated. She kept shouting at the witch, waving her away. What she said was lost in the uproar. It made no difference. The old woman floated high in private ecstasy, looking as if at any moment she would crumple to the floor. A big, beef-fed Aussie rancher emerged from the mob and guided her, gently it seemed, through the mass of jiggling whites and out the door.

The teenage black girl, still singing along with Dusty, raised a fist and screamed, "Black Power!" The big man threw her out. The second witch began to howl; he threw her out too.

The dance went on. The floor rocked, the hall shook as out-back Aussie cattle growers stamped and stomped to the big beat of the rhythm box, the thin whine of Dusty Slim singing John Denver's "Country Road."

Time for me to check on my train again, though I had little real hope it would leave as promised. As I crossed the street, I saw a writhing mass of drunken abos pushing a Ford Falcon (made in Australia) toward the south edge of town. The car was full of more abos, laughing and shouting, arms and legs sticking out the windows.

A white boy stood by watching. I asked him what was going on. He said they were pushing the car out of town to burn it. Why burn it? "Because it won't run," he said. He explained the history and evolution of the aborigines' understanding of the white man's proudest toy. When the abos first began to buy automobiles (he said), nobody bothered to tell them that it was necessary to refuel the things from time to time. The happy new owner would go roaring off into the desert in his first car, keep going until it ran out of gas, and abandon it. The used-car dealer sent somebody out with a can of petrol to recover the car, had it brought back to town, and sold it again to the next abo to come along with a pocketful of wages.

But after a while the abos caught on to this scam; they learned about gasoline. Then they would buy a car and drive it until something functional went wrong and it refused to run. Again the car was abandoned; again it was recovered, repaired, resold. The abos were not deceived for long. Now, said my informant, when their cars break down they burn them. "Give them ten more years," the boy said, "and the bloody blacks will be selling *us* cars."

I found my train actually ready to go. The rust-colored engine stood by the station house, panting. Two phlegmatic engineers stared at me, without interest, from the cab. The station master was not around, but a crewman leaning against the wall pointed out the passenger car, about a half mile down the track, still joined to the rear of the train.

I took my duffel bag and my box of food and beer and my old leather trunk that I use for intercontinental travels out of the waiting room, where I had cached them for the day. Burdened with this awkward load, I struggled down the side of the roadbcd—there was no walkway—toward my car. I had nearly reached it when the train gave a grunt, a jolt, and pulled away. I watched it trundle slowly up the tracks and stop again, the passenger car now aligned with the station house, as per regulations. The engineers stared back at me. I struggled up the roadbed and managed to get gear and myself abroad just as the train began pulling out. I found a compartment, filthy but empty, and settled down for a long journey.

First, I would sleep; later, I would open my trunk and begin my study of the collected works of a Mr. H. James. I knew we had 200 miles to go before reaching Alice Springs, the dead epicenter of Australia and my primary destination. I reckoned it would take a day, maybe two or three days, probably no more, to arrive there. Providing, of course, that the bleeding ants gave us no more bloody trouble.

4. BACK OF BEYOND

The train crept northward, under the Southern Cross, toward the Alice. Alice Springs. Into the red heart of Australia. Or the dead heart. We would see.

As usual, the train stopped frequently, for no apparent reason, at various meaningless points along the route. Looking out the open window of my compartment, I could see little but the stars, the shapes of gum trees along a wash. No buildings, no lights. The train rumbled on, then stopped again near the course of a dry riverbed. Again I saw nothing, but I smelled the oily stink of the gidgee tree. Fat globules of hydrocarbons floating on the still air. I remembered them well.

Camping one night near a thicket of gidgees (a mistake), I awoke in the morning feeling distinctly ill. But the illness went away when I did. The gidgee is notorious throughout central Australia for its odor. Even flies avoid it, and for this reason the carcass of a freshly slaughtered steer may be packed with gidgee twigs and leaves, when refrigeration is not available, to keep the flies off the meat. I thought of a story old Norm Wood had told me about himself and Dick Nunn. They were entering the lobby of a fancy hotel in Adelaide, both men tired, dusty, filthy with sweat after a long drive across the desert. Some well-dressed silver-tailed sport, lounging with friends near the entrance, said as they walked past, "I smell a bloody gidgee tree." He spoke too loud; Dick Nunn heard it, stopped. Says Dick, "Well, here's the bleedin' branch, mate," and knocked the blighter flat.

Dick Nunn despised Australia's socialite class. "Silvertails," he called them, meaning, as we would say in America, "candy-assed." Australians he divided into two classes—the silvertails, descendants of the early landowners, and those like himself, whom he called the "roughs," that is, the spawn of the convict settlements. Like many Australians, he was proud of his shady heritage. The convicts, transported from England, were mostly rebels, troublemakers, men (and sometimes women) who could not accept their subordinate place in the elaborate hierarchy of English society. *La morgue anglais.* At the bar in William Creek I heard a railroader boast to Dick Nunn that his—the railroader's—great-grandfather had arrived in Sydney's Botany Bay with only five pounds sterling (about $100) in his pockets. "Well mate," Dick says, "me own great-gran' when he got here had 200 pounds—100 on each leg." Of his fondness for older women, Dick would say, "Who looks at the mantelpiece when he's pokin' the fire?"

But Dick Nunn was now 200 miles behind me, back in Anna Creek, world's biggest and raunchiest cattle ranch. Giving up my effort to get some sleep, I joined the lads and lassie in a forward compartment, sharing their bitter beer. There were two half-breed abos named Kingsley and Brumbie, or so they introduced themselves. Brumbie means wild horse in the Strine lingo. Both were track crewmen. There was a young white chap named Greg; like the abos, he was a "ganger"; all three were getting off soon at a place called Mount Sarah. And there were a pair of young drifters, tourists like me. Hippies, you might say. The boy called himself Van; his girl, a pretty and raven-haired bird of Greek parentage, was named Themis Tunis. She spoke an elegant, BBC type of silver-tailed English; the others spoke in what I think of as the country-Cockney of Australia.

The train rocked and jolted over the Toonerville Trolley railroad track. I made some remarks about the quality of the roadbed. The gangers laughed. "Oh, this ain't our length," Greg explained. He winked at his mates. "Wait'll you get beyond Mount Sarah." They laughed harder.

All seemed intrigued when I stated my business in central Australia. "I'm a prospector," I said.

"What're you prospecting for?"

"Rare metals," I explained, "and precious stones."

"Like opals?"

"Yes." That satisfied them.

We talked about America, about Australia. "What do Americans think of Australia?" Van asked.

I hesitated over my answer. The truth would have to be that Americans in the U.S.A. seldom think about Australia at all. Then I thought of a couple I had met and talked with one night in Sydney, transplanted American journalists who have made Australia their permanent home. They were from Boston and Cleveland. I repeated to these young people what that man and his wife had said to me. Australia is a kind and gentle country, they had said. There is little class consciousness here and—except for the aborigines—almost no poverty. The unions are powerful, which makes it a good country for working people, an exasperating country for ambitious business types. Less haste, less competition, less friction between groups and ages and factions, an easygoing social atmosphere—compared with America. More tolerance, more personal liberty; nude-bathing beaches, for example, called "free beaches" here, are common near most Australian coastal cities; the Australian television, publicly owned, shows much less violence and much more female skin than would be tolerated (either of them) on American commercial television. Ah yes, the sexism, the wife had complained at that point, the women are about thirty years behind here, neglected by their men and too complacent to care; while the men with their "footy-ball" and horse racing and the beer-drinking cult are like college boys, more at home in the pub with each other than with their wives. True, the man agreed; it's still a peaceable country—none of that man-hating feminism you run into in eastern American cities. With good reason, the wife said; Australia is like America of thirty years ago—a land of sluggish slobs. Right, the husband said, like America in the forties—before the greedheads and growth maniacs took complete control; I like it here. So do I, the wife said; but I'd never marry an Aussie. Or go to bed with one. Nice but dull. They were still arguing when I slipped away. Nice people, but familiar.

Some of the above observations I repeated to the young Aussies in the train with me. They were interested, but skeptical. To them, as I gathered, Australia seems a wild, adventurous land of unlimited opportunity, offering to anyone the chance to do anything. "If you don't sell out to the Japanese and the Americans," I suggested. Themis Tunis was scornful of the charge of sexism. "I haven't met a man yet," she said, "Australian, European, or Yank, who wouldn't get down on his knees for me if I waggled my little finger."

None of us disputed the remark. Of course, a pretty girl, with that built-in, universal credit card. Van, her boy friend, grinned sheepishly and said nothing. He seemed relieved when the train slowed (even more), and Greg and his drunken abo mates announced that they were getting off. Sticking my head out the window, I saw, in the starlight, Mount Sarah looming ahead— a hillock rising 200 feet above the level of the surrounding desert. There was nothing else to see. No sign of a town; just a string of track-crew cars on the siding, a windmill and water-tank, a few big athel trees, a couple of sheds.

The train lurched, groaned, clanged to a stop. The engine panted far ahead. Greg, Brumbie, and Kingsley tramped by outside with their plastic suitcases. Greg saw me leaning out the window. "Hey, Yoink," he says, "welcome to Mount Sarah. How'd you loike to hang your hat here [. . . 'ang yer 'at 'ere. . . .]?"

"I'd rather hang myself."

"Bugger off, Yoink, and have a nice long trip to the Alice. Loike maybe two or three days, I hope."

The boys disappeared into their boxcar living quarters. The train lingered for a while, as was customary, then shuddered, groaned, and lurched forward, reluctant as a loaded camel rising from its knees. Before retiring to my own compartment, I asked Van and Themis Tunis about the ants. The girl explained. A species of army ant, she said; they like to use the railroad tracks as a military highway. They march down the tops of the rails in a column of millions, refusing to yield to any mere diesel locomotive. Crushed, they make the rails so greasy that the engine's wheels lose traction and spin. Given an underpowered, overloaded train like this, a few million resolute ants are sufficient, on a two percent upgrade, to bring it to a halt. Thus, the brakemen with brooms and sand buckets.

The sun woke me. Or was it the stillness, the train stopped again? Far to the east I could see, beyond a rocky ridge, some of the high red dunes of the Simpson Desert. Far beyond, out of sight and a hundred years ago, the Aussie explorers Burke and Wills had died out there, of starvation, at a place known as Cooper Creek. To the west lay a few low, flat-topped hills. Mesas—to me a reassuring and familiar sight. But no mountains. No rivers, no canyons. A stone building, half in ruins, stood beside the tracks ahead. Rusty tank nearby. Abminga, it said. Another watering stop for the coal-burning trains, abandoned since the advent of diesel. A man could live here, perhaps. How? Sell boomerangs—made in Hong Kong—to the tourists. Raise a few beef cows, maybe. Meditate. Starve—like Wills and Burke. You can always do *something*, anywhere.

Satisfied, I enjoyed my usual Central Australian Railway breakfast—an orange, a bag of peanuts, another orange, another bag of peanuts, some warm water from my jug, and a couple of slugs of bourbon for a chaser. The train crept on, having paused long enough to allow me to complete my ruminations on nothingness. I opened a volume of H. James. Speaking of nothingness. Speaking of the master. The master of periphrasis. The fine art of saying as little as possible in the greatest possible number of words. Until, in *The Golden Bowl*, James achieved the ultimate aim of his entire literary career, that of saying nothing at all in a book of (seemingly) infinite extension.

I shall be taken to task for this remark by Mr. Leon Edel, if ever I return to New York. If he ever reads these pages. Both being events of an extreme degree of improbability. The train crept on.

The train crept on. Wheels roll, you say, they do not and cannot creep. What do you know, insolent reader? Eh, what do you know, you crass whelp of a dingo bitch, you foal of a hunch-back camel, you sore-eyed, scab-covered noseless dropping of a syphilitic two-dollar Baton Rouge, Louisiana whore? I ask you. The train *crept* on, I say.

(The purpose of the literary device illustrated above is to suggest to the reader a state of extreme boredom without at the same time lulling the reader asleep. Henry James used it often in the middle to middling pages of his later novels.)

The train crept on through the abandoned watering stops of Alberga, Pedirka, Ilbunga, Rumbalara, Bundooma, Rodinga, Amoonguna, past Lake Cadibarrawurracanna (a dry salt bed), entering at last, after midnight, the closed-up depot of Alice Springs, Northern Territory, in the center of Australia. We had traversed some 480 kilometers, or about 300 miles, from Oodnadatta to the Alice, in twenty-six hours. A rate of travel approximately equal to twelve miles per hour. Not bad for the old iron horse.

Alice Springs is a quiet town of 12,000 souls, similar to many towns of that size in the American West, although not so blatantly ugly. Tourism, cattle ranching, a military base close by provide the principal economic supports. I found little of interest in the town itself, aside from the handsome young women still wearing the beloved miniskirts of a decade ago in the States, and the many drunken blacks tooling about town in the back seat of taxicabs. Inquiring about this latter sight, I was informed that the government provides taxi service free of charge, on demand, to any aborigine. The purpose is to discourage the black fellows from driving cars themselves. They are said to be murderously bad drivers when drunk. And—like Russians—they are always drunk.

I stayed in Alice Springs only a day, then rented from Avis a fat Ford Falcon four-door sedan (made in Adelaide), the only kind of car available with the cheap credit card supplied to me by the famous magazine that had sent me here. In the first place. Two or three weeks ago. The time *was* slipping by, like shit through a short dog. The stiff, pig-eyed bloke (wearing long shorts, knee socks, and a mustache—I hate the type) who rented me the car wanted to know where I was going and when I'd be back. "Cars rented here must be returned here," he said.

"Ayers Rock," I said, "and I'll be back in two days."

"Insurance?" he asked.

"Never use the stuff."

"Any damage to car will be charged to rentee," he said.

"No problem, I'm an American."

"I can see that," he said, adding, "no offense meant."

"Say what you like about my bloody government," I said, "but don't insult me bleedin' country."

"No offense," he said, grudgingly handing over the key.

I took the key and the car, threw in my swag, bought some food and beer (the two, in Australia, being much the same) and a couple of petrol cans, and lunged off into the sunset. Acting on impulse, as planned. I knew, from hearsay, that the west coast of Australia was only about 1,700 miles away on the other side of the Gibson and Great Sandy deserts. I figured I could make it in a week or two. Or even sooner if there were roads through the region.

I camped somewhere in the dunes outside of Alice that first night on my own again. Then rumbled on, over a washboard dirt road, across the "downs" and rolling desert plain. Lovely country—the red sand; the mottled white ghost gums, like giant eucalyptus trees, like sycamores, growing along the dry creekbeds; the waist-high, lion-colored grass; the dark green desert oaks *(Casuarina decaisneana)* that look, with their seed cones and needlelike leaves, more like pine than oak. (But the wood is hard, heavy, an excellent fuel for heating and cooking.) I passed one ranch and roadhouse at a place called Wallara; another at Curtin Springs. Otherwise, the land seemed uninhabited by humans. I did see a few cattle, a few kangaroos bounding off in the distance; the clear blue sky was, as always in Australia, alive with big birds—green cockatoos, rosy galahs, kites, crows, magpies, a few of the magnificent gold-banded wedgetail eagles.

The great Ayers Rock first appeared from fifty miles away, a tawny hump of sandstone rising from the plain. In most of Australia the air is so clean that you can see 200 miles from a high enough point. I got out of the car and climbed a dune for a better look. On the way, I passed a mulga tree with one small bird flying around it, agitated by something. I looked into the tree and saw what seemed to be, at first, a gray horned owl. But it was not an owl; it was a feral house cat with pointy ears trying to look like an owl. Impersonating innocence. It was sitting on the bird's nest, a smug malevolent smile on its furry face, having just lunched, no doubt, on the eggs or young of the bird.

There were hairy vines crawling over the sand, bearing yellow gourds. The Aussies call them paddy melons. In the American Southwest we would call them coyote gourds. They are not edible. I plucked one and lobbed it at the cat. With a chilling snarl the cat sprang from the tree, landing ten feet away on the sand, and sped off over the dune and out of sight. The nest was empty.

I contemplated the rock, central Australia's only known tourist attraction. Don't knock the rock, says the Australian Chamber of Commerce, an organization nearly as stupid, vicious, greedy, rich, powerful, and depraved as the U.S. Chamber of Commerce.

The rock rises 1,200 feet above the desert. It is a mile long, half a mile wide. One single monolithic bulge of ancient, arcane, arkose, and rugose Cambrian sandstone, 500 million years old (if you place credence in the inferential myths of geologists and paleontologists), it resembles a pink—or in different light— a rust red worm or grub, hairless and wrinkled, that has succumbed, through petrifaction, to the prevailing inertia of Being. A Being that Was—and may, someday, in some future geological epoch, stir its stumps and writhe once more toward Canberra to be recognized.

I brushed a sticky outback fly from my nose and resumed the drive, reaching the tourist village at the foot of the rock in early afternoon. I paused in the pub for a bottle of Black Swan Lager, my favorite. The barmaid who served me had the heartbreaking face of an angel: skin of a rosy perfection, violet eyes with charcoal lashes, cherry lips, a glorious crown of fair, glossy, long and flowing hair. Her fragrance, as she leaned toward me, revealing a pink swell of bosom, was sweet as wild strawberries in fresh cream. And then that delectable mouth opened, the perfect pearls of her teeth parted, and out from the angelic face came the seraphic voice, addressing not me but something beneath the bar: "Wot yer doin' 'ere, ye bloody little shit?" She kicked, hard, and a filthy, snot-smeared child scuttled for the door, bawling, "Mawwwwwww . . ."

I chatted with the girl, finishing my beer, then left the Stuart

Arms Public House, for so it is named, to go climb the rock. On the way I passed a couple of motels, a row of stinking diesel buses with motors running, and a public campground littered with beer cans, paper plates, Styrofoam cups, Kleenex, and toilet paper; from the open fireplaces rose the greasy smoke of burning garbage. The scene was heartwarmingly familiar, yet somehow a little shabbier, a little cheaper than its thousands of American counterparts; there was something *amateurish* about it all. And I realized, walking on, that anything Americans do badly the Aussies can do worse.

Climb a rock. Following the broad, well-beaten path, I found myself in the rear of a procession of pilgrims, a hundred or so, toiling up the slickrock, in the hot sun, toward a distant summit. Where the pitch is steep, there is a chain, anchored in the stone. The remainder of the route is marked by painted footprints, red and yellow. Families of Aussies from Sydney, Melbourne, Brisbane, Perth, groaned, grumbled, laughed, and kidded as they climbed, exactly like tourists anywhere. My attention was caught by a pair of smooth brown thighs in short shorts, far above; lashed on by my incurable satyrmania, I passed the halt, the lame, the fat, and the blind, until I caught up with the lure. Her name was Melissa Rhys-Jones, she came from London, she was (she told me) a dancer and a student of Romance languages. Her voice was low, soft, gentle, a comely thing in woman; and she was (of course) beautiful. For the second time within an hour I fell instantly in love. Trying to impress her, I flourished my press credentials. I was a correspondent, I said, for the *Mountain Gazette* of Boulder, Colorado, and also for the *Vulgarian Digest,* published from time to time in Wilson, Wyoming. All for naught; she would not be parted from her "group" —she was traveling with a busload of cackling, red-nosed, glass-eyed, faggoty little Tory fops from Oxford and Cambridge. She allowed me to buy her a drink that evening at the Stuart Arms and showed me, as we said goodby outside in the parking lot, how to determine direction by the constellation of the Southern Cross: "Through the center stars and four lengths beyond, then straight down to the horizon is south."

I fooled around for an hour on top of Ayers Rock. In the logbook at the summit some Aussie slob had written: Yank Go Home. I wrote after it my name and address and added: "Citizen (not subject) of the Greatest Nation on Earth. Fuck the Queen." Always a temptation to bait the poor blighters. I wrote more. "Ayers Rock is big but we make them bigger in Arizona."

What they need in this pathetic vacant lot of a country, I thought, is somebody like Morrison-Knudsen to build them some real mountains. And as I was thinking this, one of the natives, a paunchy long-faced chap from Perth on the west coast, told me that there actually is a bigger stone monolith in Western Australia, but that it lies on private property and tourists are not wanted.

I inspected the wrinkles in the great beast's hide, the parallel ravines and crevasses of stone I had noticed from fifty miles off. The first, near the end of the trail, was sprinkled with trash. Shocking! I thought; these bloody, filthy Cockney barstids. I tossed my empty beer can onto the lot and went on. Some of the little gulches were hard to get in and out of. Nor were they completely lifeless. Small mulga trees grew in here, and a shrub called snakewood, and a variety of saltbush and grasses. I found a curious trail of dark brown pellets, like sheep droppings, which I followed to a deep hole in the rock Too dark to see, but I heard something stir inside. I found a stick and poked it into the hole, gently, there was a scuffling noise, and a lizard three feet long came scrambling out, spitting and hissing. It was horned and red-eyed, with a spiny comb down its back like an iguana. Though only half my size, it seemed willing to fight. I backed off and left it alone.

God is trying to tell you something, I thought, as I lay on my back that night, looking up at Orion, also on his back, and at the Big Dipper, upside down, pointing toward an invisible Polaris beyond the northern horizon. We were only 100 miles south of the Tropic of Capricorn. For the first time I realized I was on the underside of the planet. I thought of my sweet and gentle and lovely wife, 12,000 miles away on the other side of this swollen, oblate spheroid, and hoped she was behaving better than I was. Yes, I was being unfaithful, if only in my heart. Not for the first time I realized that I was homesick again—sick with loneliness.

Well, action is the medicine for that. In the morning I drove back to the rock and had my tank and the gas cans filled at the petrol station. I asked the man about the road west from Ayers

Rock, leading across the Gibson Desert and down to Laverton and Kalgoorlie 1,200 miles southwest. He said he'd been over part of it. I asked him if this fat Ford could make it. He got down on his knees and checked the six-inch road clearance. "No, it won't," he said.

"Sell me a shovel."

"Got none to spare, mate," he says. "Besides, you need a permit."

"Permit?"

"You need a permit," he says, "to drive across the abo reserve."

"Where do I get one?"

"Alice Springs, DAA [Department of Aboriginal Affairs]."

Alice Springs was a 180 miles to the northeast. Wrong direction. I bought six quarts of oil, not that we'd need it, and went to the store and bought enough tea, coffee, and tucker to last me ten days. I also bought two five-gallon plastic water jugs. I drove to the Stuart Arms and bought a carton (twelve sixteen-ounce cans) of Black Swan. There was a poster on the wall showing a woozy cat with a mug of beer in its paws and the words, underneath, Happiness Is a Tight Pussy. I spoke to the angel behind the bar.

"I'm going to Kalgoorlie."

"Do 'ave a nice 'oliday, dearie."

"Come with me."

She was swabbing the bar. She paused for one instant. My heart stopped. "Oh no, dearie, oye cawn't do that."

"I love you."

She smiled, a bit sadly, not looking at me. "Oh yes," she said. "They all do, love."

On the way to the car I noticed an open tool shed. I swiped a short-handled spade. I'll send it back, I thought, when I get to Kalgoorlie. Or at least stash it for them in a locker and send them the key. They'll understand. I'm no common thief.

By noon, having filled everything I could or wanted to except that delicious gap in the Stuart Arms, I was on my way. Deep in the outback, into the back of beyond. Despite the pain in my groin, that feeling like a toothache where I know I have no teeth, there was exultance in my heart. Idiots like Burke and Wills might traverse the continent on foot and horse; others might do it by camel or Land Rover; but I would be the first, so far as known, to transect the western desert in a frumpy, overweight, lesbian-type, twelve-mile-per-gallon Avis rental Ford. If I did it.

Speaking of gasoline, I had cheated a little. I'd done some research, bought a map, made inquiries, and learned that petrol should be available at the Docker River settlement about 130 miles west of Ayers Rock, at the Warburton Mission about 225 miles beyond Docker River, and at Laverton 300 miles southwest of Warburton, the longest stretch without habitation. At Laverton I would be back in civilization, Aussie-style, only 70 miles from pavement and 150 miles from the city of Kalgoorlie, population 22,000.

I camped that first night near the Olga Mountains, strange hoodoo domes and humps of monolithic, barren sandstone, similar in origin to Ayers Rock but different in color and shape, a little higher, and much more extensive in total area. They looked even older than the Rock, of a disturbing antiquity, relics seen across an incomprehensible gulf of time. The geologists, the earth scientists, have given us a beautiful and elaborate picture of the planet's formation and development; they have constructed a time scheme with which they can diagram, as with an overlay, each evolutionary step in the long process. But all that, I maintain, is merely information. It is not knowledge; even less is it understanding. Knowledge and understanding, though based on information as an essential component, require more, namely, feeling, intuition, physical contact— touching, and sympathy, and love. It is possible for a man and woman to know and understand one another, in this complete sense. It is possible to know, though to lesser degree, other living things—birds, animals, plants. It is even possible to know, through love, a place, a certain landscape, a river, canyon, mesa, mountain. (Nobody ever fell in love with a rock, you say? Nonsense. Bullshit. Many of us have fallen in love with rocks. You don't think I lived for so long in the American Southwest because I wanted to be near Phoenix, or Barry Goldwater, or Glen Canyon Dam, do you?) But knowledge—I insist—is not possible through science alone.

Enough of this metaphysical gibberish. Throw metaphysic to the dogs, I say. I built a fire of finnis wood, let it burn down to a bed of flickering incandescence, then dropped a slab of beef, abo style, directly on the coals. Waiting for the entrée to cook, I gnawed—like Count Ugolino—on a head of lettuce. When the steak was done on both sides—medium rare, of course—I lifted it off the fire with the point of my combat knife, let it cool for a moment, brushed off the cinders, then devoured it, eating from my hands; naturally. The coals were still red-hot; finnis is good wood, like gidgee or desert oak or mesquite or ironwood. I placed my blackened billycan on the fire and boiling some water, made magic tea. Magic tea? Here's the *receipt,* as the melancholic Robert Burton would say: Take one large mug of hot tea, add two or three liberal splashes of bourbon, then consume, at a leisurely, reflective pace, until mug is empty. Repeat, as often as desired, until satisfaction is obtained, or oblivion achieved, or both. Begin the next day with the same, or with magic coffee, until the oblivion becomes final. If such is your desire.

I spent the next day scrambling up and down the Olgas until my curiosity was appeased. A solemn place, with deep gorges, windy gaps, hooded turrets, domes and bluffs of naked stone. No crags, sharp spires, or pinnacles; all has been timeworn to a rounded finish. I found a few natural water tanks in the drainages, but they contained only sand. I saw one pale gray kangaroo, the color of a rat, sneaking off through the brush. A few hungry-looking kites hovered above me. That evening I camped again at the same spot, watching the sunset on Ayers Rock, only twenty miles to the east. For supper I ate stew from a can—on hardship rations already—and drank, certainly, the odd mug or two of the magic tea. In the morning I woke with frost on my beard.

A few miles west of Mount Olga I came to the first fork in the desert track. One route led north, bound for God knows where; the other due west toward the low hills of the Petermann Range and Docker River. Both looked primitive, untraveled, equally inviting. Something about this fork in the road reminded me of an incident in the dim past—déjà vu— and a premonition of heartache and disaster. Prudently I took the westerly course, though it hurt deeply to leave that northward trail unexplored.

The road west was in good shape, though I had some trouble

in the sandy patches and had to stop now and then to move rocks from the high, weed-grown center of the way. The shovel came in handy, but I wished I had thought of stealing a tire pump as well. No matter. We rolled on over the wavy plain, up one sand ridge, down into the trough, and up the next. The view from each high point was splendid: the vast open desert, the golden grass, a scatter of desert oaks, far-off purple hills and lavender mesas, the immaculate perfection of the autumn sky, the sun. Dry lake beds, white with alkali, gleamed in the distance. The inevitable large birds watched from the periphery. A red-haired, bushy-tailed dingo slunk through the shrubbery. Down in the sandy washes waited the welcome shade of the big ghost gums, the less welcome caterwauling of cockatoos and galahs, and the even less welcome swarms of flies.

But no problems. Nothing but joy and delight, the freedom of solitude. I took off my shirt. I took off my pants. At high noon I went for a walk into the dunes wearing nothing but a hat and sandals. When I returned to the car, a Toyota four-by-four Land Cruiser was parked beside it, facing east, with two big-bellied Aussies nearby guzzling beer. They offered me a cold quart can of Foster's as I pulled on my pants. We talked about the road. They looked at my car, looked at each other, shrugged. "What the hell, mate," said one, "give it a go." We parted, going our opposite ways. I would not see another car or truck on the road for six days.

I camped that night somewhere in the little hills east of Docker River. I climbed one of the rocky escarpments toward sundown and looked around. Though I could see for at least 100 miles, there was not a light anywhere. The starry sky was clear of vapor trails, for I was far north of the regular air lanes. I crawled into my sack, to be awakened much later by the thump and thud of heavy feet. By the light of the waning moon I saw three camels—feral camels, wild camels—shuffling about nearby, sniffing at the ashes of the fire, nosing around the car. I threw my steel canteen cup and they hurried off, hooves clattering on the stone. In the morning I searched for the cup, found it, made breakfast—peanuts, fruit, coffee, and bourbon—and drove on.

Sometime toward noon I saw smoke ahead, a cluster of trees, the glitter of glass, metal, and other garbage. Cautiously I drove into the little aborigine settlement of Docker River, thinking about the permit I did not have. I'd have attempted to detour around the place, but my gas tank was two-thirds empty, according to the gauge. I had ten gallons in the trunk but 225 miles to go before reaching Warburton Mission.

The river at Docker River was the expected dry, sandy wash. But there was a well, a windmill, a cement tank, and the usual squalid slum of tin shanties, broken-down trailer houses, and brush shelters. Under a grove of giant athel trees was the Big House, a bungalow on stilts where, undoubtedly, the white man lived, the missionary and his family, or some governmental bureaucrat. I did not wish to see him; I anticipated a sergeant-major type, in smart shorts and knee socks, with a bristling British mustache, demanding in sneering tones, "Let me see your permit, *sar.*"

Escorted by a mob of barking dogs and naked abo kids, I pulled quietly, discreetly to a stop in front of a shed where I'd noticed a row of steel drums on a wooden platform. One broken-down Toyota pickup squatted nearby; behind it, resting in weeds, were the rusted remains of a Land Rover, with a live pig sticking its head out the window on the driver's side.

Keeping one eye on the Big House, I looked into the open door of the shed. Two old men, black as ebony, dressed in shorts and ragged shirts, lay there amid a litter of oil cans, tools, wine bottles, greasy magazines. They were playing some kind of card game. I greeted them and requested gas.

"Gas?" they said.

"Petrol," I said, "petrol."

Slowly but cheerfully one got up, began pumping petrol from a barrel into a five-gallon can. I put my funnel in the filler pipe; he poured in the gasoline. A second five gallons filled the tank. I had burned up ten gallons in only about 130 miles. Damned lesbian car. Of course, the low-gear driving through sand and over rocks had not helped. I screwed the gas cap back on. "How much?" I said.

The old man grinned, flashing purple gums, a pair of yellow fangs. "Fitty dollah?" he asked, counting on his fingers. "Fi' dollah gallon?"

"Bugger off," I said.

He grinned again. "Footy dollah?"

"Bugger all," I said. We both looked toward the Big House.
Nobody emerged.

"Thutty dollah?" the old man said. "Fair enough," I said, and
gave him the money. Grinning, he stuffed it in his pocket.

Relieved but still anxious, I got in the car and charged off, not
so discreetly now, pursued down the street by yowling curs and
joyful, shrieking brats. As I passed the bungalow, I saw a young
woman, slim, dark, long-haired, come out the front door and
peer at me through the screened verandah. She gave a tenta-
tive wave. I waved in return, but kept going, suppressing the
impulse to jam on the brakes, throw the Ford in reverse, go
screeching back over dogs and children to see if . . . to find out
if maybe . . . No, to hell with it. Consoled by virtuous thoughts
I drove rapidly ahead and plowed into deep sand five miles out
of town.

Digging out, chopping brush with the shovel, jacking up the
car, and letting it down, killed a couple of hours and cooled my
foolishness. When the car reached firm ground, I celebrated
with a can of warm beer and drove on toward the south and
west. A couple of hours before sundown (I hate to cook in the
dark), I drove off the trail and made camp in the ample shade
of a desert oak. It was then I discovered our first flat tire, a slow
leak in the right rear, where I had picked up a nail by that
grungy shed in Docker River. No matter. I'd put on the spare
in the morning. I fixed myself a supper and went for a long walk
in the twilight. Wandered far across the desert, but found my
way back to the road by following the guide of the Southern
Cross. Another cold clear night; I was glad to crawl into my
sleeping bag.

I spent two or three days in the wilderness between Docker
River and Warburton, passing Mount Aloysius, the abandoned
Blackstone Camp (another former aborigine village), and climbing a modest mountain called Squires, 2000 feet high according
to my map, that lay a couple of miles south of the road. On top
of Mount Squires I found two mature wedgetail eagles roosting
on a dead tree. Scarcely acquainted with humans, they seemed
reluctant to leave. I stepped within ten feet of them before they
took off, heavily, and soared out over the rim of the drop-off.
The sun went down. I left my calling card in a peanut jar (my
peanut jar) on the summit and stumbled back to the car in the

dark, thinking of snakes: the king brown, the death adder—both reputed to lurk in these parts, both said to be fatally venomous.

More sand, more rocks. At times the going was slow and laborious, but with shovel work I was able to continue. One evening, staring at the smoldering embers of my fire, I thought I heard the weird drone of a didgeridoo—the ancient aborigine bassoon—off in the hills to the north. I may have been dreaming. The sound was thin, vague, remote, carried in and carried away on the sigh and moan of the wind.

I recalled the depressing abo slums I had seen here and there, through central Australia; thriving on booze, welfare, and free taxi rides, the aborigines are multiplying. They are not dying out; the problem, as the white Aussies call it, will not go away. Would be nice to think that somewhere in this vast desert wilderness a little band of blacks is still living in the traditional way, by hunting and food gathering, without charity from the white man's government and churches. And indeed there are rumors of such a band, Jim's Mob it's called, deep in the terra incognita to the north, where the Tanami, Gibson, and Great Sandy deserts merge their undefined boundaries.

At Warburton Mission, another little rural slum like Docker River, I took the precaution of bypassing the village on the south, turning back onto the road and entering from the west. Still thinking about the permit business. As I parked in front of what appeared to be the petrol station—horizontal drums mounted on a rack of two-by-fours—I heard a screen door slam in the tin bungalow down the street, and the very creature of my worst apprehensions appeared, striding briskly toward me.

He wore khaki shorts, knee socks, a tan safari-style shirt loaded with pockets and straps, and a stiff-visored cap. He carried a swagger stick—in a leather case (for chrissake!)—tucked in one armpit. His eyes were a pale and fishy Anglo-Saxon blue, his hair sandy, the mustache clipped and itchy, the nose ruddy from too much gin-and-tonic solitaire. His short britches, starched and pressed, whistled as he walked. Whistle-britches. My skin crawled with loathing.

Two black men stood nearby, watching and waiting. The usual pack of children and dogs surrounded us. The flies gathered thickly, whining with pleasure.

Without a word of greeting, he lifted his clipboard and prepared to write.

"Name?"

I gave him my name.

"Address?"

I gave him the name of a hotel in Brisbane.

"Race?"

"Human."

He frowned at the levity. "Destination?"

"Ayers Rock."

He frowned again and said, "Permit, please."

"Permit?" I asked in wonder.

"You are entering an aboriginal reserve," he said, in the curt,
silvertail manner. "A permit is required."

Impasse. I confessed that I had no permit. He stated that I
would have to turn back. I argued, meekly. He was unyielding,
conceding only that I might refuel before returning across the
300 miles of desert to Laverton. Furthermore, he added, as the
blacks filled my tank and jerry cans, this car could not make it
to Ayers Rock anyhow; implying that he was actually doing me
a favor. And then, as he turned away, he invited me to his house
for a drink.

After a couple of the biggest gin and tonics I had ever seen
in my life, crackling with real ice and adorned each with half
a lemon, served in what looked like flower vases, I admitted to
my shabby little trick. He allowed to having seen me drive by
on the south. His charade in the street, he said, was for the
benefit of the "savages," who had learned recently to be quite
severe in matters of legal punctilio, especially where it served
to embarrass a white man. "They hate us," he said, "as of course
they should." He invited me to stay the night. I declined, but
accepted his invitation to dinner. A bachelor, but a good cook,
he served up excellent buffalo burgers—the flesh of a wild
water buffalo he had slain, he said, a couple of weeks earlier in
the mangrove swamps near Darwin, during his annual six-week
vacation. Heads of various animals, stuffed and glassy-eyed (like
my host), contemplated us from the walls. We talked about
hunting, the tropics, Australian politics—he was a flaming Socialist, full of contempt for the current Country-Liberal Party
administration in Canberra. A decent, affable, and lonely man.

Before leaving Docker River I had my flat tire fixed, sort of, by one of the native craftsmen. He got the tire off the rim all right, and pulled out the nail, but instead of patching the puncture (tubeless tire) he plugged it. On the first try he missed the hole, forcing his punch in at the wrong angle, and succeeded in creating an opening between plys. On the second try, he got the rubber plug in straight, and when he pumped the tire up it held air. But even as we admired his work a blister began to appear on the sidewall, swelling to the size of a walnut. What the hell. He only charged me five dollars. I threw the thing in the trunk and forgot it, glad to be getting out of that wretched outback ghetto. Gassed up (at $2.50 a gallon), running full, cool and collected, pistons popping in spastic ecstasy, me and the Ford lumbered southwest through the last big blank space on the map. Three hundred miles to Laverton.

Three days of bliss followed. I drove one afternoon onto the middle of a dry lake, firm and smooth, and wasted a gallon or two of petrol cutting figure eights in the crusted salt. I camped there that evening, listening to the dingoes howl the sun down, watching the pink hills float on heat waves, making a fire of twigs pulled from the grill and under the fenders of the car.

Next day I passed an abandoned homestead. Stone house without a roof; broken windmill and a dry cistern full of sand and thistles; the carcasses of a few dead cows lay sprawled on their sides near an empty cement tank. I thumped the ribs of one with my stick; it sounded hollow as a drum. And it was. Though hide and skeleton remained intact, the cow had been completely eaten out on the inside; the eyeballs too, of course, were gone. I could lift the entire structure with one hand; it was fleshless, odorless, and weighed no more than if made of papier-mâché. I've seen the same thing in our Southwest; once found in Utah a horse, dead perhaps for a year, hollowed-out, leaning in the corner of a fence.

On the third day beyond Warburton, after bagging another little desert peak (Mount Shenton, 1500 feet), I backed the car into a saltbush turning around and punctured the second tire. The spare with the tumor lasted half a mile. It blew as we were rolling too fast down into a rocky ravine. I did not lose control but did hit several rocks, rather hard, up front in sensitive areas of the engine. Laboring in first gear up the steep rise on the

other side of the gulch, flat tire flopping, I saw a red light wink
on, and stay on, in the instrument panel. Déjà vu.

I halted the car at the first convenient level spot beyond the
ravine. Shut off the motor. Smelled the smoking rubber, the
burning oil. Here we go again, I thought. Or more exactly, here
we do not go again. It seemed so wearily familiar. I climbed out
to inspect the damage. As I knew I would, I found a big dent
and a small crack in the bottom of the oil pan. The oil was
leaking out at a steady, though not necessarily calamitous, rate.
With the six quarts of oil in the trunk we might make it another
six, maybe even twelve or eighteen miles. If I could drive fast
enough. The flat tire, though, would be a drag.

I studied the map. Mount Shenton was only a mile to the east.
We were still a good fifty miles from Laverton. Whatever might
be there. If anything. I could wait where I was, hoping for help
to come along. But as I've said, I hadn't seen another motor
vehicle on this desert track for six days. I could load up my pack
with food and water and hike it to Laverton. Or we could rev
up the Ford one more time and *give it a go.*

First I had to seal, if possible, that hole in the oil pan. If I could
get the pan off I might be able to hammer the crack shut. But
the only tools in the car were the bumper jack and the lug
wrench. I cut a wedge from the nearest piece of green wood
and pounded that into the crack with a rock. The trickle of oil
slowed to a series of discrete droplets. I checked the dipstick:
empty. I poured in three quarts, keeping three in reserve. For
an emergency.

I started the engine, the car wallowed forward on its flat tire
and cambered rear wheel. The red "OIL" light flashed on immediately but I disregarded it. When the high temperature
light went on I would stop and let the car rest. (The son of a
bitch.) We proceeded, advancing steadily over the rocks and
sand, made 2.2 miles before the "TEMP" light began glaring at
me. I shut off the motor; moving parts clanked and sputtered
up front under the bonnet. Poor useless bloody sod of a machine. I was tempted to give it a swift kick in the kidneys. An
ungenerous thought. I opened the hood and pulled the dipstick.
Empty. I looked underneath, checked the oil pan. The plug was
gone.

Late afternoon. Time to make camp anyway. I gathered

wood, fixed myself a deluxe dinner: bacon and beans, date-nut bread from a tin, my last orange. As Sancho Panza says, "The best sauce is hunger." I uncorked a bottle of wine from South Australia—made in the shade at Adelaide—and drank it all, like a prince, and felt happy.

The huge flaming sun dropped behind a fleet of silver clouds, then behind the serrated skyline formed by the western hills. Bats flickered through the twilight. I flung my bottle high in the air and heard it crash on the rocks in the next gulch north. Two kangaroos scrambled up and bounded away into the shadows. I roared in triumph, bellowing at the luminous sky, the remote hills, the vast, waiting, listening openness of the desert. From where I stood under Mount Shenton to near the town of Broome on the Indian Ocean, a thousand miles north, there is probably not a single permanent human habitation. Exaltation! *Exultemus! Gloria in excelsis nihilo!*

I noticed my Ford slumped gloomily nearby, down at one corner, motionless, silent. That sobered me a little, not much. I checked the water supply: four gallons left. The food: enough for three days of easy walking. Laverton only about forty-eight miles away. No problem, no problem.

I passed out early and rose before the sun, poured in the last three quarts of oil and got two more miles out of the car before it shuddered to a final halt. Smoke poured from the hood. I loaded my pack, locked the rest of my gear in the trunk, locked the car, pocketed the key, and marched off down the road.

I felt good, glad to be rid of the damned car, and that evening —ten miles further—at a homestead called Cosmo Newberry I got a ride to the paved highway north of Kalgoorlie. At the junction roadhouse and petrol station I found a man with a tow truck who said he would haul my car into Kalgoorlie. His name was Ronald. My cheap credit card was acceptable. We stocked up on Black Swan and next morning drove to Mount Shenton. We hitched the car to the truck and started back. I rode in the cab of the truck with my benefactor. The Black Swan was half gone. We popped the top from two more. My friend drove very fast. At the first sharp turn in the dirt road, the car flipped on its side. We kept going, aware of additional drag in the rear but nothing more. It was a big truck. A miner passed us going the other way; he waved and honked his horn. We waved back.

"Waddeya doin' in these parts, Yoink?" said Ronald.

"Just sightseeing," I said. "Ready for another?"

"Don't mind if I do. Where ya goin' from Kalgoorlie?"

"Wolf Hole, Arizona."

"Never heard of it."

"America's a big place." I glanced in the rearview mirror on my side and saw sparks flying from the impenetrable cloud of dust behind us. Another car passed, horn blaring. I opened two more cans of beer and passed one to Ronald. Eyes fixed on the route ahead, he drove one-handed at fifty-five, optimum speed for a washboard surface, down a road that seemed all uphill.

Near the junction with the paved highway we stopped for bladder relief and discovered the difficulty. "Should've mentioned that flat tire, mate," Ronald said. "No wonder the blinkin' blighter flipped." He solved the problem by dragging the car onto a slope beside the road, where we were able to right it with the aid of a jack and a prize bar. Two doors were sprung, two jammed shut, some windows smashed, and the bright new finish a bit worse for wear, but otherwise everything looked shipshape. Even the trunk was still closed; I jimmied it open with the bar and rescued my baggage. We replaced the flat in the rear with one of the wheels from the front of the car and drove on.

We stopped at the roadhouse on the highway for cocktails and dinner. I telephoned the airport at Kalgoorlie and made reservations for the next flight to Sydney. The plane departed at ten; if we drove at a smart pace we should make it with a few minutes to spare.

Onward, through the evening, south into the hills of a famous mining region—nickel, silver, gold. We reached the outskirts of Kalgoorlie at nine thirty, feeling a bit tired but cheery. "Where to, mate?" says Ronald.

"Well, the man said I had to return the car to where I rented it."

"Where'd you rent it?"

"Avis."

"Righto. The airport it is."

Ronald knew the way. We got there in a few minutes and dragged the Ford into an empty slot in front of the Avis sign. Ronald got out his imprinting device and took my credit card.

I gave him the shovel I had borrowed from the Stuart Arms; he promised to see that it was returned, sooner or later. He un-hitched the car from his truck, we shared the last can of Black Swan, shook hands, parted. Ten till ten. I entered the terminal, bought a ticket, checked my baggage, and rushed for the gate. On the way I passed the Avis desk, where I dropped the car keys and the rental papers, mileage filled in, all in order.

"Was everything satisfactory, sir?" asked the pretty wench in the trim red uniform.

"Oh quite," I said, sweating, stinking, drunk, filthy, and happy, "quite, quite," and took off, disappearing forever into the Southern Cross.

5. A DESERT ISLE

Isla de la Sombra is a small island off the coast of Mexico. Twenty miles long, five to ten miles wide, with 4,200 feet of vertical relief, it has no human inhabitants whatsoever. Not one. And this for the very good reason that la Sombra, so far as is known, lacks any trace of spring, seep, or surface stream. Except for a few natural stone basins—*tinajas*—high in the canyons, which may hold water for a time after the rare winter rains, la Sombra is absolutely waterless. It is a true desert isle.

Naturally we had to go there. Me and Clair Quist, a friend from Green River, Utah. Clair is a professional river guide by trade, a jack-Mormon by religion. He doesn't talk much, but says a lot when he does. I like that.

To get us to the island, we hired Ike Russell, a veteran bush pilot out of Tucson. There are no recognized landing fields on the island, but Ike had landed there a couple of times earlier anyway and thought he could do it again if conditions were favorable. Loaded with twenty gallons of drinking water and other baggage, we took off one morning from Tucson in Ike's old Cessna 185, a refurbished aircraft fitted with oversize tires, reinforced landing-gear struts, and other special equipment. We rose about thirty feet in the air and dropped back to the runway. Power failure.

Half an hour later, with twelve new spark plugs installed, we tried again. Made it. On the way south, Ike landed and took off twice from a small dirt strip in the desert, for practice. The plane carried a heavy load: 160 pounds of water, food for ten days, and two passengers weighing nearly 200 pounds each. We landed again at Nogales, Sonora, to be cleared through Mexican Customs. Easy enough—Ike paid the customary bite, *la mordida*, about five dollars to each official lounging around the office—but it made me nervous all the same. I always get scared when I enter Mexico. Something about those short, heavy mestizo police with their primitive stonefish eyes—the way they look at you—and the bandits loafing along the highways with stolen assault rifles, picking their teeth with lizard bones. I don't know which I fear most, the cops or the bandits. In fact, except for the uniform, I can't tell one from the other.

But we were flying 6,000 feet above it all, across the cowburnt wastelands of Sonora, toward the blue Pacific and a remote, uninhabited island. Nothing to worry about.

We reached the coast and flew across some fifty miles of rough open sea. The island came in sight, dark and craggy through the haze—la Sombra. We circled over the south half of the island, close above the rugged mountains. They looked like the mountains of Death Valley—barren, volcanic, with the color and form of rusty, mangled iron. Down in the narrow canyons we could see wild palms and other small trees, but no water.

Ike made a pass over one possible landing place, a 700-foot strip near the beach and the mouth of the palm canyons. He had landed there before, but not with such a big load. He flew five miles farther to a dry lake and put us down. The lake was a little muddy beneath its dried crust, and we made a very short stop. We got out, glad to be on land again. From beyond the waves of gravel and pebbles, piled like a dike along the shore, we could hear the surge and uproar of the sea. The wind was blowing hard.

We agreed that the area near the first landing strip would

make a nicer base camp. To lighten the load, we removed five gallons of water from the airplane and decided that Clair and I would walk back to the first strip. Ike took off with most of our food, the rest of our water, and the camping gear. Clair and I cached the water jug and started walking.

Late afternoon: The sun stood low over the western hills. Though the distance was short, we had to climb three coastal ridges and find our way by starlight through a cactus jungle before Ike's bonfire guided us to his airplane and our camp. As we arrived, a huge full moon—a little late—rose out of the sea, looking ruddy as an orange through the eastern mists. Happy to find our pilot alive and his plane right side up, we celebrated with Ronrico 151 and three mighty steaks grilled on an ironwood fire.

Early next morning Ike took off, promising to return in ten days to take us home. Clair and I were alone on the island.

On our island. We could hear the seagulls shrieking and cackling by the shore. We saw a file of brown pelicans sail by, sedate, dignified, skimming low above the waves in graceful and perfect unison. Far above, a hawk patrolled the lonely sky.

Clair wanted to go look for lobster. He has this dream of lobster unlimited, fresh from the boiling pot (a quick death, they assure us; I hope so), of sinking his fangs in that tender sweet meat from claw and tail. But I was thinking of water. Fresh water. We had fifteen gallons with us. Enough for ten days, probably. If we were careful with it. If nothing went wrong. If Ike returned on schedule. I suggested, therefore, that for our peace of mind—my peace of mind—we might take a little walk up into the canyons before doing anything else. To look for water.

Clair knows a paranoid when he sees one. He takes a hundred of them down through the Grand Canyon every summer. So off we went, into the desert, toward the mountains. I carried a daypack over my shoulders, with cheese, nuts, oranges, and a gallon of water. We trudged up the sand and gravel of a dry wash, into the mountains, following what we thought was the main drainage. Though early February, the heat seemed intense—and the seaside humidity even more unpleasant. We found ourselves sweating heavily as we climbed, mile after mile, through the sand, around and over boulders, higher and higher into the narrowing canyon. We paused several times to drink from my canteen. Despite the grandeur of these desert mountains, the strangeness of the desert plant life, we thought of water rather often. We weren't finding any. One likely pothole after another, on inspection, turned out to be full of nothing but dry sand. Cheap, leaky, volcanic rock, full of fissures and vesicles: The winter rains had apparently percolated right on through into the substrata.

We passed a few small fan palms but found no trace of water on the surface. Palm trees suggest oasis, but this boulder-choked gulch we were ascending was hot, arid, and waterless. Palm trees are also supposed to indicate the presence of permanent water beneath the surface, but we saw a few of these palms growing high on rocky ridges, hundreds of feet above any possible water source. It would seem that the wild fan palm, like the cactus, the mesquite, the ironwood, has adapted to a situation where water is available only intermittently.

Halfway up the mountain, sitting in the shade of an overhanging cliff, Clair and I ate our lunch, drank the last of our canteen water, and contemplated the bright blue sea 2,500 feet below and four or five miles away. A long dry march back to camp. We had about given up hope of finding water and were feeling a bit discouraged. Then I thought I heard a dove calling, farther up in the canyon.

"Dove," I said.

"You're crazy," Clair said.

But we heard it again. The soft, sad coo of a mourning dove; *hey . . . hoo . . . hoo . . . hoo.*

Dove means water. We scrambled farther up through the rocks and, about fifty yards higher, deep in a grotto under the shade of a palm, we found a beautiful basin in the bedrock half-filled with the precious and lovely stuff. Good water—clear, cool, fresh—left there, no doubt, by the last rain. Filling the canteen, I slipped and fell in, not ungracefully. The pool was knee-deep, about three feet wide by four feet long. Fifty gallons at least; enough for a month of survival, if necessary. If the damned doves didn't drink it all first. Several of them sat about on nearby rocks and trees, staring at us reproachfully.

"Wish I had my shotgun," said Clair.

"Such ingratitude."

"Law of the jungle. Kill or be killed."

Refreshed and reassured, we climbed on to the saddle of the mountain. We were now about 3,000 feet above the sea, up among the century plants and ocotillos. We descended into the canyon beyond, scrambling down bluffs and scarps of the rottenest rock I've encountered anywhere. We didn't care. We were pleased with ourselves and our island. We reached the sandy floor of the canyon and checked out a narrow gorge beyond. The rock here was solid and monolithic, some kind of consolidated volcanic tuff, pale yellow with red and brown nuggets of jasper embedded in the matrix.

We walked into a corridor carved through the stone over centuries by rare but violent desert floods, and made our best discovery of the day: a pool of drinkable water, ten feet wide, twenty feet long, of unknown depth. There were probably more tanks beyond, around the bend of the gorge, but we would have had to swim the pool to find out. The walls on either side were smooth, polished, overhanging. Deep in the shade of the gorge, too cold for a swim. And besides, as everyone knows, it is not good manners to swim in a desert pool. Well-brought-up desert rats such as ourselves, sweaty and greasy, do not go paddling about in what may be the next man's drinking water. This pond might last for several months, before evaporation took it all.

Canteen full and bellies gurgling with water, Clair and I made tracks for camp. At an easy pace; we knew the moon would be up, sooner or later, to light our way. No longer concerned about water, we paid more attention to the novelty of the plant forms along the route. The ironwood trees, for example, alive and dead. The dead ones, looking each a thousand years old—and perhaps they were—resembled metal sculpture. This wood is so hard, dense, and heavy that it sinks in water. On the hillsides grew stands of the elephant tree—a short, thick, grotesque plant no more than ten to fifteen feet tall, with bright green waxy leaves and peeling white bark. We named it the leprosy tree. An unfair name, maybe; in their way, these things are beautiful, particularly in contrast to the rust red cliffs behind them. We saw many more of the palms, some of them up to forty feet tall. Their high fronds, rustling in the sea breeze, sounded like running water. Some were bare-trunked; most were clothed in thick skirts of dead fronds reaching from near the top to the ground. A kind of fruit, grapelike bunches of green berries the size of cherries, dangled within reach on the females. I bit into one: bitter, hard, almost all seed.

We thought of food, now that our water supply was assured. So far we had seen no sign of any possible game, except the doves—and there *is* something about the piteous bleating of those little chickens, as they flee before you, that makes a man want to reach for a shotgun. I understand and sympathize with that reaction. But the doves were few, and we were unarmed. We had not seen the tracks or scat of any mammals larger than mice—no trace of deer, bighorn sheep, rabbit, hare, coyote, fox. This, more than anything else, convinced us that la Sombra truly is a barren isle. The doves, when the potholes dried up, would fly back to the mainland; but mammals, all but a few species of desert rodents that manufacture their own water, metabolically, must have a reliable, permanent supply of surface water. Furthermore, if springs or seeps had ever been found here, the Indians and then the Mexicans would have moved in, together with their goats, pigs, cattle, and burros.

We saw plenty of chuckwallas, however, on the walk. The chuckwalla is a big, fat, ugly, remarkably stupid lizard. A vegetarian, it grazes on the leaves of such desert plants as brittlebush and creosote. We saw dozens of chuckwallas scurrying out from perfectly good hiding places, rushing across our path and trying to hide again between or under rocks, digging in frantically. The animal's only defense seems to be the heavy tail, which it switches back and forth like a whip. Wedged in a crevice, it puffs itself up, hoping to become inextricable. The Indians, so I've heard, would deflate them with a sharp-pointed stick, pull them out, take them home alive. Adequate, if not good, eating. How are they cooked? The same way you cook a lobster. I suppose, if starving, I could do it. Neither Clair nor I felt near that hungry yet.

Into twilight. We stumbled home through the dark—moon late again—over the rocks and among the cholla, passing a forest of the giant cardon cactus on our right. Monstrous forms of bronze and thorn, twenty, thirty, forty feet high, the biggest cactus in the world. When swollen with moisture, as these were, each must weigh many tons.

We heard and then smelled the sea. Dark ridges loomed against the 2,800 visible stars in the sky. Where the hell were we? Wait for moonlight or go on? We guessed the correct direction and went on. Another fifty feet and we walked right into the ashes of our morning campfire.

The moon rose. We built a little fire. Clair set two cans of beans, unopened, in the flames. I lit my cigar, backed off a bit, and waited for the explosion. The cans went *bleep! . . . bleep! . . . bleep!* At the third bleep, Clair pulled them out, opened them. The beans were ready. Neither of us thought of cooking anything more. We don't go into the wilderness to cook fancy meals, for chrissake. We ate our beans and smoked our smokes and drank some more Ronrico and were content.

Next morning Clair took his snorkeling outfit and a pair of leather gloves and went lobster hunting down where the surf was pounding against the slimy rocks. I walked for miles down the rocky, pebbled shore, naked except for sandals and a hat. The seabirds hollered at me, and once a big bull sea lion came wallowing up out of the waves, staring at me with huge eyes like those of a basset hound. I tried to coax him ashore; nothing doing. He lay on his back among the billows, loafing; then dived and vanished. Cormorants, frigate birds, pelicans, and gulls sailed by. I found a small sandy beach in a sheltered cove, took a swim, stretched out on the warm sand, hat over my face, and let the sun blaze down on my body. The sun, the sand, the clamoring sea, my naked skin. Close to peace for the first time in weeks, I began to think of women. Of this one, that one, all the lovely girls I've found and known and lost and hope to find again. That girl in Tucson, for example: her light brown hair, her docile eyes, the glow of her healthy flesh.

"Take me to Mexico," she had said.

"I'd rather take you tonight," I said.

God damn it. Really a mistake to come to a perfect place like la Sombra without a good woman. If for no other reason than this: Having a woman along helps keep a man's mind off sex. God damn it all. I committed adultery with my fist and went back to see how Clair was doing.

Powerful, shaggy, and dripping, he looked like Triton emerging from the waves. But no lobster in his grip. I borrowed his mask and cruised the surface for a while, admiring the schools of green-gold coral fish streaming over the underwater rocks. I saw a small stingray rise from the pale sand and dart away, terrified. Both of us. And starfish. And one dark somber creature hovering in place below me, not more than three feet long but with the unmistakable outline of a shark.

The tide went out. We crawled upon the damp rocks, searching the tidal pools, pursuing long-legged crabs. Never got near them. Thousands of primitive looking bugs, with long antennae, many short legs, and the forked tails of earwigs swarmed over the rocks before us, hustling out of our way, making suicidal leaps. I suppose they were feeding on microorganisms left behind by the receding water.

We played all day in the Sea of Cortez and walked home near sundown to our camp. That camp consisted of two flat stones with a pile of ashes between; of two bigger stones for sitting on; of a skillet, coffeepot, and two tin cups nearby; of a cloth sack of food off the ground in a limber bush (*sangre de dragón* in Mexican); of three water jugs under the bush; of Clair's bedroll over there and mine down yonder and Ike Russell's "airport" in between.

We thought now, in the cool of the day, that we might do a little work on the airport. Ike had thoughtfully left behind, as a hint, one shovel, one hatchet, and a pinch bar. He had marked out a 1,000-foot runway he hoped we would clear, but—all rocks and shrubs—it looked like a week's work to us. Instead, we pried loose a few boulders at the head of the old strip, chopped down some limber bushes at the lower end (those bushes with their bright red sap—blood of the dragon!) and made it ninety feet longer. We agreed that we preferred a possible death by airplane smashup to certain death by hard labor under a desert sun—an easy choice.

"What's for supper?" said Clair a half-hour later.

"Whose turn to cook?" I said.

"Yours."

"Beans."

Days passed; nothing happened. No boat appeared on the sea. One morning we found a dead sea lion on the beach, rapidly decaying amid the wrecked turtle shells, driftwood, lost cordage, sun-blued rum bottles, pelican skulls, broken clam shells, spiny blowfish, limestone starfish, and other castoff wrack from the ocean. Not the same sea lion I had seen before, this one looked smaller, younger. The big eyes were already gone, pecked out by the shore birds. Always the best part first.

I sat down on a log and thought about sea lions. Those remote cousins of ours, returned to the beginning. I thought of the big one I had seen a few days earlier, staring at me from the waves, and wondered if these oceangoing mammals ever felt a twinge of nostalgia for the land world they had left behind, long ago. (At night I often heard strange forlorn cries coming up from the shore.) The whales, the dolphins—do they feel a sense of loss, of longing, exiled forever from the land, the open air, sunlight? Or—the obvious counterthought—do they feel pity for *us*? After all, theirs is the larger world, perhaps the more rich and strange.

Useless speculations. The melancholy of the sea—the "bitter, salt, estranging sea"—getting into my nervous system. Clair had vanished, somewhere around the headlands, still exploring the underwater realm. I went for a walk into the place we named Paradise Valley. (And, in fact, we were privileged to name every place on this forgotten, enchanted isle.) Paradise Valley was full of flowers—purple lupine, glowing like candelabra, the coral-colored globe mallow, yellow brittlebush, many others I could not identify. Light green vines—the type known as dodder—briefly resurrected by the winter rains, crawled upon the giant cardons and wreathed themselves about the walnut brown shapes of old-time, long-dead, rugose ironwood trees. Smokethorn floated on the heat waves in the sandy wash. The fishhook cactus sported its delicate lavender blossoms; some were already bearing fruit. I ate a few of the red morsels, their flavor like wild strawberries. Butterflies and hummingbirds also explored this wild, perfumed garden. Under a man high shrub spangled with blue flowers, I found a rattlesnake coiled in striking position, observing me. It looked fat, fresh, and dangerous: scales a coppery pink, coon-tailed rattles whirring vigorously. I teased it for a minute or two with a long stick, then left it in peace. Ravens croaked on the crags. High above, a red-tailed hawk screamed, the sound of its cry—as the *koan* says—exactly like the form of its fatal beak.

Death Valley by the sea. Salmon-colored clouds float over the water. Reflecting that light, those images, the sea, now still, looks like molten copper. The iron, wrinkled, savage mountains take on, briefly, a soft and beguiling radiance, as if illuminated from within. Canyons we have yet to look at—deep, narrow, blue black with shadow—wind into the rocky depths. Sitting on a hill above our camp, listening to the doves calling far out there, I feel again the old sick romantic urge to fade away into those mountains, to disappear, to merge and meld with the ultimate, the unnameable, the bedrock of being. Face to face with the absolute—whatever it is. Sweet oblivion, final revelation. Easy now. What's the hurry? I light a cigar instead.

Old moon in the morning, worn and pale as a beggar's last peso, hangs above the western skyline. Last day before departure—if the plane gets here. Coffee and oranges for breakfast. Clair and I sit in silence on our rocks by the fire of ironwood coals and contemplate the conflict in our heads. Regret to be leaving—the longing to be gone. We resolve the conflict by making plans for a return next winter by boat, with loads of water and food and, of course, women. What women? Our women. Good women, what else? What other kind is there?

Time for one more walk up the canyons. Clair has other notions. I go alone, across the wash, kicking sluggish chuckwallas out of my way, past tiny pink flowers shining in the sand, through the cardon forest over a field of tough, tawny grass. Unspeakable beauty, unbearable seasick loneliness. Murmur of the shore, distant cries. I climb a long ridge and find, at the end of it, on a good lookout point, a circle of flat stones set on edge in the ground. The circle is five feet in diameter, big enough for several small human bodies. For Indians. By the look of the stones, the growth around them, they've been here for centuries. Silence.

The day seems very hot. I notice that my heart is beating rapidly, that I feel slightly giddy, as if veering toward heatstroke. I sit down in the shade of a giant elephant tree and drink some water, eat some lunch. A hummingbird comes close to inspect the red bandana around my neck. Feeling better, I get up, go on, tramp into the dry stillness of a new canyon.

I enter a thick grove of wild palms. A dozen ladies in thick grass skirts, their green living fronds hang thirty feet above my head. Birds are poking about up in there. The loose stones clatter under my feet like broken glass. I walk through a funnel

of solid rock, like the stem of a wineglass, like the passageway
to birth, into the womb of the mountain.

Sunlight again and the oppressive heat. More palms, many of
them, both dead and living. Some appear to have been struck
by lightning, burned alive. I clamber over boulders polished by
floods, inlaid with mosaics of garnet and obsidian. I sit again in
the shade of a palm, drink the last of my water, and listen to
what sounds like a mockingbird singing nearby, concealed in
the top of another palm tree. It moves. I see it—the white wing
patches, the long tail and slender bill. It is a mockingbird: What
is a mockingbird doing here? What am I doing here? Indifferent
to my presence—or is it performing for my benefit?—the bird
sings on and on, a sweet clear song with subtle variations. This
bird and I, companions in the wilderness, going gently insane.
I don't mind. Far away and far below, beyond the deep notch
of the canyon, the blue rim of the sea glitters under the sun.

The bird flickers away. I wait. What *am* I doing here? Who
cares? I can't think of any other place I'd rather be, despite the
sensation in my heart of panic and dread. Of fear. Fear of what?
I don't know.

Going on, thinking of water now. There should be water up
in here somewhere, and the search for it gives a purpose to my
meaningless wandering. At the head of a second stony corridor
in the canyon I come to the end, a wall of rock fifty feet high
that, at first glance, seems to block any further advance. I tramp
across the sandy basin under this dry waterfall and look up at
the smooth polished chute of the pour-off. Above, in that basic
bedrock, there will be, almost certainly, a series of natural
tanks, some of them containing water. The pattern is obvious.
At the side of the chute, where the stone has not been worn so
sheer, I find, on closer examination, a number of possible hand-
holds and toeholds. The pitch is climbable. Clair, a good
climber, would go snaking up there with little hesitation. But
he is not here.

I start climbing, putting my fingertips into little holes in the
vesiculated rock that would make ideal scorpion dens. Halfway
up or more, about thirty feet above the base, I pause to survey
the route beyond. Still looks like it will go, but already I am
dreading the necessary return and descent, which will be much
scarier than the climb. I look down; always a mistake. A long

way down. Not a fatal fall, perhaps, but worse—crippling. Should go on up before I lose the rest of my nerve. Instead, I stand there, on a tiny ledge a couple of inches wide, embracing with both arms the column of stone in front of my chest. The taste of fear on my tongue—a green and sour flavor. The blue green corrosion of an old battery terminal. Catastrophe theory: the quantitative description of discontinuous functions, as of a heavy body falling from point to point. Of course, Clair will come looking for me, tomorrow. Should have told him where I was going.

The mind whimpers on, tormenting itself. What a lonely place to die. But death is a lonely business. Let's go on. Maybe we can find some other way down. Climb the ridge into the next canyon, maybe.

Resolving to climb, I reach for a higher handhold and discover that the rock I've been clinging to is loose, attached by gravity and nothing more to the pedestal on which it rests. That settles the matter. I abandon any notion of going higher on this murderous, rotten, decaying rock. Instead, I descend. How? Very carefully. Back down to the relative safety of the canyon floor. Back down the gorge, back down through the canyon, back down to the sea and the shore and the long walk homeward through the dark, guided by the screeching laughter of seabirds on my right and Clair's towering signal fire against the stars.

Last day. We cleaned up camp, cached what was left of our food (coming back someday), cleared a few more boulders from the landing strip, and waited for Ike and his airplane. Clair stood on the knoll nearby, surveying his island one last time. A curious osprey circled several times above his head, nearly close enough to touch. I went down to the beach and gathered some pretty shells for my daughter. The dead sea lion was still there, still recognizable, but leaving us cell by cell, atom by atom. I took one last tumble in the roaring surf and went back to the airport.

Between the wild clamor of the sea and the hot mystic stillness of the desert, we waited for the return of the aluminum bird of the north. The bird came, precisely on time, and carried us aloft and away. Our bright lonely island, with its red mountains and golden fields, encircled by blue, became smaller and smaller behind us until it was lost in the vastness of the sea.

6. SIERRA MADRE

Our pilot is Ike Russell. Again. We're flying in his old wrinkled Cessna from Tucson and Nogales south-southeast to a little logging town known as Creel in the state of Chihuahua. Named for the Mexican entrepreneur and politician who helped establish the Ferrocarril de Chihuahua al Pacífico—that fabulous railway which runs from Chihuahua City across the western Sierra Madre to Los Mochis and Topolobampo (perfect name) on the west coast of Sonora.

The sky is extremely hazy this afternoon in spring, full of windblown dust and the smoke from forest fires to the east. Northwest Mexico, like the American Southwest, has been suffering a prolonged drought. Below, I see the barren desert hills rising gradually toward the crest of the Sierra Madre Occidental. Brown, burnt, sere, denuded hills, stripped of grass and largely waterless. Somewhere down in there, in the meager shade of cactus and mesquite, the cattle are dying by the thousands from thirst and starvation. The Sonora newspapers call it, appropriately, a disaster area.

The hills become bigger, rougher, with deep vertical escarpments facing the west. We fly over the trenchlike canyons of the Rio Moctezuma, the Rio Papagochic, the Rio Yaqui, mere threads of water winding among the foothills. Somewhere up around the headwaters of the Rio Yaqui there may be—maybe—a surviving remnant of the once-numerous Mexican grizzly population. No one seems to know for sure. The great bear survives mostly on rumor.

Although the approaches are rugged, the range ahead of us lacks any prominent peaks. Some points rise 10,000 feet above sea level, but from the air this part of the Sierra Madre ("Mother Mountains") presents only long ridges and high plateaus with a rolling surface, all trending in a northwesterly-southeasterly direction. There are no snowy summits here or any snow in sight at all. Arid, arid country. The scenic grandeur of the region lies not in the mountains but in the canyons or *barrancas* carved by the rivers, where the vertical relief may often exceed 5,000 feet. According to unverified report. Northwest Mexico has never been mapped in a thorough and scientific manner. Stories of canyons deeper than Arizona's Grand Canyon must be regarded with suspended judgment.

We fly over the forests now, thin but extensive growths of jack pine, scrub oak, yellow pine. Everything I can see appears to be well logged; the land is overlaid with an intricate network of dirt roads. According to Russell, who has been flying over, exploring, and prospecting the Sierra Madre for twenty years, there is almost no virgin forest remaining.

Fires are burning in many places, apparently unattended. As an old-time fire lookout, my instinctive reaction is to grab the radio mike and sound the alarm to all points—but down here, who knows? Maybe nobody cares. Let them burn. In any case, we are beyond my jurisdiction. Furthermore, Ike tells me, while some of the fires below were probably lightning-caused, the majority are deliberate, started by the Indians to clear the ground for the planting of their corn and beans, the slash-and-burn economy.

That forested range below is plainly not uninhabited. Everywhere I look, I see not only the logging roads and fires but also the milpas of the Tarahumara Indians, small clearings of one to two acres scattered about on every bench and swale of land with a slope of less than fifty degrees off the perpendicular. You might call it wild or primitive country, but as in most of Mexico, the land is occupied to the limit of its carrying capacity by human beings—and by their cattle, burros, goats, dogs, chickens, pigs. To the limit and then some.

Ike flies on, holding his course steady. We pass above the tracks of the Chihuahua al Pacífico, and suddenly more great breaks appear—the barrancas. Hard to make much of them through the smoke, the dust, the glare of the midday sun. I see craggy drop-offs, the serrated edge of rimrock, brushy slopes descending at precipitous angles into obscure depths, out of which a few buttes and pinnacles rise into the light. Water glints far below. The cornfields, the corrals and granaries, the little stone huts of the Indians are perched on the edge of the barranca and on the open slopes far down within it. Barranca del Cobre, Ike tells me; "Copper Canyon." That faint hint of water down in the shadows must be the Rio Urique.

To call it a canyon is not quite exact. There is a distinction of meaning between *barranca* and *canyon*, both of them, of course, Spanish words. The term "canyon" refers to a long and narrow defile, well defined, walled in by cliffs, usually though not necessarily, with a stream running through it. "Barranca" means, literally, a "break"; in Spanish landform terminology the word functions as a broader, more inclusive term than canyon, denoting any area where the land falls off steeply from one level to the next in an irregular, very rough, highly eroded fashion. For example, Santa Elena in Big Bend is clearly a canyon; Bryce Canyon in Utah is not a canyon at all, but something that better exemplifies the word break (like Cedar Breaks, also in Utah) or barranca.

The Barranca del Cobre, as I can see from the air, huge as it is in itself, is only one barranca among several in the vicinity. Easy to see why this portion of the Sierra Madre has been for so long a formidable barrier to east-west traffic. Even today, from the Arizona line down to the Durango–Mazatlán highway, a distance of 700 miles, there are no paved roads across the range. The railroad is still the only reliable transportation from one side to the other.

We make a pass over the right-angled bend of the Rio Urique, then turn north past the town of Creel for a quick aerial look at the Cascada de Basochiachic on the little river called Chinipas. Basochiachic is a waterfall with a straight pour-off a thousand feet down, making it one of the highest single-jump falls in North America. But it's been a dry winter in the Sierra Madre, and the waterfall, as we approach it, is not in good form. The volume of water that pours from the brink of the falls is not sufficient to reach the plunge pool below; blown sideways by the wind, the veil of falling water dissolves into vapor halfway down.

Banking east and south again, we return to Creel. Ike buzzes the Hotel Nuevo twice, hoping to rouse the management to the advent of gringo tourists without reservations, then drops us off at the airstrip five miles south of town.

There is nothing here but the strip itself, a limp windsock, a few Indian huts, a few gaunt cattle munching weeds. The Indians stare. The dogs bark. Ike takes off and disappears. My wife Renée and I shoulder our packs, climb the hillside to the road, and start marching toward town. We've walked a mile when a flatbed truck comes grinding along, headed our way. I stick out a thumb and we've got a ride. There are four or five adults in the cab of the truck, and as many more plus children in the back. We join the crowd on the bed.

One of the passengers is an old man, a Tarahumara, with a big gray Zapatista mustache. His handsome, leather-skinned face looks as if it has faced the mountain sun and mountain winds for a century. He wears the conventional Tarahumara dress: straw hat, white shirt, red bandana around the neck, and a loose white baggy sort of dhoti around the loins. His lean brown legs are bare; on his feet he wears homemade thong sandals, the soles cut from discarded auto tires. Huaraches.

I am fascinated by his feet. The old man owns the most beaten-up, stone-battered, cactus-cured, fire-hardened pair of feet I have ever seen on a human being—so cracked, splayed, and toughened they almost suggest hooves. No doubt he has gone barefoot most of his life, the sandals being for dress-up occasions, for Saturday night in the big town: Creel, population . . . 2,500?

The Tarahumara are famed for their long-distance running. Their races are said to go on for fifty miles, sometimes 200 miles. This old man whose feet I am gaping at may be, in his world, a once-great racer.

Though it's rude to stare, I cannot help but look again at his weathered face, the map of his soul. The expression there is attractive and appealing—serene, far-seeing eyes; a calm and easeful smile. Where have I seen that kind of face before? And I remember: yes, among old folk in Appalachia, in west Texas, in Norway, in Calabria. The sign of honor, an interior victory of some kind that cannot be won in less than seventy years—the Biblical threescore and ten. The faces of beautiful old men and women around the world.

We enter Creel, a little mountain logging town 7,000 feet above sea level. We pass the mill, its conical sawdust burners belching woodsmoke, with little boys stacking boards, dragging slab lumber out of the sheds as spinning buzz saws bite with a snarl into fat logs of ponderosa.

Into the town. Rutted dirt streets. Stone cabins, slabwood shacks, log huts. Children swarming everywhere—filthy, ragged, snot-nosed *mucositos,* shouting, screaming, laughing, and happy. Despite the food shortages, the alarming rise in the price of such staples as corn and beans, these children seem to be adequately fed, active, irrepressible. What does it take to sober a child? I don't want to know.

Renée and I check in at the Hotel Nuevo, opposite the railroad station. Despite the name, it is the oldest hostelry in town, definitely second class, maybe third. Still it has that south-of-the-border— what shall we call it?—style? Authenticity. Reputation. (Friends in Tucson had insisted on it.) The rooms are small, dank, dingy; the beds sag like hammocks; the lighting is erratic; and the hotel food (American plan)—ah, that Nuevo cuisine— perturbs the imagination. Peculiar looking vegetables, unidentifiable. Stringy bits of flesh, obscure in origin, wrapped in limp and greasy folds of dough. Everything disguised, the flavor—if any—buried beneath a mucous membrane of melted cheese and last week's tomato sauce. You can always count on the tomato sauce: Every dish comes immersed in it.

I am glad we've brought with us a week's supply of dehydrated All-American ersatz. Once we get out in the woods we'll *eat.* But there was a better reason for that than mere gringo caution and fastidiousness: By bringing in our own food we will not be competing with the natives for something to eat, will not be helping to force up the price of local foods. The *rico* tourist may think, when he pays the extravagant bill at a Mexican restaurant, that he is at least contributing to the welfare of the workers in the local economy. False. A few will benefit, but the majority, deriving no income whatsoever from the tourist racket, find they are paying higher prices for their daily tortillas.

Turismo is always and everywhere a dubious, fraudulent, distasteful, and in the long run, degrading business, enriching a few, doing the rest more harm than good.

Next morning we are joined by old friends. Bill Hoy and his Argentine wife Marina arrive by train from Ciudad Chihuahua. The four of us plan a walk together down into the Big Barranca —el Cobre—by a new and unknown route. We spend the day packing our packs, inspecting Creel, eating the Hotel Nuevo dinner, recovering, going to bed. Next morning, early, we are off in the hotel jeep for a ride to the head of a side canyon— unnamed on our map—that leads to the Rio Urique and Barranca del Cobre. Our intention is to hike down this canyon to the river, follow the river upstream to the next tributary canyon, and walk out to the Creel–La Bufa road, completing the loop. We carry food for five days.

The trek begins down a Tarahumara footpath along a pretty stream. On either side of the stream are the corn patches and bean fields of the Indians—tiny, cultivated plots that don't look big enough to support a flock of chickens, let alone a human family. Early May: The corn is a foot high, green and fragile. There is no attempt at irrigation; all depends on the summer rains. Each miniature field is fenced in with brush, rocks, or logs, presumably to keep out the animals—the burros, pigs, cattle, and flocks of voracious goats that swarm like hooved locusts across the hillsides. Subsistence agriculture, close to the margin of survival: One must credit the courage and faith of these peasant Indians. Each year they gamble their lives on a few acres of sand and dust, a rocky hillside for their beasts, the rainclouds. An earnest and serious wager, for there is no public welfare system in the Republic of Mexico. The losers simply disappear.

We tramp in single file between their fields, four big gringos with grotesque packs on our backs, while the Indians near their huts review our parade, shyly, furtively, from a safe distance. Quite likely they have never seen such a procession before. We are shy ourselves, fully aware of the incongruity of our presence here (Vietnam!), the pounds of luxury foods in our backpacks, the goosedown sleeping bags, our big solid boots, the Vibram tracks we leave on the trail. The Indians squatting around small fires, cooking their pinole, or cornmeal mush, in handmade clay pots, watch without a word as we go by. But their yellow curs bark vigorously enough, vicious yet prudent.

What the hell *are* we doing here? Sightseeing? Not very dignified. Call it exploration. Science, that's the word. We are exploring a canyon that, according to the manager of the Hotel Nuevo, no gringo has ever trod before. Certainly no self-respecting Mexican would come down here. And even the Indians' trail will peter out long before we come in sight of the Rio Urique.

Onward, over the goat dung, through the dust, over the shelves of smooth volcanic rock that skirt the stream. I notice that the fields are protected from floods by flimsy barricades of brush. I think of the heavy logging now taking place in the upland forests, of the vast excavations for a new truck and tourist highway, of the hordes of hungry cattle scouring the clearings and hillsides for a blade of grass, a bite of browse. What will happen when the dry spell breaks and the rains finally do come? When all that runoff water and all that grazed-off soil come pouring down these narrow canyons in a flood of muck and mud? The 35,000 Tarahumara have survived in this rough, beautiful "undeveloped" land for centuries, with their hard and beautiful way of life; but things are happening to their country now that they have never had to deal with before.

Indians, Indians, the goddamned Indians. As if we don't have enough to worry about without them on our hands, and hearts and minds as well. The one thing we could do for these people, I am thinking as I trudge along at the rear of the column, the one and only decent thing we could do for them (and by "we" I mean mainly the Mexicans and the Mexican "authorities," but include gringo Americans and Europeans, too), is leave them alone. Throw out the teachers, the missionaries, the government doctors and public health technicians; close off the roads and stop the road building; stop the logging; shut down the mines; burn down the hotels; tear up the airstrips; throw out the totalitarian fanatics from so-called Third World politics; ban all tourists, including us; and let these people alone. *Leave them alone.*

But leaving them alone is the one thing we will not do. So the Indians are doomed. The Tarahumara, unless saved by a quick collapse of the world industrial megamachine now moving in on them, haven't a chance. Like the Tupi of the Amazon, like the Kurds of Iran and Iraq, like the herdsmen of Tibet, like the Hopi of Arizona, like a hundred other small and once-independent tribes around the globe, these Indians are going to be . . . incorporated. Assimilated. Extinguished.

Well, it's not my problem. We march steadily on and soon leave the Indians and their milpas and their tedious troubles far behind, out of sight, out of mind. The goat paths continue on for a few more miles, but the huts become fewer and fewer, and the few we see appear to be unoccupied. We have a final glimpse of a goatherd—a woman—trying to hide from us in the brush; she is the last Indian or other human being of any variety that we shall see for days.

The stream descends, growing bigger, augmented by springs, seeps, and tributary runs, through a canyon walled by ragged, brush-covered formations of volcanic origin—consolidated tuff interbedded with thin strata of conglomerates. Dark, broken, craggy rock reaching far above us, perhaps 1,500 to 2,000 feet high. I am reminded of the canyons in the Gila Wilderness of New Mexico. Every slope short of bare-rock vertical cliff is terraced by animal paths. Domestic animals. Not surprisingly, we find little sign of wildlife, except for lizards and a few minnows in the pools and the birds.

Many birds. A multitude of birds. Some of them, like the coppery-tailed or elegant trogon and the solitary eagle (their proper names), I have never seen before, anywhere. Marina Hoy, a keen observer, the most able birdwatcher among us, will identify sixty-three different species before this walk is done.

The trogon, as its full name implies, is a striking and colorful bird. But shy: We catch only glimpses of it flitting among the trees. A pair of nesting solitary eagles (for even the solitary must sometimes mate—and these, like other eagles, mate for life) give us a much better show. We lie on our backs at the side of the path for half an hour, watching them soar and circle over the cliffs, alighting on trees and taking off again, screaming from time to time, no doubt disturbed by our presence, even though we are hundreds of feet below the focus of their domestic operations. We apologize for the intrusion, but they are beautiful birds in their black-and-white regalia, hard to give up watching. Furthermore, it takes the four of us, passing binoculars back and forth and consulting Marina's field guide, that much time to determine to our satisfaction that we are indeed looking at solitary eagles and not at their similar-looking cousin, the Mexican black hawk. Birdwatchers are a fussy, eccentric lot, especially perpetual beginners like myself, who seem condemned never to find a bird, anywhere, that corresponds precisely to its description and illustration in the bird books. A failing, on the part of the bird, difficult to forgive.

Finally, we go on, leaving the eagles in peace. Our bird list continues to grow. Even I spot a few I can recognize: a robin, a common flicker (all flickers are now classified as one species by the avian authorities), some kind of hummingbird, and a buzzard. Marina helps me find some of the more special, unusual, or beautiful: a caracara, a Cassin's kingbird, a crested flycatcher, a Townsend's solitaire, a painted redstart, a black-headed grosbeak, a red crossbill. But those rarest and most spectacular of Sierra Madre birds—the thick-billed parrot and the imperial woodpecker—are nowhere to be seen. It is possible that the imperial woodpecker is now extinct and the thick-billed parrot close to extinction.

Despite decades of heavy overgrazing and overbrowsing, a great variety of plant life still survives in this nameless side canyon of Barranca del Cobre. There is yellow pine *(Pinus ponderosa),* Arizona cypress, manzanita, alligator juniper, tamarisk, willow and bamboo along the creek, silverleaf oak, a fig tree (introduced) growing by an ancient stone hut, Apache pine, the wine-colored madroña, Emory oak, palmetto, a few small aspen on the slopes (this surely must be near the southernmost extension of the aspen's range), some type of maple, some species of locust. And on the lower, south-facing, hotter and drier slopes, a mixture of typical desert flora: prickly pear, hedgehog cactus, aloe, sotol, flowering agave, and yucca. We see a woody shrub blooming with what look exactly like sunflowers. Impossible but true. And air plants, orchids, flourishing on the pines. And many other plants, the identity of which we can hardly even guess at.

"What is it?" we ask, meaning what is its name? This odd quirk of the human mind: Unless we can name things, they remain for us only half-real. Or less than half-real: nonexistent. A man without a name is nobody. A man's name can become more important than his person. A plant, an animal, a thing without a name is no thing—nothing. No wonder we humans like to think that in the beginning was—the Word. What word? Any word. Any word at all, anything rather than the silence and terror of the nameless.

We don't get far this first day. We spend more time ogling birds or bushes or the rocky walls upstairs, or talking and eating and resting, mainly resting, than in serious businesslike hiking. Compatibly indolent, we call a halt in midafternoon and make our first camp, much earlier than strictly necessary, on a nice, pebbly beach with sand pockets, sleeping-bag size, by the side of the stream.

After our supper of reconstituted freeze-dried glop, we lie about the evening fire sipping rum, listen to the poorwills and whippoorwills (both), and watch the little lights that float through the dusk around us. *Molto misterioso.*

The first light I saw, from the corner of my eye, startled me. Unimagined and quite unanticipated, a small globe of furry luminescence drifts unblinking toward my face. For a moment I think I'm seeing one of Carlos Castaneda's Don Juan magic-button spooks: a spirit from some separate reality incarnated for my very own spiritual benefit in the form of a low-wattage bug. No, not so; the bug blinks, and I recognize our old friend, the firefly.

Alas, occult visions seem to come only to those who believe in them beforehand. First the faith, then the hairy little miracle. First the pill, the tab, the wafer, the space capsule—then come the ruby-eyed, six-legged alligators swimming through your psychedelic dome.

To hell with mysticism.

Next day we push on, at a comfortable pace, downward and deeper into this jungle-brush, jumbled-rock side canyon. Where is the Rio Urique? There is no longer any trail, only a welter of animal paths following the contours of the terrain and winding among the boulders that nearly choke the stream bed. No easy way. We follow the rock shelves, we climb over and around the boulders, we scramble up and down the brushy slopes, our hands on tree trunks for support. At one point, far beyond the last of the Indian fields, we discover a long-legged boar wallowing in the water, enjoying himself. Half-wild or maybe wholly wild, he scuttles off like a javelina when he finally sees us. I dislodge a stone; a red scorpion scurries under the leaves. Four piebald burros high on the slope watch us pass; they have long dark eyelashes, like movie starlets or cocktail waitresses; they do not bray but *cough* at us.

We are not making much progress, I suspect, and God only knows where the Rio Urique and the Big Barranca are; but it doesn't seem to matter. There's plenty to look at and feel, plenty of time to think about where we are. The growing consensus among the four of us is, "If we get there we get there and if we don't we don't." To hell with science too. Thus the ambience of Mexico infects our nervous systems: Montezuma's revenge in its subtler form.

In late afternoon we come to the loveliest scene yet: a series of pools big enough for swimming, joined to one another by noisy cascades pouring through sculptured grooves and polished chutes in the rose-colored bedrock. Tall willow trees shade the sand and stone at the water's side. Thickets of oak on the slope higher up promise good fuel for cooking. Against the blue, on either side of us, behind and ahead, rises a metropolitan skyline of towers, blocks, pinnacles, and spires of unknown height, though the pine trees on the rim suggest by their scale that the distance must be at least 3,000 feet.

A good, clean well-furnished campsite, with a view. Here we shall camp tonight, and the next night and yet another. Too fine a place for only an overnight stop. We unload the pig iron from our backs, strip, and plunge into the clear green pools, then sit in the sun on the smooth pink andesite and study our creased, coffee-stained topographic map, trying to determine where we are. The map is a Xerox copy of a copy, printed in Mexico on recycled tortilla paper with iguana piss for ink. Hard to read. We end up guessing we may be halfway to the Urique. No matter. No sweat. We build a fire of oakwood in a cove in the stone, cook supper, uncap the Ron Bacardi, contemplate the coagulation of twilight and the assembly of our organic lanterns afloat on the warm currents of evening—the fireflies, the lightning bugs. I remember from childhood that a firefly stays luminous even when ducked under water—it should lure trout? But there are no trout in the tepid waters of this creek; nothing but chub, carp, dace, mudsuckers. The biggest fish we've seen so far was six inches long.

Morning. We have decided to make this stopping place a base camp. Hoy and I, leaving our packs in camp, plan a fast reconnoiter down-canyon to see if the river and main barranca are within reach; Renée chooses to spend the day at home; Marina accompanies us part way, then drops back for photography. Bill and I go on alone.

We find that the canyon gets rougher the farther we go. A few miles beyond base camp it becomes a narrow gorge, walled in by rotten-rock cliffs a couple of hundred feet high. Above the cliffs are benches and talus slopes covered with brush and forest, then the higher cliffs. The complexity of the landscape, with its lavish growth of vegetation, reminds me of scenes depicted on Chinese tapestries. Hoy, the shutterbug, cannot resist pausing for more picture taking. Click, click—we hasten on.

Fallen slabs big as boxcars lie tumbled and heaped across the creek, jamming the gorge from wall to wall. We climb over and through cracks between and under them. The gradient becomes steeper, which may or may not mean we are getting close to the Urique. Waterfalls tumble ten, fifteen, twenty feet down to emerald basins. We belay one another off the vertical pitches, climb down trees, in one place descend, chimney-style, between a giant slab and the canyon wall.

We realize that we are not going to crawl down through here with full field packs on our backs plus a pair of girls not too keen on bouldering. Our proposed loop expedition is hereby canceled for this year. Bill and I go further, but by two in the afternoon, after rounding several more bends without seeing any hint of the main canyon through the hazy vistas beyond, we admit defeat. We are not going to reach Barranca del Cobre by this particular side canyon. That much is clear.

In cheerful ignominy we stop, rest, eat some gorp and jerky, then turn back without regrets, retracing the route up rocks and trees and chimneys, boulder hopping back to camp. Taking our time. We don't talk about it, but I'm sure Bill is as conscious as I am of the trouble we'd be in if one of us bent a bone or tore a cartilage in here. Why, you couldn't get even a burro down into this shattered maze.

We spend two more days and nights in Little Eden Camp before starting the long walk back to the Indian farms, the dusty road to Creel. On our return, we pause to examine more closely a Tarahumara plow, left leaning against the wall of an unoccupied stone hut. The plow has been carved—whittled, rather —from a single big chunk of oak, with one root still attached serving as the handle, much like the one-handled plow that Hesiod tells us the ancient Greek farmers used. The plowshare is simply the frontal tip of the oak, chipped to a point and hardened in fire. In the center of the beam a square hole has been cut or burnt (somehow); inserted in this hole is a square peg by which, apparently, the implement is drawn when hitched to an ox. Primitive? From the Indians' point of view, quite up to date: The plow was introduced into Mexico by the Spanish only 470 years ago.

A day later we're riding the *ferrocarril*, the "iron road" from Creel to the west coast of Mexico. But we stop for two days at a point on the rim of Barranca del Cobre called Divisadero, meaning "overlook." Before hiking off into the woods, we check out the local facilities. Divisadero is the Grand Canyon Village of Mexico and that is bad, but not the worst thing I can say about it. Perched on the extreme rim of the barranca, just like Bright Angel Lodge, is a brand-new hotel, built Holiday-Inn style for the accommodation of tourists. A fat black sewer hose, leading from the hotel, dangles over the cliff in full view of the principal lookout point, dripping its contents onto the next terrace down, about a hundred feet below.

The air is filled with the roar of a diesel generator nearby, busy making electricity for the lodge, bellowing continuously night and day. The building is surrounded by a barbed-wire fence, seven strands high—obviously a people fence, meant to keep out the Indians who have gravitated here in hopes of selling their clay pots and wooden fiddles and other trinkets to the passing trade. Against this fence the wind has piled a solid layer of papers, trash, junk.

We go into the hotel restaurant for cold beer. The Cerveza

Bohemia is good—Mexican beer is better than most American commercial beer—but we foolishly make the mistake of ordering sandwiches to go with the beer. Half an hour later, after long whispered consultations back in the kitchen, the *mozo* in his red monkey jacket brings us each what is meant to be a gringo sandwich: two slices of pale Kleenex balloon bread, exact imitations of our own back-home unspeakable Holsum, Wonder, and Rainbo, between which are concealed a transparent sliver of tomato, a film of mayonnaise, and a token wisp of cheese; with each sandwich we get one green olive impaled on a toothpick.

The tab for this affront (including the beer) comes to eighty-four pesos—$6.72. Adding injury to insult. Got to learn Mexican for "rip-off." Walking out, I inquire, from curiosity only, how much the rooms are; the desk clerk says thirty dollars a night for two. Fred Harvey would love this place.

We clear out, evading the temptation to provoke an international incident, hoist backpacks, and walk several miles along the rim until we are well beyond sight, sound, smell, and taste of Divisadero. We set up camp on a slab of rock cantilevered over the edge of a 500-foot drop-off. There we relax, perusing from above the impressive depths of the Barranca del Cobre.

How deep is it anyway? As I mentioned before, no exact surveys have been made in this part of Mexico. Boosters of the barranca claim it is 6,500 feet deep in the Divisadero area; Arizona's Grand Canyon is a mile deep, if measured from the South Rim, 6,000 feet deep if measured from the North Rim. The trail from near Divisadero to the Rio Urique in the bottom of the barranca is eighteen miles long, according to Michael Jenkinson in his book, *Wild Rivers of North America*—making it comparable to the walk down to the Colorado River from the North Rim. Of course, the length of the trail has no necessary correlation to the depth of the descent.

To me the barranca does not look as deep as the Grand Canyon. But Bill Hoy thinks it does. Subjective, chauvinistic prejudices play a role here: The Grand Canyon, for me, is part of my backyard, home; Hoy is queer for Mexico and all things Mexican.

Which is bigger? The Grand Canyon is 285 miles long from Lee's Ferry to the Grand Wash cliffs; the Barranca del Cobre is approximately 150 miles long. If its length is added to that of the neighboring barrancas, however, we get a combined barranca system that may be four times the length of the Grand Canyon.

Which is more impressive? They are different. The Grand Canyon descends steeply and dramatically to its inner gorge, revealing more varied and colorful rock strata than the barranca, which is wider, generally brushy, and formed mostly of dark, broken volcanic rock.

Which is wilder? Once again, such comparisons are difficult and maybe useless. The Grand Canyon, except for Phantom Ranch, Supai village, and the nearly continuous stream of tourist boat traffic on the river during half the year, is uninhabited. The Barranca del Cobre and the other barrancas are settled in every tillable nook and cranny by the Tarahumara Indians. But the Grand Canyon is surrounded by the general asphalt-covered, electrified terrain of industrial U.S.A. The barrancas of the Sierra Madre make up a far vaster area, mostly roadless (except for logging and mining roads); most of the interior is far, far from any town, telephone, or Park Service comfort station.

We spend the evening with our feet hanging over the edge of the abyss, spying on the Indians down below. How slowly they seem to move among their huts and fields and stone corrals, along the winding threadlike paths that lead from one tiny settlement to the next. A life in slow motion. Illusions of distance? But what's the rush? The Tarahumara live deliberately, wasting no movements; and when they run, they run all day, all day and half the night. We hear roosters crowing, dogs yapping, the tinkle of goat bells, the sound of somebody playing a tune on a wooden flute. I think of southern Italy, Crete, North Africa.

The Rio Urique, studied through field glasses, looks from our perch on the rim like a trickling stream hardly larger than the one we'd followed down the side canyon a few days earlier. It has indeed been a dry winter. The barranca floor is full of rocks, boulders, fallen debris, through and under which the water moves. A river of rocks. Parts of the Urique have been run by boaters with kayaks, in early spring after a winter of normal precipitation in the mountains, but the feat looks impossible now.

As the evening settles in, we become more aware of the fires burning around us, miles away in all directions, on hillside and ridgetop, enormous bonfires. Smoke and haze overlie the barranca and the rolling high country beyond. Tangerine-colored flames creep through the brush and jack pine: all that potential forest going up in gaseous waste. My lookout's reflexes are agitated by the spectacle. In vain. Useless to remind myself that fires are perfectly natural phenomena, good and necessary for the long-term health of the forests. But these are not natural fires; these are man-made, the intentional extermination of the plant cover of an entire region.

Well, none of my business. Mustn't get involved. I'm sure the Indians and the Mexicans know what they're doing. Maybe they *want* to eliminate the forest and wash the topsoil down into the dammed-up rivers of Sonora. Maybe they *want* to starve. Maybe it's part of the machismo thing.

The demographers tell us that the population of Mexico has risen from 15 million in 1900 to 60 million today—a fourfold increase in three generations—and that it continues to increase at a rate of 3.5 percent per year, compounded annually. Machismo! Half the present population of Mexico is under the age of seventeen. A nation of babies, kids, and horny adolescents. Youthful vigor! Dare one mention—would it be impolite and impolitic?—the name of the real and true specter haunting this glamorous land, a dilemma that no amount of *turismo* and no amount of *industrialismo* is going to solve? May one?

No. One may not. We are guests here, and the reply, if one were reckless enough to provoke it, can easily be anticipated: *No, gringo, mind your own focking beez-ness and geev me peso or I cut your focking gringo throat.*

There is another India aborning on our southern borders: Juarez, Nogales, Tijuana (where, as they say, all old whores go to die) will be the cactus Calcuttas of the year 1999. No wonder a million desperate wetbacks, a million hungry aliens attempt each year to infiltrate our southern defense lines. Living bodies hang on the coils of concertina wire, hands clutching at the barbs.

Nightmares. Impossible. The violet green cliff swallows whizz past our rock, flaunting their aerial supremacy. Little do they care what happens to humankind, the little feathered bastards.

The red sun goes down in smoke and flame. Great ball of fire!

The red sun rises through the smoky dawn. Lying in my sack, I hear trogons barking from the oak thickets under the rimrock. Yes, they bark, the elegant trogons. Then I hear the Tarahumara roosters crowing from the hamlets far below. Now there's a barbaric yawp if I ever heard one. The call of the male chicken, if not so familiar, would seem to us like the wildest, most thrilling cry in all of nature.

We cook breakfast during the smoky sunrise while a little yellow dog sniffs around camp, watching us with beggar's eyes, the same wretched, mangy, starved cur—abject and unwelcome, vicious and pathetic—we see everywhere south of the border. He must have followed Hoy all the way from Ciudad Juarez. The magical dog, with who knows what supernatural powers? Don Juan's dog. Mescalito, or Son of Mescalito, or Mescalito's dog. Throw him a tropical Hershey bar, somebody, or a salami rind, a pair of peanuts, a bag of Crunchy Granola, something, anything, quick! Got to appease them gods. This here's Mexico, you know, not Georgetown. Not Shaker Heights. Home of the taco bender, the bloody sacrifice, the gay *pistolero*. Give him a stick of jerky and take no chances. Then let's get the hell out of here.

And so we bid farewell to carefree, colorful, romantic Mexico. *Adiós, amigos*—and keep your flies with you.

We hang around the rim for another day, tramp back to the railway station, and ride the rails down through the tunnels, down through the terrific chasms of the western Sierra Madre to Los Mochis ("The Flies"), north to Nogales ("Walnuts") on the night train, cross through the Berlin Wall, and ride a bus back to Tucson and the Great Big Cafeteria of the North, counting our money.

I don't know. Take your choice. For my own part, I regard all these American nations with extremely moderate love. Best to stay in Wolf Hole, behind the Virgin Mountains, near Dutchman Draw and Pakoon Springs, the kind of place where an atavist belongs. The world is wide and beautiful. But almost everywhere, everywhere, the children are dying.

7. ON THE RIVER AGAIN

Big Bend, Texas

We are going to float by river—the Rio Grande—through the centerline of the borderlands, through the Santa Elena and Mariscal canyons, in Big Bend, with Mexico on the right bank, Texas on the left, freedom in the middle. Our guide and outfitter is Ken Sleight from Green River, Utah, one of the best of western river guides. Our oarsman is Kim Crumbo, a young Vietnam veteran with many river trips on the Colorado, the Green, and the Snake to his credit. Also coming along, for the fun of it, are Vaughn Short of Tucson and Susan Daniels of Moab, Utah; Jim and Marty McKnight of Salt Lake City; and John McComb, Southwest representative of the Sierra Club, and his wife Joanna.

We assemble at a trading post called Lajitas, at a point two miles outside the northwestern corner of Big Bend National Park. Launched on the river, our fleet is varied and colorful: My wife Renée, myself, and Short ride an eighteen-foot silver-painted pontoon boat of the type known as Green River, with

Crumbo at the oars; Sleight and Susan each row an orange plastic Sportyak, a kind of rowboat the size and shape of a bathtub; Jim, Marty, and McComb paddle kayaks; Joanna McComb paddles a bright yellow two-man inflatable raft. Mexicans watch from the riverbank, straddling the rumps of their burros. None of us except Sleight has been down this river before.

On the first day, beginning at noon, we float, paddle, and row toward the great uplifted fault block of cretaceous limestone known as Mesa de Anguila, through which the Rio Grande has cut Santa Elena Canyon. A considerable gorge: For most of its eighteen-mile length the canyon is 1,500 feet deep, about 500 feet wide at the rim, and in some places only 30 feet wide at river grade. Like most such canyons in the American Southwest, Santa Elena is what geologists term an "entrenched meander." The river was there first, winding toward the sea. Crustal movements in the mid-Cenozoic era raised the surface slowly, and as the ground rose the river, having no alternative, eroded its passage deeper and deeper into the rising rock. For the most part the walls are sheer, nearly vertical, with a terrace or setback halfway up. Under the zigzagging band of blue that canyoneers call the sky, the river flows red and brown at floodtime, in winter and spring a pea-soup green.

In late afternoon we approach the entrance to the canyon. The river winds through low hills of rock and gravel that support a sparse desert growth of cactus, mesquite, candelilla, agave. On either shore are jungles of water-loving phreatophytes—tamarisk, willow, bamboo. There are few cottonwoods in sight, or any other tree. Beyond this mixed foreground of river, thicket, and arid hills stands Mesa de Anguila, walls rising straight up from the foothills, a dark and barren plateau of inhospitable aspect. Until we come within actual sight of the canyon entrance, it is difficult to believe that the river flows into, rather than around, this formidable obstacle.

Anguila means "eel" in Spanish. Since it seems unlikely that eels ever inhabited this mesa in historical times, the name *anguila* is probably an Anglo corruption of the Spanish *aguila* ("eagle"). The eels are long gone; the eagles are still here.

We can see the portal now, a tall and narrow slot in the limestone walls, into which the river rushes in a turmoil of riffles, crashing over boulders fallen from the walls, pouring in slick green spillways between them. Running this first bit of white water without difficulty, we make Camp No. 1 on the sandy beach immediately below, just inside the opening of the canyon. We will hear the roar of complicated waters all night long, falling through our dreams. But we sleep good, and get up at dawn.

"I would rather wake up in the middle of nowhere," says the actor Steve McQueen, as quoted in an interview, "than in any city on earth." Amen.

We breakfast in the canyon, but still within sight of the outer, open world. An hour later the outer world is gone; we float on the dreamlike river down into a subterranean country of water and walls, with fluted gray limestone at the river's edge, tumbled boulders, banks of sand where the mesquite grows (leafing out in spring green), clusters of bamboo twenty feet tall, thorny acacia in golden bloom spicing the air with a fragrance like that of apple blossoms, everything illuminated by a soft, filtered, indirect, refracted light.

A tunnel of love, while it lasts. But soon we come to a rapid known as the Rockslide, and the day's work begins. The Rockslide looks at first like no more than a pile of rubble reposing against the wall on the Mexican side of the river. Just beyond, however, are boulders huge as bulldozers obstructing the current, with only the narrowest of gaps among them. The river is choked by this jumble of debris; the water finds its way through in a maze of drop-offs, boils, blind alleys, suckholes, and undercut walls. Many river parties have lost boats and equipment here; possibly lives as well. In high water the Rockslide is considered extremely dangerous and the Park Service (always concerned for our well-being) forbids boating at such times.

We beach our motley assortment of river craft on the American shore upstream from the Rockslide and climb above to reconnoiter. There is no easy way through. Some of the passageways are wide enough for canoe or kayak, but nothing bigger. We are going to have to maneuver the Green River pontoon edgewise through the openings or else deflate, fold, and portage it over the rocky shore around the rapids. We elect to attempt the former method.

McComb goes through first in his kayak, then Jim, both

making it safely without a spill, though the course looks peril-
ous. Marty capsizes, but rolls upright. None of the other boats
can get through. Crumbo maneuvers the big pontoon as far as
he can, to a point where it becomes wedged between boulders. One-third of the river roars through beneath the boat,
heaving under the rubbery bottom. We unload the boat, passing oars, duffel bags, ammo cans, food boxes, water jugs, shov-
els, ropes, Dutch oven, tents, tarpaulins, and other parapher-
nalia of a river expedition up the side of a slippery boulder to
its rounded summit, where baggage and passengers are un-
steadily perched.

The smaller boats—the two plastic Sportyaks and Joanna
McComb's raft—are passed from hand to hand over and across
the pontoon, lowered to the water below, and lined by rope
down to the next launching point. Now we climb to the top of
the boulder—barely enough room for our feet—and heaving on
the lines pull the pontoon boat onto its side and pull and push
it through the narrow opening. The boat is lowered, leveled,
reloaded. The operation sounds simple, but takes two hours.
Two hours to advance seventy-five yards.

Once beyond the Rockslide the course is easy, or at least
appears to be. There are places where the river, rushing into
grottos in the undercut cliffs, can overturn a boat or knock your
head off if you're not alert, but with foresight and effort, they
can be avoided. I discover for myself, when I trade places with
Sleight and take the oars of his Sportyak, that it is not enough
to drift along with the current. When the mainstream sweeps
you toward an overhang, you must row backward, across the
current, keeping a safe distance from the trap.

For the most part the voyage through the remainder of Santa
Elena Canyon is a dream, a lark, and a wonder. Down the river
in a fantastic echo chamber 1,500 feet deep, blue gray cliffs
above and the air full of swallows, the scent of flowers, the sound
of stillness, we glide and turn and row, silent with awe. The
current is swift but smooth, broken here and there, now and
then, by boils and crossrips, enough to keep things interesting.
Far off beyond the rimrock dark clouds gather—glints of lightning, distant thunder. A great blue heron flaps along before us,
alights, waits, takes off again, leading us on. A graceful bird, but
not too bright. Canyon wrens. Rustle of feet and claws in the dry

bulrushes on the bank. Lizards climb the walls. Hungry Mexican buzzards soar on the clouded sky.

We pause to explore tributary Fern Canyon, find hedgehog cactus and prickly pear about to bloom, a running stream, a dank cave with scarlet monkey flower and clusters of calcite crystals. Onward, down the river, we pass rusted canteens, torn boots, silver driftwood wedged in crannies in the stone at flood line. The limestone walls are veined with pegmatite and quartz; they gleam like polished marble. Twilight closes in on us, and with it a storm: time to seek a place to camp. We emerge abruptly from the mouth of Santa Elena as the rain begins to fall. We camp on the broad sandy beach at the side of Terlingua (*tres lenguas,* "three languages") Creek. Far to the northwest I can see lightning crashing among the clouds above Rough Run, Goat, Calamity, Crystal, and Javelina—feeder creeks to the Terlingua. Storms advance over Solitario Peak, Study Butte, Contrabando Mountain, and the Terlingua Monocline.

We build a fire in the rain, cook supper, pitch tents, and rig up shelter halves in a downpour. The rain abates to a steady drizzle; we stand around the fire singing foul songs, reciting unspeakable limericks, before drifting off one by one or two by two into the darkness. A troubled night; the rain resumes, heavier than before, and at dawn a flash flood comes rolling down the Terlingua—a thick mucous onrush of water, liquefied mud, silt, clay, bentonite, and diatomaceous earth that almost carries away the boats. Crumbo and Sleight, sleeping near the shore, rise in time to rescue most of our equipment, but a few items, including the fourteen-inch cast-iron Dutch oven, are swept away or buried under the muck.

Our morning camp looks like a disaster area. Sleight's Navy has suffered its first setback. Trees and bushes near the camp are soon draped with wet sleeping bags, mud-soaked garments. The sun comes out. All hands accounted for, we shove off onto the river. Yesterday the Rio Grande was pea-soup green; today it is the color of Terlingua soup: mustard yellow, nausea gray, slime lime. Today no one has the heart for water battles, not even McComb; the river looks thick enough to suffocate catfish. Maybe the Dutch oven simply floated away. The current is much faster.

Late in the morning we reach Castolon, where I'd once

begun a disastrous auto journey into the desert, many years before. We stop for early lunch, visit the Castolon store, and restock our drinking water and beer supplies. The river is rising rapidly, gaining momentum from the many floods that come from last night's storm. Unusual to see flash floods in March— but here they are. Sleight decides to take advantage of the speeded-up river and make the hard run through open desert to Mariscal Canyon, forty miles southeast. We begin a long day of steady rowing.

The sky is bright, half-clouded with towering thunderheads. The muddy river gleams like brass, like copper, *mucho calor,* under the sun. The waters foam past the jungles of willow on either shore. Often we catch a glimpse of startled beaver slipping down their mudslides ahead of us and hear the sharp *whack!* of their flat tails slapping the water. Except for birds, we see no other wildlife.

The flat country is overrun with half-starved Mexican cattle. They infest the thickets on both shores of the river and graze, browse, and trample the desert for miles into Big Bend National Park. Eating up our national heritage, as the boatman Kim Crumbo says. What to do about it? Stock the park with jaguars, mountain lions, and wolves, says Renée. Plant the river with alligators, crocodiles, piranhas, and hammerhead sharks, say I. But we well know that nothing will be done. The Mexican cattle, like the Mexican people, suffer from lack of the same thing: a good five-centavo contraceptive.

My turn at the oars of the big boat. I commence operations by getting caught in the current under willow trees overhanging the bank, nearly swamping the boat. Row across the current, I remind myself, when it pulls you toward the jungles. But some obstacles are unavoidable. I nearly collide with a herd of illegal cows swimming across the river; the big pontoon plows through the middle of the herd.

A mile behind, as we later learn, Vaughn Short in one of the Sportyaks is swept beneath the trees, tips the boat, and is forced to save himself by climbing out of the water into a big willow. Sleight rescues the boat and Short, but a case of Cerveza Superior and most of our kitchen gear is lost. A half quart of Old Crow also disappears, but is recovered, bobbing along in the current, half a mile below the accident.

For much of the afternoon we are so walled in by willow, salt cedar, and bamboo that we cannot see the desert beyond; it is as if we were cruising a canal through a Louisiana bayou. Then the river turns, the hogbacks of uplifted limestone rise from the water, and we gain far-ranging views of the Chisos Mountains and Mule Ear Peaks, the Mesa de Anguila and Sierra Ponce slowly receding to the northwest, the grand wall of Sierra del Carmen advancing from the east. Mariscal Mountain rises closer by, to the southeast, ten miles away, where the river carves its second big canyon in Big Bend. But we'll not get there today, despite the flood and the swift current.

We make camp after dark and cook supper in tin cans taken from the garbage sacks, eating from our drinking cups. A good meal. Any meals are good meals on a good river. A clear night, more stars, no floods: All hands sleep well and rise in the blue dawn for an early start.

The approach to Mariscal Canyon is sudden and dramatic. The mountain stands before you, 2,000 feet high, a wall of limestone directly blocking the course of the water. Absurd to think the river can go through that apparently monolithic mass. But it does. A sharp turn in the current, some muddy riffles, another turn, and the canyon is magically revealed—a dark defile in the mountain ten times higher than the river is wide. Into this shadowy cleft, as into a funnel, the Rio Grande pours.

We have hardly time for a look at the inside of this new canyon before we come to a roaring impediment called the Rockpile. (Not the Rockslide.) Ken Sleight, in the lead with his plastic bathtub, glides straight into it without hesitation. McComb follows in his kayak, then the McKnights, then Joanna in her raft and Susan in her Sportyak, then the rest of us in the pontoon with Crumbo at the oars. We get through without mishap.

A half mile further and we come to the second obstacle, a wide black boulder in the middle of the river with a five-foot gap on the left, a ten-foot gap on the right, and in the center, flowing over the boulder, a waterfall. This is the Squeeze. Though not so difficult as the Rockslide in Santa Elena Canyon, the Squeeze can be dangerous, for the current piles up against another rock about twenty feet beyond. Following Sleight's lead, we land all boats on the grassy beach above the Squeeze.

We find castaways on shore, two young men who'd tried to get through here in a rowboat. They hit a rock, were dumped, lost the boat and most of their supplies, and have been stranded here for three days without food. They are glad to see us.

We feed them, then explore the hermit's nest of wired-together bamboo poles somebody has built against the cliff on the Mexican side of the river. The hermit, whoever he may be, is not home this afternoon. It seems odd to find, in so remote a place, little statues of Jesus and the Buddha mounted on the rock, candlesticks, and a stack of moldy 1972 *Look* and *Life* and *Ladies Home Journal* magazines. An anchorite with mediocre tastes, that's about the best I can say for him. His icons of organized religion look out of place here, irrelevant and incongruous in the wilderness.

We go on into the Squeeze with the castaways, dropping without incident through the slot. There are no more rapids. We sail into the vast halls of the quiet canyon on a current smooth as glass. There is plenty of time to ship oars and paddles, lie back, gaze up at the towering walls, the trees perched far above on the rimrock, the swallows and bats flitting through the twilight. Mariscal and Santa Elena canyons are similar in origin, structure, and dimensions. Mariscal has more color in the rock, a little more plant life; it seems not quite so somber and silent and precipitous as Santa Elena. Since there is no need to choose, we find them both beautiful.

Last night in the canyons. We camp halfway through Mariscal at a transverse rift known as the Break. Ancient Indian trails lead through it from north to south. In historical times the Comanches crossed the river here, and today it is a favored crossing of contemporary smugglers of firearms, drugs, liquor, candelilla wax. The candelilla, boiled and rendered with sulfuric acid, yields a wax commercially valuable as a component in the manufacture of shoe polish, floor wax, candles, and phonograph records. In many places along the river, on the Mexican side, we have seen ricks of the candelilla stacked up to dry, and nearby the small steel vats and ovens used in the separation process.

We see no smugglers tonight. In fact, after a time, few of us see much of anything. One member of our party, Dr. Marty McKnight, is a lab technician and mad scientist; soon after supper she passes from hand to hand a laboratory flask of Harvey Wallbanger spiked with 170-proof alcohol; the genteel gathering around the campfire degenerates into hooliganism, madrigal, entropy.

Next morning we leave Mariscal Canyon, floating on a melancholy, slower river past the adobe ruins of a smugglers' motel, out into the open desert again. On a sand bar in the middle of the river, we find an aluminum canoe, battered and warped, but still buoyant. With a borrowed paddle and help from Renée, I negotiate the salvaged hulk the last ten miles downriver to our destination at San Vicente Crossing in the southeast corner of Big Bend National Park.

End of journey.

8. A WALK IN THE PARK

Canyonlands National Park in southeast Utah is one of the nation's newest national parks. Established in 1964 by Act of Congress, carved out of public lands formerly under the administration of the Bureau of Land Management, the park has been a source of controversy and hard feelings, regionally anyhow, since the Year One of its official existence.

Maybe we should have left the place to the cows, the coyotes, the turkey vultures, and the uranium miners. The miners—ah yes, there's the catch. With the Southwest plagued by another uranium rush, we can easily imagine what those Texas oil companies and Oklahoma drilling outfits would be doing to the Canyonlands if they had there, as they have most everywhere else, a free hand. One definition of happiness: watching a Texan headed home with an Okie under each arm. Undesirable elements, like plutonium and strontium.

Well, the "undesirable elements" are everywhere. We're all undesirable elements from somebody's point of view.

What really rankles the Utah business community, as it calls itself, is this: Having grudgingly consented—through their privately owned state politicians—to the creation of the new national park, the businessmen are embittered by the fact that Canyonlands, so far, has not been developed in the intensive, comprehensive style of Grand Canyon or Yellowstone. There is only one paved highway into the park, and it expires, near a place called Squaw Flat, into a forbidding jeep road. Nothing beyond but rock and sand, whiptail lizards, and skid plate grooves on the sandstone. For mass motorized traffic this is no better than a dead end. Unacceptable.

Furthermore, it now appears that back in the fifties and early sixties, when negotiations for the park were under way, the Interior Department made some kind of deal or "understanding" with the Utah congressional delegation—then as now the most primitive in America—that Canyonlands National Park would be fully developed for automobile tourism in the traditional grand manner, with hotels, motels, and visitor centers on panoramic headlands and a system of paved highways leading into and out of the park at different points. There is something in our automated American souls that cannot abide the dead-end drive; we demand that our scenic roads curve across the landscape in great winding loops, freeing us from the detestable necessity of motoring through the same scene twice.

Such roads have not been built—so far—at Canyonlands National Park. As a result the tourism business has not been nearly so expansive as local businessmen had expected. Remembering the promises made back in the sixties, they regard the failure to build the roads as a double cross by the Park Service. They are understandably outraged. The walkers, meanwhile, and the trail bikers and jeep herders continue to enjoy the park in their own relatively modest fashion, noisy enough at times, but on a scale of numbers too small to satisfy the great expectations of the Utah Chamber of Commerce.

This situation simmered along for a decade or so, changing little, the Park Service apparently ignoring its road-building promises, the commercial natives growing ever more restless. In the fall of 1977—after extensive public hearings—the Park Service released its Draft Management Plan for Canyonlands National Park. The plan makes no provision for the building of new roads within the park, although it does suggest an upgrading of at least one existent road. Citing a change in public attitudes to road building in the parks, the need for conservation of natural resources, and "irreversible environmental damage," the plan dropped completely a long-time pet project of Utah tourism developers: the proposed Confluence Overlook road.

The Confluence Overlook is a pile of sunburnt sandstone and limestone some 1,000 feet above a point in the heart of Canyonlands where the Green River from the north meets the Colorado River from the east. Here the two rivers merge to form the augmented master stream that used to be known as the Grand River. (At the insistence of Colorado politicians the Grand River became the Colorado River.) The point of the road proposal is this: If the Park Service could be persuaded to build a paved road to the Confluence Overlook, it would then be feasible, politically and economically, to continue the paved road south through the park to a junction with Utah State Highway 95 near Natural Bridges National Monument, thus completing the grand loop drive design so dear to the heart of its Utah promoters. A group that includes, naturally, not only the Chamber of Commerce but also the Utah State Highway Department. With a through-highway bisecting the park, the developers could hope to see an unbroken torrent of gas-guzzling Detroit machinery pouring through the Canyonlands. A river of gold. Waterfalls of money pooling behind the eager-beaver dams of commerce.

This great vision has been stalled, however, by public opposition to more road building in Canyonlands National Park. When the Park Service management plan became known, the tourism developers in Utah set their congressmen on the bureaucrats, with Representative Gunn McKay leading the pack. His insistent complaints led to a personal appearance in the town of Moab, Utah, heart of the heart of the canyon country, by William Whalen, President Carter's newly appointed director of the National Park Service.

After a briefing by local Park Service officials and a quick survey of the Canyonlands scene, the new director presented himself at a public meeting in Moab. Carefully noncommittal, promising only to reevaluate the road-building controversy, Whalen asked for comment from the crowd. He was followed by other officials and by Sam Taylor, editor of the local newspaper, all of them asking for thoughtful, reasonable, "nonemotional" suggestions for Whalen's consideration. (Those who get emotional about money are considered "practical.") These repeated requests for public opinion used up the first half hour of the one-and-a-half-hour meeting. When the men in business suits finally sat down to listen, it became apparent immediately that old rifts had not healed.

First to speak from the floor was Ray Tibbetts, a former cattleman, now a Moab realtor, uranium prospector, and clothing store owner, and a proud, outspoken conservative. ("What's wrong with being right?") As expected, he demanded more and better roads in the park. "We want the people of the world to see this beautiful country. . . . The present roads out there are a disgrace. . . . The working taxpayer [deliberate dig at nonworking eco freaks in the audience] is on a tight schedule and should be able to drive his car into his national park. He shouldn't have to put on a backpack to do it. I've lived here all my life and still haven't seen all the park." (Rude voice from the back of the hall: "That's because you never get out of your car." *Crude laughter.*) "The Park Service," Tibbetts went on, "is being infiltrated by the worst kind of radical environmentalists." *(Delighted laughter.)* "Let's put the parks back on a paying business basis. . . . We want everybody to visit them, not just the welfare backpackers." (Tibbetts sat down to a sitting ovation, mingled with hoots, jeers, and laughter from the grungy crew in the rear of the hall.)

Sam Taylor, acting as moderator, stood up to quiet the crowd, chiding certain elements for indecorous behavior. He then advanced his compromise solution to the problem of environmental damage. The Confluence Overlook road would necessitate a multi-million-dollar bridge over what is called Big Spring Canyon. Taylor proposed that the bridge be redesigned and lowered so it could not be seen from a distance. He also suggested that paved roads do less damage to a national park than foot trails, since motorists tend to buzz quickly through a park while hikers stray all over the place, lingering for days and polluting the countryside. (Unstructured activity.) This led to a demand by another pro-development speaker that backpackers be required by law to carry chemical toilets. The same man complained of too much "wildernessization" in southern Utah. Somebody read a letter from former Utah senator Frank Moss advocating more and better roads. It was a different Utah senator—Orrin Hatch—who once said to a friend of this reporter: "But Miss McElhenny, you're much too pretty to be an environmentalist.")

After a while the road opponents got in their say. The burden of their argument was that, since neighboring parks like Arches, Deadhorse Point, Natural Bridges, all in southeast Utah, have already been developed for motorized sightseeing it might be wise to let Canyonlands National Park remain in its relatively primitive condition. One little old blue-haired lady in heavy boots stood up to say that she no longer took friends to see Deadhorse Point, since the State Parks Commission had "ruined" it. Wild cheering from the rear.

Joe Stocks, a small miner (five foot eight), independent operator, and mining claims speculator, friend of the road builders, made a brief but moving plea. (Many moved out of the hall during his talk.) "When I was in the army," he said, "I carried an eighty-pound pack all over Georgia and Vietnam. I can't see much in this backpacking. . . . I've got a Mom and Dad in their seventies, and they don't have their health and they want to see Canyonlands. This confluence road is their only chance to see the confluence. . . . My ten- and twelve-year-old kids want to see it too, and they can't carry these backpacks. . . ."

So it went. The assembly broke up in total disarray. As usual, no minds were changed; many were hardened. William Whalen went back to his Park Service office in Washington presumably enlightened but less anxious than ever to make a decision. Either way he'll make few friends but plenty of hearty enemies. The bureaucrat's lot is not an easy one.

One thing positive emerged from the meeting. Joe Stocks's concluding remarks reminded my daughter Suzie and me that we had never seen the confluence of the Green and Colorado either and that if we were going to get there before Joe Stocks *en famille* we'd have to walk it. But could we do it? After the talk about the hardships of desert hiking, we were a little uncertain. My daughter Suzie is nine years old, a child by profession, slightly built, not the rugged outdoor type. I am forty-nine and a half years old (and will be for the next decade or two), beer-

bellied, broken-nosed, overweight, shakily put together, with a
bad knee—lost the cartilage years ago.

Could we do it? It's a good five miles from trailhead to trail's
end. The same coming back. I put the question to this kid of
mine.

"Isn't there a road?" she said. "Why do we have to walk?"

"Shut up," I explained, "and tie your shoes."

We climbed in our friend Frank Mendonca's pickup—he
would photograph the exploit—and drove out to the end of the
Squaw Flat "scenic drive." Drove a hundred miles in order to
walk ten. Anything to make a point.

The paved road ends abruptly on the very rim of Big Spring
Canyon; giant red and white warning barriers alert the motorist
to the terminus of the asphalt roadway. You see at a glance that
the road builders never meant to stop here. The foot trail begins
a few steps beyond. The sign says: Confluence Overlook 5.1
Miles, 8.1 Kilometers.

"Which is shorter?" I asked Suzie.

"Kilometers are shorter," she explained, "but there's more of
them."

We walked down into the canyon. A pretty place, cottonwoods leafing out in April greenery, the great red walls of sandstone standing vertically beyond them. Would take a lot of
blasting to ram a highway through here. The trail is a winding
path among the boulders, stepping down from ledge to ledge,
crossing beds of sand. Where the route looks doubtful, the way
is marked by small cairns.

We reached the bottom of the canyon, a few hundred feet
down from the parking lot. "How much farther?" Suzie wanted
to know. I guessed we had come about one-twentieth of a mile,
leaving 5.05 yet to go. "Yuck," she said. We started up the trail
on the other side. "This is the part I hate," she said, "this uphill
stuff."

We topped out on the rim beyond. Looking back, we could
see Frank's truck and a couple of other vehicles parked in the
circle at the end of the pavement. Beyond were the sandstone
monoliths of nearby buttes, then the mesas and plateaus, then
the snow-covered La Sal Mountains fifty miles away by line of
sight, twice that distance by road. Frank set up his tripod and

camera to make some pictures. Once again I gave thanks to my good sense in never getting hooked on photography. While he prepared his heavy, expensive, and elaborate equipment, I took a pen and notebook from my shirt pocket. As I say to my friends Eliot Porter, Ansel Adams, and Philip Hyde, one word is worth a thousand pictures. If it's the right word. The good word.

Two young hikers climbed past us, heavy-laden, panting too hard to do more than nod in greeting. A man and a woman, both wearing nylon track shorts. We watched them go on and out of sight. I made an unkind remark. "New Yorkers," I said.

"How do you know?" Frank asked.

"They both had hairy legs."

Suzie was kicking a bush. "What kind of bush is this?"

"Just an ordinary bush," I explained. "Stop kicking it around."

"But what do you call it?"

"We call it—single-leaf ash. But what it really *is* no man knows. No, nor woman neither. Leave it alone."

"I think it's yucky."

I pointed to a small, green, spiky plant nearby. *"That* is a yucca."

The sun came out of the morning clouds. Feeling gay as the day was bright, we marched on. We reached a high point on a stone ridge. An unobstructed view in all directions. We could see three separate mountain ranges, sublime with distance and snow and the patient grandeur of high, lonely places. In the middle ground, south, stood the labyrinth of sandstone spires called the Needles. Suzie thought they looked more like noodles. They have that coloring, we agreed. Close by, growing out of cracks in the rock, glowing under blackbrush and from behind hedgehog cactus, were clumps of Indian paintbrush. We tried to pin down their color. "Fiory orange," I suggested. "Day-Glo cadmium," said Frank, "with here and there a shade of burnt magenta." "Paintbrush red," said Suzie.

Onward. The footpath, maintained only by the feet of many walkers before us, as a national park trail should be maintained, followed little sandy drainages among patches of sand. Untrod by cattle for many years, the sand bore on its surface a type of dark primitive moss called cryptogam. Dry, crunchy, but alive, this humble plant is one of the first to begin the transformation

of bare sand into organic soil. (Don't step on the cryptogams!)
Growing on top of the cryptogams, carrying the earth-making
process forward, were clumps of gray and bluish lichens.

"Why do lichens always grow in bunches?" asked Suzie.

"Lichen attracts lichen. Symbiosis." We covered another half
mile trying to explain that term to her. I think she understood
it better than I do. We stopped in the shade of a juniper for
water and a snack. In her pack Suzie carried a quart of water,
an orange, a hunk of cheese, a jar of soy nuts, a chocolate bar,
spare socks, a sweater. I carried a gallon of water and more food.
Frank carried food, water, and the technology.

We went on, descending from the high rock into the first of
a series of grabens—long, narrow, parallel sinks in the ground
big as canyons, some of them with no outlet to the river only
a few miles away. The grabens are hot, dry, with little plant life,
rather dismal places compared with the slickrock gardens of
flowers and trees above. A century of overgrazing has not
helped.

Our footpath intersects the old jeep road leading to the Confluence Overlook. One mile to go. The trail brought us to the
rimrock above the rivers. We passed a Park Service warning
sign: Unfenced Overlook Ahead. Use Extreme Caution. Par-
ents, Control Your Children.

Suzie yelled with delight and sprinted forward. When Frank
and I arrived at the overlook point, we found Suzie waiting in
the shade of a boulder, her toes six inches from the edge of a
500-foot drop-off. It's all right; I'm used to it; we are both incurable acrophiliacs.

Down past the drop-off and a talus slope, 1,000 feet below, are
the two rivers confluencing. The Colorado comes in from the
great canyon on the right, the Green from the left. The
Colorado is chocolate brown today, the Green a muddy yellow.
The colors do not blend at the meeting point, but flow on for
several miles before becoming wholly a watery one. The division between the two is marked not only by the different colors
but also by a thin line of floating driftwood. The rivers are high,
in flood; a large beach near the confluence is completely under
water.

Frank takes pictures. Suzie and I eat lunch. The rivers make
no sound, sliding gently around the bend, flowing along side by

side. I hear ravens croak on the rim over yonder, on the other side, near that high point of rock that leads to the Maze, the Standing Rocks, Candlestick Spire, the Fins, the Black Ledge, the Orange Cliffs, Land's End. North of us stands Junction Butte and Grandview Point. Far off are the snowy mountains. Above is the same imperial blue sky that Major John Wesley Powell saw when he explored these canyons from the river in 1869. The same sky that sheltered one Captain J. N. Macomb over a century ago, when he stood where we are standing and wrote in his diary: "A more profitless locality than this can scarcely be imagined."

A sound of yodeling far below, echoing off the canyon walls. Two rubber rafts float into sunlight from the deep shade of the Green River's Stillwater Canyon, drift toward the confluence. We watch them pass slowly by until they go out of sight below the rimrock. Naked boat people floating with the stream, half-asleep in their reverie. Cataract Canyon, not far downriver, will wake them up.

After a long siesta under another comfortable juniper tree, we begin the walk back. "How far now?" asks Suzie. Still 5.1 miles, 8.1 kilometers. We make the return an easy stroll, with many stops for pictures and side explorations over the slickrock humps and into narrow corridors of stone where nothing grows but your sense of stillness. The enchantment of late afternoon in the desert retards our steps. We are loth, *loth to depart*—as old Walt Whitman said of his life.

"Maybe we should stay out here," I suggest to Suzie.

"But there's nothing to do."

"You're right. There's absolutely nothing that has to be done."

We were back at the road and Frank's truck before sundown. We drank a couple of cold beers while Suzie climbed up and down the barrier signs and practiced her cartwheels. Still bored and restless, that child. Next time I'll make *her* carry the big pack.

On the long drive home we interrogated the kid. "Look here, Suzie," we said, "should we let them build that bridge? Should we let them build their paved highway to the Confluence Overlook?"

"No," she said.

"But why not? What are you, some kind of elitist? How do you expect people to get in there if they don't have a good road?"

"They can walk."

"Suppose they're too old to walk? Too young? Too fat, thin, arthritic, decrepit, scared, ignorant, lazy, rich, poor, dumb? How about crippled war veterans who fought for their country —are you going to deny them the right to see the Confluence Overlook from the comfort and convenience of their Ford LTDs?"

"Everybody can't have everything."

"Is that so? You think you should have anything *you* want. If you can get it. Who do you think you are? Do you think you're better than most people?"

Suzie thought that one over for a moment. "Well," she said, "a little better."

9. DOWN THERE IN THE ROCKS

We're driving these two little boats down Lake Powell in Utah, Clair Quist and his girl friend Pamela Davis in one, me and Mark Davis in the other. Mark, Pam, and Clair are professional river guides, boatmen, characters, honest folk. They work for an outfit called Moki-Mac (or Murky Muck) Expeditions out of Green River, Utah. Work for it? Hell, Clair and his two brothers own the damn thing. Whatever it is. What it is, is one of the three or four best river-running outfits in the West.

Nobody's working today. This is a holiday outing for the four of us. Our goal is Escalante Canyon and its arboreal system of branch canyons. We're going by way of the so-called lake because we plan to explore a few side canyons, the mouths of which are now under water. Starting at Bullfrog Marina, our course takes us south-southwest past old familiar landmarks. Halls Creek Canyon, the south end of the Waterpocket Fold, the Rincon, the mouth of Long Canyon. Around that next bend will be the opening to the Escalante.

Bright blue above, the golden sun at high noon. On either side the red walls of what once had been—and will again be—Glen Canyon. No use fretting about it anymore. We throw our orange peels overboard to feed the fish. These hatchery fish will eat anything. Clair and Mark amuse themselves by steering as close as they can, without quite ramming them, to the buoys marking the channel. There's nothing much else to do out here on this smooth expanse of flat and stagnant water. Pam reads a book; I stare at the cliffs, and at the domes, plateaus, and mountains beyond, remembering what I sometimes wish I could forget: Glen Canyon as it was, the wild river, the beaches, the secret passages and hidden cathedrals of stone, the wilderness alive and sweet and charged with mystery, miracle, magic.

No use fretting. I throw my torn beer can into the lake, where it sinks and disappears. We clear the corner and plane up-canyon into the broad Escalante. Sheer, slick vertical walls of Navajo sandstone rising on either side, one wall in blue shadow, the other in radiant light. But nothing lives along those stone barriers; all that was living and beautiful lies many fathoms below, drowned in dead water and buried under slime. No matter. Forget it.

Cabin cruisers roar past; we wallow across their wakes. A houseboat like a floating boxcar comes toward us, passes. The people on board stare, then wave tentatively, unsure whether or not we, in our little open boats, deserve the dignity of recognition. That doesn't matter either. We wave back.

A few miles up the canyon we go ashore in a cove without a name. Others have been here before, as the human dung and toilet paper, the tinfoil, plastic plates, abandoned underwear, rusty fishhooks, tangled lines, discarded socks, empty Coors cans, and broken glass clearly attest. But on the shores of Lake Powell, Jewel of the Colorado and National Recreational Slum, you have no choice. All possible campsites look like this one. There is no lower form of life known to zoological science than the motorboat fisherman, the speedboat sightseer.

We have stopped here because we want to climb an old stockman's trail that leads to the rim from this vicinity. We tie the boats to a rock, load our packs, and ascend the humps of bare slickrock toward the skyline 800 feet above. Halfway up we find traces of the long-abandoned trail—wide, shallow steps chiseled in the sandstone, sufficient to enable a horse to climb or descend.

Over the rim, out of sight of the lake and its traffic, we make camp for the night. In the morning we march north and west over a petrified sea of stone waves, across sandy flats studded with juniper, yucca, single-leaf ash, scrubby Gambel oak, and up monolithic ridges that seem to lead right into the sky. Far beyond are the salmon pink walls of upper Stevens Canyon, the Circle Cliffs, and the incomprehensible stone forms, pale rose and mystical, of the great monocline known as Waterpocket Fold. We'll never get there; this is merely a reconnoiter, a scouting trip, and we're not even sure we want to get there. Perhaps a few places are best left unexplored, seen from a distance but never entered, never walked upon. Let them be, for now.

At some point out there, among a circle of sandstone mammaries hundreds of feet high, we find a deep groove in the endless rock. Down in the groove stands a single cottonwood tree, alive and golden with its October leaves. Alone in all these square miles of desolate grandeur, this dry Elysium, it is the tree of life. We find a way down to it, and sure enough, as we had hoped, we discover a series of deep potholes, some of them half-filled with sand, but others with water. Old rainwater, but clear and cool and heartening. We fill our jugs and bottles and camp nearby for a couple of days.

Campfire of juniper and scrub oak. The smell of coffee, the incense of burning wood. Vast, lurid sunsets flare across the sky, east as well as west, portending storm and winter, but we don't care. Showers of meteors streak across the field of the stars, trailing languid flames. An old, worn moon goes down as the rising sun comes out. In the chill mornings we make a breakfast and track off again in another direction. What direction? Any direction.

One afternoon we sit by a pool on the lip of stone that overhangs the head of one of the Escalante's many side canyons. The drop-off must be 1,000 feet straight down. Down . . . and . . . down and . . . down, your mind falls to the green pool in a sandy basin far below. Perennial springs flow there, under this overhanging spout we lie upon; we can see the glaze and glitter of a stream snaking through jungles of willow, box elder, redbud,

and Frémont poplar toward the Escalante River somewhere
beyond, hidden in its profound meanders.

We see a natural stone arch below, under the west wall, and
balanced rocks, free-standing pillars, pinnacles, alcoves, grottos,
half-dome amphitheaters. The pathways of many deer curve
with the contours of the talus slopes. A redtail hawk rides the
air, soaring *beneath* us. Ravens clack and croak and flap around,
quarreling over nothing. Over anything. Over nothing.

In the shallow pond at our side are hundreds of tadpole
shrimp, the grotesque, helmet-headed *Apus longicaudatus,*
swimming back and forth, pursuing one another, the large cap-
turing and devouring the small. They look like tiny horseshoe
crabs—or like miniature trilobites from the earliest seas of all,
come back to haunt us with the memory of the earth's long,
strange, splendid, and meaningless history. The spiral of time.
The circle of life. The vanity of death. The black hole of space.

The hot radiance of the sun, pouring on our prone bodies,
suffusing our flesh, melting our bones, lulls us toward sleep.
Over the desert and the canyons, down there in the rocks, a
huge vibration of light and stillness and solitude shapes itself
into the form of hovering wings spread out across the sky from
the world's rim to the world's end. Not God—the term seems
insufficient—but something unnameable, and more beautiful,
and far greater, and more terrible.

My friends and I touch one another, smiling, and roll a few
boulders into the canyon, only for fun, meaning no harm. We
listen, and when the bedrock stops trembling, and after the last
far-off echoes of our thunder die away, we shoulder our packs
and start the long tramp back to where we came from, wherever that was. It makes no difference. Willing or not, ready or
not, we'll get there.

Behind us, back at the canyon's head, the sun blazes down on
the shallow pool. The hooded grope things swim writhing
through the water. One thousand feet beneath, the spring continues to flow and the little stream to snake its shining way
through canyon jungle toward the hidden river. The hawk
soars, the ravens quarrel. And no man sees. And no woman
hears. No one is there. Everything is there.

POLEMICS
AND
SERMONS

10. SCIENCE WITH A HUMAN FACE

Science with a human face—is such a thing possible anymore? We live in a time when technology and technologists seem determined to make the earth unfit to live upon. According to C. P. Snow, scientists are happy in their work, especially when contrasted with poets, novelists, artists, philosophers, all those customarily lumped together in the category of the "humanities." The humanitarians? The term connotes self-mocking futility, reflecting accurately the trend and tempo of the age. But I want to ask Mr. Snow this question: "Sir Charles, sir, if the scientists, technicians, researchers, whatever you wish to call them, are so happy in their work and so pleased with the world they are creating, why are they also and at the same time so earnestly devising ever more efficient ways to blow it all to hell?"

The mad scientist, once only a comic figure in a specialized branch of fiction, has now come luridly to life in a hundred thousand forms. Together with his co-workers in big government, big industry, and the military, he dominates our lives.

United, they will tyrannize the planet. H. G. Wells, prophet and visionary, described the type exactly when he wrote: "Intelligences vast and cool and unsympathetic watched our world with envious eyes . . . and made their plans."

Of course, Wells called them Martians; we know today they are our own, sons of our fathers, the busy men with white smocks and clipboards who are planning our future. *For* us. "The World of Tomorrow—and You." And *you,* of course, are never consulted on the matter. Like the imaginary Martians in Wells's novel, the engineers and technicians have no interest in our personal preferences except as data to be tabulated and attitudes to be manipulated. They love us no more than we love them; and they certainly have no love for the earth. What is perhaps most sinister of all is the fact that in this worldwide drive to reduce all life, human and otherwise, to the limits of a technetronic system, there is not even a mind at work. Many brains, but no mind. Nor heart nor soul. There is no intelligence directing this enormous and enormously complex process; merely the cumulative efforts of thousands of specialists, experts, each sequestered in his tiny niche in the technological apparatus, each unaware of or indifferent to the investigations of all but his closest colleagues, each man in his way an innocent. How can we think of a man who spends years studying the behavior of hamsters in an electrified maze as anything but a harmless idiot? Yet the results of his study, combined with the studies of many other similar harmless idiots, may result in knowledge useful, let us say, to a central police agency concerned with the problem of controlling an urban populace in revolt.

And in the evening, after a fruitful day in the nausea-gas lab, the innocent scientist goes home to the arms of his wife and children and after supper plays with his model railroad in the rumpus room. As Hannah Arendt has pointed out, the most destructive men of our time are distinguished chiefly by the banality of their characters and private lives. Harry S Truman liked to boast that he had never lost a night's sleep over Hiroshima and Nagasaki; Lyndon Johnson and General Westmoreland, with the blood of hundreds of thousands of Vietnamese peasants and American adolescents on their hands, were perfectly capable of getting down on their knees every Sunday morning and praying to what they guilelessly believed is the God of Love. And Adolf Eichmann, as he correctly pointed out, was only following orders, as millions of other men have done for their respective "authorities"; the Nazi leaders were punished because they had the misfortune of ending up on the losing side. Political and military leaders win the publicity, but the fantastic crimes they have committed against humanity in this century were made possible for them by the achievements of our scientists and technologists.

What I have written so far will seem to sober-minded professors of the scientific method (the type I remember from my own student days) as an irrational and hysterical outburst of misapplied indignation. They will scarcely credit my insistence now that I am, despite the horrors of the twentieth century, fully in sympathy with the basic and traditional aim of science, which I define as the pursuit of knowledge. Knowledge—not power. That I think of men like Democritus, Galileo, Copernicus, Kepler, Newton, Lyell, Darwin, and Einstein as liberators of the human consciousness, intellectual workers whose insight and intelligence have expanded our awareness of existence infinitely more than all the pronouncements of all the shamans, gurus, seers, and mystics of the earth, East and West, combined. The simple telescope, for instance, has given us visions of a world far greater, lovelier, more awesome and full of wonder than that contained in an entire shipload of magic mushrooms, LSD capsules, and yoga textbooks.

But having made this disclaimer, I can only repeat the charge, itself a banality but no less true for being so, that science in our time is the whore of industry and war and that scientific technology has become the instrument of a potential planetary slavery, the most powerful weapon ever placed in the hands of despots. Nothing new in this discovery, of course; the poets, with their fine sensitivity to changes in the human weather, have been aware of the danger from the outset, for 200 years. It may even be the case that the situation has so far deteriorated that the only appropriate question now is whether or not technology will succeed in totally enslaving mankind before it succeeds in its corollary aim of destroying life.

In this general condemnation of the prostitution of science, we must allow exceptions. Many will assert that science, *true* science, cannot be held responsible for the aberrations of uncontrolled technology. Others will point out that some men of science, such as Linus Pauling, Leo Szilard, Karl Morgan, Otto Hahn, Norbert Wiener, and many of their younger students in the universities have been among the first to attempt to organize resistance to the technological culture, both in America and in the Soviet Union. The latter statement is unquestionably true but, so to speak, not true enough; the defenders of freedom and sanity among professional scientists have been far outnumbered by the Herman Kahns, Glenn Seaborgs, Hans Bethes, Edward Tellers, and Dr. Barnards ("the operation was a success although—sorry—the patient died") of the scientific world.

Is science responsible for the perversions of technology? To what extent can science and technology be separated and distinguished from one another? Can either exist independently of the other? These are intricate questions of history, method, and practice that I am not competent to answer with more than this diffident opinion, humbly offered: Pure science is a myth; both mathematical theoreticians like Albert Einstein and practical crackpots like Henry Ford dealt with different aspects of the same world; theory and practice, invention and speculation, calculus and metallurgy have always functioned closely together, feeding upon and reinforcing each other; the only difference between the scientist and the lab technician is one of degree (or degrees)—neither has contributed much of value to our understanding of life on earth except knowledge of the means to destroy both. Einstein is reputed to have said, near the end of his career, that he would rather have been a good shoemaker than what he was, a great mathematician. We may take this statement as his confession of participatory guilt in the making of the modern nightmare.

The denunciation of science-technology that I have outlined here, simple-minded and oversimplified though it may undoubtedly be, should be taken seriously at least as an expression of the fear and detestation millions now feel for the plastic-aluminum-electronic-computerized technocracy rapidly forming around us, constricting our lives to the dimensions of the machine, divorcing our bodies and souls from the earth, harassing us constantly with its petty and haywire demands. What most humans really desire is something quite different: liberty, spontaneity, nakedness, mystery, wildness, and wilderness.

In such a climate of thought and emotion it is not surprising that a large-scale revolt against not only science but even reason itself is under way in Europe and the United States. Because of the filth, ugliness, slavery, and mass murder it has engendered, the scientific-technological establishment faces a deep-seated reaction against the whole Western tradition of rational thought, which is (or was) the foundation of science. The addicts of the occult and the Eastern religions have always been among us, but probably never before have so many abandoned realism and naturalism and rushed to embrace the fantasies of astrology, the life weariness of Buddhism, the world negation of Hinduism, the doper's heaven of institutional Christianity. As an antidote to a poisonous overdose of technology and crazy rationality, I can understand why so many of the spiritually tired have switched to Zen, om, I Ching, and tarot. As an approach to effective resistance against the on-coming tyranny of the machine, however, these worn-out doctrines and obscure little magics will prove as futile as the machine can prove fatal. In fact, there is no reason why psychedelics and occultists, for example, and the most sophisticated technetronic system cannot comfortably coexist—the former inside the latter. They do; and they will. I find it pathetic as well as ironic to see the enthusiasm with which hairy little gurus from the sickliest nation on earth are welcomed by the technological idiots of all-electric California.

In this embrace of easily reconcilable opposites I wish to stand apart, alone if need be, and hold up the ragged flag of reason. Reason with a capital R—Sweet Reason, the newest and rarest thing in human life, the most delicate child of human history. Reason without technology, if that seems best; reason without science, if that seems necessary. By "reason" I mean intelligence informed by sympathy, knowledge in the arms of love. (For knowledge without conscience is the ruin of the soul, sayeth the Proverb—and the oldest wisdom is usually most reliable.) By "reason" I mean fidelity to what alone we really know and really must love—this one life, this one earth on which we live. I find myself equally opposed to the technological mania of the West and the occult morbidity of the East: Both are the enemies of reason, and of life, and of the earth.

The scientist is accused of the reductionist fallacy when he identifies a thing with its constituent elements, saying that a rock, for example, is *nothing but* a certain slow-moving system of molecular particles. But his mystagogical opposites are guilty of the same fallacy when they personify the world, or things within that world, and identify the sun or trees or a river with aspects of human personality. To look at nature in that way is to reduce it to the dimensions of the human intellect—to make it small indeed. Both approaches are fallacious; both exemplify a poverty of the imagination.

The orthodox scientific view reduces the world to measurable and predictable units, to that which can be charted, graphed, statistically analyzed; the traditional religious or mystical view reduces the world to a reflection of human, anthropomorphic desires and intuitions. Both have in common the psychological compulsion to scale down the world to humanly comprehensible limits, and both have in common, also, at their most profound level, the tendency to think of the world as essentially (and only) a *process* that lies beyond direct sensory perception. At this point the Yogi and the physicist come close together, and both, I would like to suggest, are mistaken. Mistaken, that is, insofar as either insists on the fallacy that existence, nature, the world, is *nothing but* the flow of process, and that the beings of this life whom we know and love—a woman, a child, a place, a tree, a rock, a cloud, a bird, the great sun itself—are mere ephemera, illusory shadows, nothing.

They are wrong. Even a rock is a being, a thing with character and a kind of spirit, an existence worthy of our love. To disparage the world we know for the sake of grand verbal abstractions, whether they are called mesons and electrons or the vibrations of an endlessly slumbering and reawakening Brahma, is to be false to the mother who sustains us. The highest treason, the meanest treason, is to disavow and deny this lone but gracious planet on which we voyage through the cold void of space. Only a fool, milking his cow, denies the cow's reality. Be true to the earth, said Nietzsche.

For what do we really know? I think of a lightning-blasted but still living shagbark hickory in the pasture back home on my father's farm in Pennsylvania; I think of a twisted juniper on a ledge of sandstone at Cape Solitude, far above the Colorado River; I think of the pelicans that sail along the shores of the Sea of Cortez; I think of a thousand other places I have known and loved, east and west, in North America and Australia and Europe, and all the creatures great and small that live there—each a part of a greater whole, but each an individual as well, one and unique, never to be known again, here or anywhere, each as precious as the vivid moment in which it first appeared on earth.

Don't talk to me about other worlds, separate realities, lost continents, or invisible realms—I know where I belong. Heaven is home. Utopia is here. Nirvana is now.

Walking up the trail to my lookout tower last night, I saw the new moon emerge from a shoal of clouds and hang for a time beyond the black silhouette of a shaggy, giant Douglas fir. I stopped to look. And what I saw was the moon—the moon itself, nothing else; and the tree, alive and conscious in its own spiral of time; and my hands, palms upward, raised toward the sky. We were there. We *are*. That is what we know. This is all we can know. And each such moment holds more magic and miracle and mystery than we—so long as we are less than gods—shall ever be able to understand. Holds all that we could possibly need— if only we can see. There are no further words.

11. THE RIGHT TO ARMS

If guns are outlawed
Only outlaws will have guns.
(True? False? Maybe?)

Meaning weapons. The right to own, keep, and bear arms. A sword and a lance, or a bow and a quiverful of arrows. A crossbow and darts. Or in our time, a rifle and a handgun and a cache of ammunition. Firearms.

In medieval England a peasant caught with a sword in his possession would be strung up on a gibbet and left there for the crows. Swords were for gentlemen only. *(Gentlemen!)* Only members of the ruling class were entitled to own and bear weapons. For obvious reasons. Even bows and arrows were outlawed—see Robin Hood. When the peasants attempted to rebel, as they did in England and Germany and other European countries from time to time, they had to fight with sickles, bog hoes, clubs—no match for the sword-wielding armored cavalry of the nobility.

In Nazi Germany the possession of firearms by a private citizen of the Third Reich was considered a crime against the state; the statutory penalty was death—by hanging. Or beheading. In the Soviet Union, as in Czarist Russia, the manufacture, distribution, and ownership of firearms have always been monopolies of the state, strictly controlled and supervised. Any unauthorized citizen found with guns in his home by the OGPU or the KGB is automatically suspected of subversive intentions and subject to severe penalties. Except for the landowning aristocracy, who alone among the population were allowed the privilege of owning firearms, for only they were privileged to hunt, the ownership of weapons never did become a widespread tradition in Russia. And Russia has always been an autocracy—or at best, as today, an oligarchy.

In Uganda, Brazil, Iran, Paraguay, South Africa—wherever a few rule many—the possession of weapons is restricted to the ruling class and to their supporting apparatus: the military, the police, the secret police. In Chile and Argentina at this very hour men and women are being tortured by the most up-to-date CIA methods in the effort to force them to reveal the location of their hidden weapons. Their guns, their rifles. Their arms. And we can be certain that the Communist masters of modern China will never pass out firearms to *their* 800 million subjects. Only in Cuba, among dictatorships, where Fidel's revolution apparently still enjoys popular support, does there seem to exist a true citizen's militia.

There must be a moral in all this. When I try to think of a nation that has maintained its independence over centuries, and where the citizens still retain their rights as free and independent people, not many come to mind. I think of Switzerland. Of Norway, Sweden, Denmark, Finland. The British Commonwealth. France, Italy. And of our United States.

When Tell shot the apple from his son's head, he reserved in hand a second arrow, it may be remembered, for the Austrian tyrant Gessler. And got him too, shortly afterward. Switzerland has been a free country since 1390. In Switzerland basic national decisions are made by initiative and referendum—direct democracy—and in some cantons by open-air meetings in which all voters participate. Every Swiss male serves a year in the Swiss Army and at the end of the year takes his government rifle home with him—where he keeps it for the rest of his life. One of my father's grandfathers came from Canton Bern.

There must be a meaning in this. I don't think I'm a gun fanatic. I own a couple of small-caliber weapons, but seldom take them off the wall. I gave up deer hunting fifteen years ago, when the hunters began to outnumber the deer. I am a member of the National Rifle Association, but certainly no John Bircher. I'm a liberal—and proud of it. Nevertheless, I am opposed, absolutely, to every move the state makes to restrict my right to buy, own, possess, and carry a firearm. Whether shotgun, rifle, or handgun.

Of course, we can agree to a few commonsense limitations. Guns should not be sold to children, to the certifiably insane, or to convicted criminals. Other than that, we must regard with extreme suspicion any effort by the government—local, state, or national—to control our right to arms. The registration of firearms is the first step toward confiscation. The confiscation of weapons would be a major and probably fatal step into authoritarian rule—the domination of most of us by a new order of "gentlemen." By a new and harder oligarchy.

The tank, the B-52, the fighter-bomber, the state-controlled police and military are the weapons of dictatorship. The rifle is the weapon of democracy. Not for nothing was the revolver called an "equalizer." *Egalité* implies *liberté*. And always will. Let us hope our weapons are never needed—but do not forget what the common people of this nation knew when they demanded the Bill of Rights: An armed citizenry is the first defense, the best defense, and the final defense against tyranny.

If guns are outlawed, only the government will have guns. Only the police, the secret police, the military. The hired servants of our rulers. Only the government—and a few outlaws. I intend to be among the outlaws.

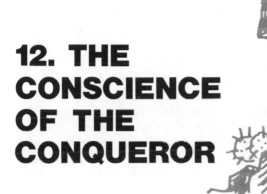

12. THE CONSCIENCE OF THE CONQUEROR

If, as some believe, the evolution of humankind is the means by which the earth has become conscious of itself, then it may follow that the conservationist awakening is the late-flowering *conscience* of that world mind. A vainglorious exaggeration? Not at all, if in conservation we can see a logical extension of the traditional Christian ethic—and that of the other world religions—beyond narrowly human concerns to include the other living creatures with whom we share this planet. Not only those obviously beneficial to us, but even those that might appear to be competitors, even enemies. The broadening of the ethic cannot stop at this point; once we become generous enough in spirit to share goodwill with living things, we can advance to the nonliving, the inorganic, to the springs, streams, lakes, rivers, and oceans, to the winds and clouds, even the rocks that form the foundation of our little planet.

All is one, say the mystics. Well, maybe. Who knows? Some of us might prefer to stress the unique, the individual, the diversity of things. But it now seems well proven that all things,

133

animate and inanimate, living and (as we say) nonliving, are clearly interdependent. Each form of life needs the others. We see ourselves, the human race, as the apex of a pyramid of life, the point of it all—and not without justice. Through humanity the earth finds its voice. But we in turn are merely raw material for others; the microorganisms that thrive in our bodies while we live, the bacteria that feast on our flesh after death, the plants that draw nutriment from our bones would be entitled to believe that God created the human race to serve their needs. The very concept of a special creation should give pause to those Christians who hold the view, still widespread and dominant in our society, that everything on earth exists for the sake of man.

This is not to say that the Peaceable Kingdom can or ever should exist on earth. Conflict within and between species is inevitable, necessary, and up to an optimum point, desirable. When the lion lies down with the lamb, it must be for the purpose of sharing a dinner, a dinner in which one eats and the other is eaten. Otherwise the lion would starve to death. The lamb itself eats grass, those green, tender, delicate beings with who knows what fine emotions and refined aspirations of their own. The moralistic vegetarian is a hypocrite; no self-respecting herbivore would share such a doctrine for a moment.

Competition within the species is likewise desirable—to a point. An absolute leveling of men and women would reduce humankind to the status of the social insects; good enough for ants, bees, and termites, but inappropriate to our kind and a serious injustice to those among us with the special qualities and abilities that give variety, vigor, zest, progress (yes, there is such a thing as progress), and finally glory to the human enterprise. Any Utopia, any Golden Age of Unlimited Power and Plenty, whether mythical, pastoral, or technological, where the needs and pleasures of life can be obtained without effort, would be a world of insufferable boredom, downgrading humans to the sloth and torpor of swine in a luxury sty; unworthy of us, the death of our nature.

Nevertheless, the opposite course leads to an equally fatal result. Unlimited struggle within a species would destroy that species; the human race has now reached a stage in its clever- ness where, for example, we can continue to have war or science, but no longer both. The industrial way of life implies the risk of mass-produced death.

Nor are we wrong to strive for justice within a society, the fair division of wealth, charity toward the weak, the old, the foolish. Stand up for the stupid and crazy, said Whitman. Amen. The mad may be saints, the crippled may be artists, magicians, craftsmen. Human society is based on mutual aid, cooperation, sharing—without those attributes it would perish. Will perish.

What the conscience of our race—environmentalism—is trying to tell us is that we must offer to all forms of life and to the planet itself the same generosity and tolerance we require from our fellow humans. Not out of charity alone—though that is reason enough—but for the sake of our own survival as free men and women. Certainly the exact limits of what we can take and what we must give are hard to determine; few things can be more difficult than attempting to measure our needs, to find that optimum point of human population, human development, human industry beyond which the returns begin to diminish. Very difficult; but the chief difference between humankind and the other animals is the ability to observe, think, reason, experiment, to communicate with one another through language; the mind is our proudest distinction, the finest achievement of our human evolution. I think we may safely assume that we are meant to use it.

What are the alternatives to reason and the conservationist conscience? There seems to be only one: go on as we are going now, submitting to the blind growth of human domination over the planet, the mindless increase in population, the greed and gluttony of the rich nations, the desperate need of the poor, leading in turn to one of the two most probable resolutions.

First, an intensification of the conflicts within each nation and among the nations as the competition for dwindling natural resources becomes more severe. We can see early symptoms of this conflict in the United States, where industrialists have begun to recognize conservationists and environmentalists— not labor leaders, not government, not Marxists—as their chief antagonists in shaping the character of the American future. Business leaders have succeeded already in creating an unjustified hostility between elements of organized labor and the environmental movement. This conflict can be resolved only in a society based on a mature, stabilized political economy that functions so smoothly we can take its health for granted, becoming aware of pain only when something is going wrong. The endless-growth economy, contrary to orthodox belief, is a diseased economy.

If efforts at internal reconciliation fail, if the environmental movement fails, we will see conflict increase, becoming more bitter as classes, factions, ethnic groups, and races compete with one another for as much as each can take from what economic wealth remains available in North America. In the course of the struggle luxuries such as wilderness and wildlife, public lands, and personal freedoms will begin to vanish, as they have already largely vanished from most of Europe, Asia, Africa, and South America. At the same time the competition among the nations will drive all closer to the edge of war, with each nation seeking to promote its own economic growth in the only way it can: at the expense of other nations. The result will be, as history demonstrates with tedious repetition, war and civil war, accompanied by famine, plague, and the descent, once again, into another dark age.

So much for the familiar and popular disaster hypothesis. The second possible outcome of population growth and industrial growth would be the creation of a planetary technocracy, a technological superstate in which we surrender our individual lives to some kind of international, computerized, scientifically engineered despotism. In a planetary order combining the best features of Huxley's *Brave New World,* Orwell's *1984*, and Stanislaw Lem's *The Futurological Congress,* we can imagine the transformation of Spaceship Earth into an orbiting food machine, automatically processing rock, air, seawater, and sewage into snack packets for a population of 10 billion drug-pacified, comatose, semihuman inhabitants. *They*—the technologists— say it can be done. But who wants to live in their world?

Commonplace nightmares. Perhaps we will find a way to muddle through and between the gruesome horns of our dilemma. The American nation (including Alaska) is one of the few places left on earth where it is still feasible to make a stand against the growth fanatics, the graph-paper mentality of the GNP economists, the replenish-and-forever-multiply theology of the Latter-Day Native-American Yahoo Church—all the descendants of those hordes of avaricious peasants (our forefathers) who swarmed across the Atlantic to fall, like a plague of locusts, upon the sweet, lovely, defenseless, virgin lands of America.

In any case, America offers what may be our final opportunity to save a useful sample of the original land. It is not a question merely of preserving forests and rivers, wildlife and wilderness, but also of keeping alive a certain way of human life, a wholesome and reasonable balance between industrialism and agrarianism, between cities and small towns, between private property and public property. Here it is still possible to enjoy the advantages of contemporary technological culture without having to endure the overcrowding and stress characteristic of this culture in less fortunate regions. If we can draw the line against the industrial machine in America, and make it hold, then perhaps in the decades to come we can gradually force industrialism underground, where it belongs, and restore to all citizens of our nation their rightful heritage of breathable air, drinkable water, open space, family-farm agriculture, a truly democratic political economy. Why settle for anything less? And why give up our wilderness? What good is a Bill of Rights that does not include the right to play, to wander, to explore, the right to stillness and solitude, to discovery and physical freedom?

Dreams. We live, as Dr. Johnson said, from hope to hope. Our hope is for a new beginning. A new beginning based not on the destruction of the old but on its reevaluation. It will be the job of another generation of thinkers and doers to keep that hope alive and bring it closer to reality. If lucky, we may succeed in making America not the master of the earth (a trivial goal), but rather an example to other nations of what is possible and beautiful. Was that not, after all, the whole point and purpose of the American adventure?

13. MERRY CHRISTMAS, PIGS!

Scrooge was right. What I like best about Christmas in the desert is the conspicuous absence of Christmas. By late December the cone-nosed humbugs are gone and all the horny elf toads retired into their burrows for the season. When somebody asks me what I think of Christmas (nobody ever does), I reply, "Not much." Easy to avoid it out here in the rocks.

Think about Ebeneezer Scrooge and Bobby Riggs, the twin patron saints of us middle-aged cryptoliberals. Cryptoliberal? Well, sure, why not? I have been called other names even worse. Misanthrope. Sexist. Elitist. Crank. Barbarian. Anarchosyndicalist. Wild conservative. And my favorite, from a Maoist lady in New York—she called me a creeping Fascist hyena. Quite true, so far as it goes (you can't please everybody), but they forget to add that I am a pig lover too.

The pig I'm talking about is the one known also as peccary or javelina, the wild pig of the Arizona desert; not a true pig exactly, according to zoologists, but a good approximation—a close relation. Close enough for me, and the javelina, commonly defined as "a wild piglike animal," is the best kind of pig. Though that definition, come to think of it, is a shade too broad. Some of my best friends qualify as wild piglike animals without half trying. But that's another issue. The fault of the permissive social atmosphere, the Bill of Rights, the general weakening of moral fibers everywhere you look.

Back to my topic: Christmas and wild pigs. Have you ever stood alone under the full moon in the prickly cholla-mesquite desert on the night before Christmas and found yourself surrounded by a herd of hungry, snuffling, anxiety-ridden javelinas? I have, and it's a problematic situation: Some of those little fifty-pound beasts carry tusks and have been known to charge a full-grown man right up the hairy trunk of a saguaro cactus. That's the story I've been told by old-timers around here.

In any case, this part is true. I was surrounded by javelinas while O'Ryan chased the Seven Sisters around the Big Bear and the moon looked kindly down. To say that I was nervous would be an overexaggeration. Though unarmed and on foot, I was happy, at ease, and comfortably drunk.

The herd of javelinas was aware of my presence. The mind of a wild pig is unpredictable. These couldn't make up their minds whether to run or stay. After a while, since I made no move, they stayed. I could see them plain in the bright moonshine: parody pigs with oversize heads and undersize hams, each one bristly as a wire brush. They trotted from bush to bush and cactus to cactus, anxious restive fellows, all fits and starts, busy, busy. I was accepted, but not welcome; they hoped I wouldn't stay. As I watched, I heard the sound of their vigorous jaws at work—a crunching of jojoba nuts, the munching of prickly pear. In all nature there's no sound more pleasing than a hungry animal at its feed. Ask any cattleman or farmboy

Down by Aravaipa Creek I heard the barking of a fox. An owl called. Everybody out shopping for supper.

There was a good strong odor in the air, the rank and racy musk of half-alarmed javelinas. I like that smell, just as I enjoy the smell (at a comfortable distance) of a skunk out looking for trouble. Associations: The wild tang of skunk brings back October nights, raccoons and baying hounds, the big woods and foggy hills of Old Pennsylvania. That smell means Arizona too: a border wolf, a desert bighorn, a mountain lion crouched on a ledge above the deer path in the chaparral. Good smells, good things, important, hard to find on Speedway Boulevard in Tucson or Central Avenue up in Phoenix.

Now and then one of the larger javelinas, suffering from curiosity, would come close to me, sniff, advance, and retreat, trying to figure out exactly what this thing is that stands there like a bush but breathes, smells like Jim Beam, moves a little. Suspicious; from time to time a ripple of panic passed through the herd like a wave through water. They knew something was wrong, but didn't know what. One minute they're on the point of exploding in all directions, pig fashion. A minute later and they forget the danger, start feeding again.

Then what happened? An angel came down from the stars in a long white robe to give us a lecture on the meaning of Christmas? No. I'll admit I have a weakness for simple fact, even if it spoils the story. Maybe that's the main difference between a serious literary artist like me and one of your ordinary sports columnists, say, who writes for the newspaper. But I don't want to make any hard judgments here; this is supposed to be the season of goodwill toward people. Sports columnists too. And wild pigs.

As my hero Ebeneezer says, if the spirit of Christmas is more than humbug then we're obliged to extend it to all creatures great and small including men, women, children, foreigners, Mexicans, coyotes, scorpions, Gila monsters, snakes, centipedes, millipedes, termites, and the wild pigs of the Arizona desert. That's the reason the Arizona Game and Fish Department puts off javelina season until January. Out of a decent respect for that annual outburst of love and goodwill we call Christmas.

As for the herd of javelinas snorting around me, the truth is, nothing much of anything happened. In fact, I got bored first, tired of simulating a saguaro cactus. I picked up a couple of rocks, in case one of those husky boars with the tusks came at me, and tiptoed off through the prickly pear. I did not wish to disturb my friends, but they took alarm anyway, erupting in various directions. Would take them an hour to reassemble. None charged me. Despite many meetings with javelinas, I have yet to come eyeball to eyeball with one. Even though I've charged *them* a few times, out of meanness, just to see them run.

If I were good and hungry, would I eat a javelina? Yes. I'd roast its head in a pit of mesquite coals and scramble my eggs with its brains. I have no quarrel with any man who kills one of God's creatures in order to feed his women and children and the old folks. Nothing could be more right and honorable, when the need is really there. I believe humanity made a serious mistake when our ancestors gave up the hunting and gathering life for agriculture and towns. That's when they invented the slave, the serf, the master, the commissar, the bureaucrat, the capitalist, and the five-star general. Wasn't it farming made a murderer out of Cain? Nothing but trouble and grief ever since, with a few comforts thrown in here and there, now and then, like bourbon and ice cubes and free beer on the Fourth of July, mainly to stretch out the misery.

Sermons aside, the javelinas and I parted company that moonlight night with no hard feelings, I hope, on either part. They had the whole east slope of Brandenburg Mountain to ramble over, and I had my cabin to crawl back into, where I keep my bearskin and this neurotic typewriter with a mind of its own. Christmas or no Christmas, it does my chilly Calvinist heart a lot of good to know those javelinas are still out there in the brush, pursuing happiness in their ancient piglike manner. What would Arizona be without a Game and Fish Department? Without a Sportsmen's Association? Hard to say. I wonder. But what would Arizona be without wild pigs? Why, no wonder at all. Arizona would be another poor, poached, puny, poverty-struck antheap like California, not fit for a man or his dog.

Happy Christmas, brother and sister. Long live the weeds and the wilderness. Merry New Year, pigs!

14. THE WINNEBAGO TRIBE

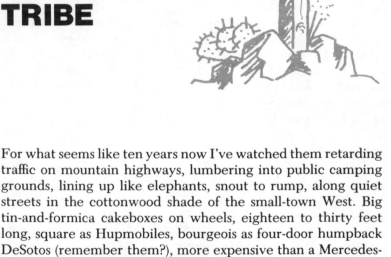

For what seems like ten years now I've watched them retarding traffic on mountain highways, lumbering into public camping grounds, lining up like elephants, snout to rump, along quiet streets in the cottonwood shade of the small-town West. Big tin-and-formica cakeboxes on wheels, eighteen to thirty feet long, square as Hupmobiles, bourgeois as four-door humpback DeSotos (remember them?), more expensive than a Mercedes-Benz with solid gold valve tappets—that's your Winnebago Motor Home. Together with its many imitations and look-alikes, the Winnebago tribe seems on some days to be all over the landscape, multiplying like maggots.

Those of us whose idea of camping still involves the antique notion of a frypan full of bacon and beans held by hand over a wood fire, a sleeping bag unrolled on the ground, for shelter in rainy places a tarp slung over a line between two trees, have naturally tended to laugh at the bumbling Winnebagos. We feel only pity and scorn for the poor souls behind the pale faces peering through the tinted picture windows. That's camping? What has a Winnebago to do with camping? We always thought, and rightfully so, too, that you'd get closer to the natural world living in a cold-water railroad flat in Hoboken, New Jersey; there at least the wildlife is real, scrambling over the teacups in the cupboard, crawling under the wallpaper, stampeding for safety when you light the oven, dodging your fist, your foot, your rolled-up newspaper when you try to launch a counter-attack. (I can still hear, in my dreams, the *banzai* cries of charging cockroaches coming at me across the rolling plains of the kitchen linoleum.)

Why the very sight of a Winnebago is ridiculous. Look at them, blundering down the asphalt trails of a hundred national parks, most of them loaded and overloaded not only with Mom and Pop and seven kids, but also with a motor launch on the upper deck, a brace of trail bikes strapped to the rear, a Jeep or a Bug or an Opel or some such small auxillary motorcraft towed behind. Hilarious and pathetic, these pastel-painted barges of the Interstate Freeway System. Last summer, at Glacier National Park in Montana, one of these monsters side-swiped a rock wall on the park's famous Going-to-the-Sun Highway and jammed shut its only door. An ultramodern air-conditioned unit, like most of them, it had no openable windows big enough to pass a human body. To rescue the family trapped inside, the rangers had to pry the door open with crowbars. Some of us, when we heard about it, laughed ourselves sick.

I mean—sick. And then one day in the fall, pausing at a campground along the Colorado River, I talked with the owner and operator of a genuine twenty-two-foot Winnebago. She was a widow, sixty-five years old, sweet, plump, white haired, healthy and happy looking, sitting in the shade of her motor home and knitting something for a distant grandchild. We talked, and I learned. When her husband, a Montana farmer, died six years ago, she rented out her house near Billings, the one nailed to its foundation in what had been her family's community for a century, bought herself a metal and plastic Winnebago with the old man's insurance money, and trundled off into nomadism. For her, the Winnebago is not a vacation vehicle but a home. Period. Nor does she any longer *take* vacations; she is always on vacation. "I'll never shovel snow again for as long as I live," she said.

Like a bird, she spends her summers up north, her winters down south, and the intermediate seasons in between. She avoids the big cities and the heavy traffic. She stops wherever and whenever she feels like it, never spending more than two months in any one place. Doesn't she miss her old home? "Never," she said. "Wherever I go now, there's my home." Lonely? Not at all. When she wants to, she visits relatives; the rest of her time she travels and camps with other elderly nomads, a circle of gypsy friends she has formed in the past few years. "It's a nice way to live," she said, "but don't tell the world about it." She smiled at me. "We can't have everybody doing this, you know."

PERSONAL HISTORY

15. MY LIFE AS A P.I.G., OR THE TRUE ADVENTURES OF SMOKEY THE COP

The Smokey we're talking about is not the natty chap in the sharp sombrero, bane of truck drivers, who lurks behind billboards along the Interstate. No, the one under discussion here is the fellow in the suit of forest green who hands you the ticket, leaning out of his box office, when you buy your admission to Yosemite, Grand Canyon, Yellowstone, Great Smokies, or any one of our many national parks. The Crown Jewels of America, as someone once said. No doubt. Guarded, patrolled, looked after, explained more or less by the rangers of the National Park Service. Also known, formerly, as tree fuzz, tree pigs, or Smokey Bears—no kin of that other Smokey Bear (the famous ursine bore) who used to serve as a fire-fighting symbol of the Forest Service until he died (of tertiary syphilis) in a Washington, D.C., zoo.

Perhaps there are still some people who don't know the difference between the National Park Service and the U.S. Forest Service. Let us review the question one more time. The Park Service is an agency of the Department of the Interior, entrusted with the care and management of the national parks, national monuments (such as Death Valley and the Statue of Liberty), and what are called National Recreation Areas—Lake Mead, Lake Powell, etc. The Forest Service is a branch of the Department of Agriculture, alas, and was given charge, long ago, by Congress, of our national forests. The parks were established primarily as wilderness areas, to be kept so far as possible in a state of nature, but open (in some manner) to the enjoyment of the people. The forests, on the other hand, have been meant for various uses—watershed protection, wildlife habitat, human recreation, livestock grazing, logging, even mining. Since World War II the last three uses have become predominant, usually at the expense of the first three.

There is a certain built-in antagonism between the two agencies. Park rangers sometimes refer to forest rangers as "tree farmers" (this was once considered an insult); while the latter like to call the former "turkey herders" or "posie sniffers." No matter. The difference between one service and the other, and between national parks and national forests, is not so great as it once was. With mass motorized recreation becoming a bigger and bigger industry in itself, the national parks have been subjected to increasing commercial development: paved roads, motels, hotels, marinas, gas stations, stores, banks, hospitals, cloverleaf intersections, parking lots, traffic lights, even jails. I know of no place in the national forests that has suffered the grotesque and incongruous development of Yosemite, Grand Canyon, Yellowstone, Great Smokies.

In any case, I myself have worked for both agencies, in both kinds of places, and can testify from ample personal experience that the difference between the Park Service and the Forest Service is more nominal than real: Both labor under the domination of the GNP, the NAM, the corporate pursuit of pecuniary happiness. "Business means America and America means business," says your friendly U.S. Chamber of Commerce. "America's business *is* business," said John Calvin Coolidge, our last honest president, and he was never more right than now, here, in the Sick Seventies, when even sex therapy and spiritual fulfillment have become growth industries. (My cousin Gus told me the other day, with barely subdued excitement, that he has nailed down the Transcendental Meditation franchise for Win-

kelman, Arizona. Better than Pizza Parlor or Midas Muffler—
a gold mine.)

What has all this whining and complaining to do with Smokey
the Cop or the out-of-doors, that other world *out there*, beyond
the expanding labyrinth of walls that cuts us off from what we
long for, more and more, as it recedes into our past? Not much.
Very little. But some.

For seventeen seasons, off and on, I have worked as a ranger,
as a fire lookout, as a garbage collector, for the Park Service,
occasionally for the Forest Service. Since most of these jobs
involved, to some extent, what is called "protection" (law enforcement) as well as "interpretation," I too have played the
role, or more exactly played *at* the role, of Smokey the Cop. I
wore a uniform and a badge, I carried a .38 in the glove compartment of a government pickup, I sometimes harassed people, especially hippies. And shot two dogs and a number of beer
cans. In self-defense.

An odd part to play, you might think, for one who fancies
himself a libertarian, an anarchist, a dedicated scofflaw. Perhaps
not. I've never known a serious policeman who had much respect for the law; in any well-organized society the police con-
stitute the most lawless element. Policemen are not legalists;
they are moralists, stern believers in good and bad, right and
wrong. I too am a moralist, not a legalist, and thus fulfill the
basic qualification for cophood.

My career as a PIG (Pride, Integrity, Guts) began not with the
Park Service, however, but during my stint with another over-
grown governmental bureaucracy affiliated with the Department of Commerce—I refer of course to the U.S. Army. One
morning I was coming down off a boat onto the bomb-wrecked
docks of Naples, Italy, when this man I'd never seen before
tapped me on the shoulder and asked how tall I was. I told him
I was six foot two on a warm day but contracted a bit in cold
weather. "You're a cop now, wiseass," said the man. He was a
second lieutenant in the military police; the boat I'd just left
(traveling tourist class) was a troop ship; I was an eighteen-year-
old acne-haunted draftee rifleman in the infantry; and on that
particular day every replacement six feet tall or taller was being
shunted, willing or not, into the military police.

Typical of the army; keep the big men in the rear; let the little guys do the fighting. Actually the war was over; the Japanese had surrendered the day I finished basic training; but our wise, spunky Harry Truman was doing his best to get a fresh war started with Russia, Yugoslavia, Korea, Arkansas, anyone available.

My feelings were hurt at being assigned to the MPs, since my true military ambition was to become a clerk-typist like James Jones and Norman Mailer. But it did no good to object. Some sergeant put a black and white Nazi-like armband on my sleeve, a white helmet liner on my head, a nifty red scarf around my neck, and a club and a .45 automatic in my hands. At once I began to feel mean, brutal, arbitrary, righteous. "Let's stop coddling criminals," I wrote home to mother, that first night in Napoli; "let's put father in jail where he belongs." (My father was the village Socialist back in Home, Pennsylvania.)

After that first day I never saw an MP officer. The officers were down in Sorrento, shacking up with contessas, living off their black market profits. Our boss was Sergeant Smitty, a lifer and a drunk, who'd received his police science training, like most other MP noncoms, in the army's Disciplinary Training Center at Pisa. There he had served first as an ordinary inmate (rape, larceny, assault, murder), then as a trusty, then as a guard, emerging fully qualified to enforce the law. Smitty was proud of the two years he'd put in at Pisa; not only had he avoided front-line combat, but he had also learned, as a routine part of the required training there, how to polish his mess kit with a needle. With a needle? Why yes, with a needle. That's the way it was done at old ivy-covered DTC.

Smitty became my hero. "Did you ever kill a man, Smitty?" I asked him once, stars in my eyes. He grinned his evil, wolfish, yellow grin. "Naw," he said modestly, "not really. Couple of niggers, that's all. A few Germans. I'm kind of a tender-hearted fella." And he gave me the fearsome grin again and put me down for the vice squad.

"Dear Mother," I wrote home after my third day in Napoli, "last night I raided my first whorehouse." Not entirely true, I wrote no such thing. But I did raid the whorehouse, and it was certainly my first. In fact I was still a virgin. In many ways. I had never before seen, for example, one man beat another with a club. Sergeant Smitty showed us—me and another rookie—how it is done. We arrested several whores and one AWOL soldier, the black man Smitty had clubbed into unconsciousness. That soldier, I later learned, was sent to Pisa, where he too would learn to polish his mess kit with a needle.

I requested a transfer to the motorcycle squad. "What's the matter, kid, you cherry?" Smitty asked. "Yellow?"

"Well sir," I said, "that night work . . . I don't know."

"Can you handle a Harley?" he said.

"No problem," I said. I wasn't sure what a Harley was, but figured that anyone, like me, who knew how to harness a team of horses or crank up a Farmall could probably put a bridle on a Harley.

"Well, stick around," Smitty said, "we're having the tryouts in a few days."

There were three positions open on the bike squad. Six of us showed up for the tryouts, which were held on a racetrack outside the city. Sergeant Smitty—wreathed in whisky fumes—wrote our names down on his clipboard sheet. "Okay, Abbey," he said, "you're first." (I was at the head of every list in the army.)

I approached this olive-drab machine parked on the cinders, a huge Harley-Davidson loaded with red lights, a siren, chrome-plated crash bars, and a tailpipe fashioned from a German 88-mm cannon shell, the brass polished to a golden gleam. I straddled the seat and turned the switch. I'd been doing some homework and sneaking around and was pretty certain I knew how to start this type of machine. Spark in the left grip, throttle in the right, kick starter, gear shift lever and clutch pedal just like a car. Easy. Nothing to it. Nervous all the same, my sweaty thumb slipped onto a button on the handlebar. The siren began to growl. "Shut that thing off!" Smitty bellowed. Okay, okay, I fumbled around, got the shift lever into neutral, my foot on the starter, and kicked. The motor roared like a dinosaur. Frightened but determined, revving the engine, I slipped the lever forward into first *(clunk!)* and slowly, cautiously engaged the clutch *(clang!)*. The bike leaped forward like a spooked horse, bearing straight ahead.

Paralyzed with terror, I clung to the handlebars, trying to think what I was supposed to do next. Shift into second? Of course. But we were already approaching the first turn in the track. How do you steer this thing? To me the handlebars seemed rigid, welded to the frame. It never occurred to me that I must lean into the turn. Locked together, the Harley and I crashed through the wooden fence on the outside of the track, plowed into a dirt bank, stalled out, keeled over. Still gripping the handlebars, I heard, above the scream of the siren, the outraged bellowing of Sergeant Smitty staggering down the track toward me. "Back to the vice squad, Abbey! Back to the whorehouse for you!"

One week later I was riding my Hog, loaded with siren and chrome, up the wide streets and down the cobbled alleyways of Napoli, a proud, full-fledged member of the motorcycle squad. A traffic cop. A bona fide Smokey. A genuine Pig.

How did I do it? Simple. On the day of the tryouts, after my disastrous debut, while Smitty was watching the others (he flunked them all), I crept back to the bench where he had left his clipboard and when he wasn't looking wrote in "passed" after my name. Shit-faced and falling-down drunk, he never knew the difference. A few secret hours of practice and I was on the squad.

My eight months as a motorcycle cop in the balmy, crazy, sunny, utterly depraved city of Naples was the most educational time of my life, so far. Glorious days breezing along the bay and up the Via Roma toward Salerno, charging up and down marble stairways on our bikes into Mussolini's Palazzo di Esporza where we made our barracks, weekend passes to Capri, Ischia, Amalfi, Vesuvius, Pompeii. Long siestas with my girl friend in her filthy villa high on Posillipo, the Harley hidden under the orange trees. Yes, I'd finally discovered sex. (I was a retarded child.) And the black market. And the pizza pie. And grand opera: Puccini! Rossini! Verdi! Ravioli! Claudio Monteverdi and His Green Mountain Boys! And good wine. Real cheese. Honest bread. Once stopped and cited an air corps colonel—and his dark-eyed sweetheart—for speeding (85 in a 15 mph zone) and driving one-handed. "Use both hands, sir," I reminded him, leering at his girl. "I'd like to," he replied, "but I need one hand to steer with." I wish we could have another war like that one. Whatever happened to Hitler and Tojo anyhow?

There were little catches to the hitch. The weekly quota of traffic tickets, for instance. But I learned to solve that problem.

Once a week I'd stop a military supply convoy outside the city, give the first thirty truck drivers citations for some violation or other—dust on the headlights, dirt on the bumper markings, worn windshield wipers, etc. The drivers didn't give a damn; most of them didn't speak English; they were Germans, POWs, Nazis. If I'd managed to catch Himmler or Hess or Bormann or Ehrlichman (excuse me, Eichmann) among them, I'd have written him up too, just like anybody else. I was a good cop.

But it couldn't last. Something went wrong. Various things. Foolish mistakes, like giving Italy back to the Italians—once the Allied High Command had made certain the Italian working people would not be allowed to take over the country. And personal mistakes. Like getting caught once too often failing to salute an officer. You're saluting the uniform not the man, they had taught us in basic. Really? I'll salute a *man* anytime, but damned if I'll salute a *uniform*.

The war ended for me much as it began, mopping floors and peeling potatoes in an army mess hall. From the military police back to the kitchen police. And then—discharge. Out. I never did get to be a corporal like Norman Mailer or James Jones. All I salvaged from my career as a military cop was one Colt automatic, chrome-plated by skilled Ginzo craftsmen in Naples, which I smuggled past the MPs at the exit gate of Fort Dix, New Jersey. Good thing I got it past; otherwise, I'd have been polishing mess gear with a needle myself.

Well sir, about ten years later, armed with my more or less honorable discharge and my five-point veteran's preference, I began a long series of sometime seasonal jobs as a ranger with the National Park Service. (I am one of the few veterans of World War II who has yet to find a steady job.) My first was in Arches National Park in Utah, then quite a primitive place, where I enforced the law (natural law) by pulling up survey stakes from a new road the Park Service was attempting to build into *my park*. That didn't do much good; I moved on.

I spent three winters as a ranger in Organ Pipe Cactus National Monument in southwest Arizona, a lovely place swarming with rattlesnakes, Gila monsters, scorpions, wild pigs, and illegal Mexicans. The only useful work I did there was rescuing rattlesnakes discovered in the campground, catching them alive with my wooden Kleenex-picker before some tourist could cause them harm, dumping them in a garbage can and relocating them by stuffing them down a gopher hole six miles out in the desert.

At Petrified Forest, the worst job I ever held in our National Park Service, I worked the box office. That is, I sold tickets to tourists entering the park and interrogated those departing. The latter task we carried out in this manner: the tourist, obeying the stop sign, would rein his car to a halt beside my station; looking him straight in the eye I would say, "Sir, have you or any members of your party removed any rocks or other objects from this National Park?" Looking me straight in the eye, the man at the wheel would reply, "Oh no, just looking," and his wife, at his side, would nod in solemn agreement. Then one of the little kids in the back seat would say, "But Daddy, what about that big log we put in the trunk?"

So that's why the rear bumper was scraping the asphalt; and here I'd thought it was just another Punkmobile. I'd radio at once for reinforcements; we'd open the trunk, remove the petrified log (worth about $3,000 on the curio dealer black market), club the driver into insensibility while his family stood around screaming, arrest them all, generally have the husband and wife locked up for five to fifteen years, and pack the kids off to an orphanage where they'd probably get better balanced meals anyway. But such diversions seldom occurred more than two or three times a day. In general, the job was a bore; if it had not been for the financial rewards I would have quit much sooner. Financial rewards? True, a seasonal park ranger then was paid about $2.50 an hour. But the tickets! Each time I sold a tourist his admission ticket, I would remind him to keep that piece of paper in plain view at all times, verifying his right to be in the park. (Really. For Petrified Forest, like Grand Canyon or Yosemite, is a *national* park—not a people's park.) When the tourist was leaving the park, I would lean out my window, extend my hand, and say, "May I see your pass, sir?" The tourist would give me his ticket, I'd look it over, say, "Okay sir, thank you," and he'd drive away, glad to be gone, and I would resell the same ticket to the next mark coming in off the Interstate. In that way I'd clean up about $500 to 600 on a good day, sometimes more on weekends when the action was lively.* But as I said, the job was a bore; I moved on.

On, to Everglades National Park down in Florida, where I was given a souped-up Plymouth Interceptor with siren concealed behind the grill and a big red light on the roof. Once again I found myself a traffic cop, a highway patrolman. Night shift. I wrote a few warning tickets, out of meanness, but spent more time careering down the Pine Island–Flamingo Park highway, late at night, lights flashing, to see what the Interceptor would do (115 mph). Sometimes I had to halt traffic on the highway for a few minutes in order to assist one of those eight-foot sawgrass diamondbacks across the pavement. A routine chore was checking doors at the visitor center, chasing skunks and drunks and alligators out of the rest rooms, which were left unlocked at night. But the best part of the job was lying in wait for 'Gator Roberts, the most famous alligator poacher in the state of Florida, maybe in the whole Southeast; a legendary figure, phantom outlaw, folk hero, and a bone in the throat of Everglades park rangers. We hated him.

We had an informant, a waitress who worked at the Redneck Café near Pine Island; she had connections with the alligator underworld and would tell us from time to time (for a price) exactly where old 'Gator Roberts was planning to strike next. We'd stake out the place—some stinking, stagnant slough deep in the dismal swamp—and wait there through the night, sweating, cursing, scratching chigger bites, slapping mosquitoes, fondling our guns. He never appeared. Next morning we'd learn that sixteen skinned alligator carcasses had been found at the other end of the park, forty miles away, with a note attached: "You Smokies aint got the brains Gawd give a spoonbill duck, regards, Gator."

One winter in that low-rent bog was enough. Retiring phase by phase from the law enforcement business I returned to Arizona and got myself a job as a fire lookout up in a sixty-foot tower on the North Rim of the Grand Canyon. The good rim, where the Mormon girls come every summer to work at the lodge. Strictly forbidden all vices but one, those bountiful handsome girls always make the most of that one, which may be the

---

*This actually happened—once—at Grand Canyon National Park. The culprit (not me) was caught, I am happy to say, convicted, and duly electrocuted at the federal penitentiary in Leavenworth, Kansas.

reason Utah has the highest birth rate and the highest VD rate in the nation. Strict family types, those Utahns, stern believers in woman's traditional role. "Woman's place?" said Joseph Smith; "why woman's place—is in my bed!"

I'd sit there in my lookout waiting for Kathy or Susan or Sharon—all those girls seemed to be named Kathy or Susan or Sharon—waiting for one or the other to come and climb my tower. As far as I can tell, it never did any of us harm. Although now that I think about it, looking over what I've written here so far, I'm not so sure. (Were you ever awakened at night by the sound of crashing brain cells, whole tiers and entire galleries of corroded gray matter coming loose and thundering like an avalanche down into the abyss of your cerebellum?)

The last I heard of Smokey the Cop was over the short airwaves, through the Park Service radio in my lookout tower. It seemed that some scruffy types from California, degenerate hippies, were smoking a controlled substance somewhere in the vicinity of Indian Gardens under the South Rim. Far out in the wilds, as they doubtless imagined, far from the fuzz, the law, and those who call themselves "the authorities." So they thought. But they were wrong. A humble maintenance man, fixing a waterline, saw them, smelled the sweet stink of *Cannabis,* and radioed park headquarters. Minutes later a helicopter —a helicopter!—with armed rangers inside was sent down to make the bust. I can see those hippies now, in my mind's eye, sitting naked and cross-legged in their little circle under the shade of a juniper, passing the pipe of peace from hand to hand, each one far out in the cool of inner space; I see them becoming gradually aware of a giant dark bird with whirling wings hovering above, shrieking at them in the voice of steel and power and outrage—God is the great black spider in the sky!—coming down, down, down upon them. . . .

Was it then I finally gave away my Smokey Bear hat? The one with the four dimples in the high crown and that wide, flat, rigid brim, hard as iron, with which you could chop a man's head off if necessary? (We kept the brim flat by installing the hat under the seat of a toilet bowl each night; the same way your friendly state police do it.) Don't remember. Can't seem to recall things as good as I used to. As the French say, *quel dommage du brains.* But I did give it away, to a short boatman with a big head. Fellow named Stewart, I think. He ruined it by wearing it head-first through the Big Drop in Cataract Canyon down in Utah.

But I still remember some things. I remember the old Park Service Bizet-inspired fight song that we sang at night around the campfire at the Horace Albright Training Center (not quite the same thing as DTC in Pisa):

> *Toreadora*
> *Don't piss on the flora*
> *Save our wild decóra . . .*
> Etc.

And I remember a few other things I'd rather forget. Only a few but they're enough. That's why I live out here where I do, where none but the wedgetail eagles and the buzzards will ever find me, here on this rocky butte with the 200-mile view in all directions, here in the heart (but the desert has no heart), here in the skull of the Hoodoo Desert. Paranoid? Yes, I'm paranoid; anyone who's not should have his head examined. What? What's that, Doctor? Well, yes sir, you're right, I don't know *exactly* who my enemies are, I can't *name* them, if that's what you mean. But Doctor, can't you see?—that's what frightens me: *I don't know who they are.*

As for Smokey the Cop and all his friends—those jolly policemen of various types—state, federal, secret, private, uniformed, plainclothes, foreign, and domestic—I stay away from them. I also avoid muggers, rapists, hijackers, terrorists, politicians, murderers, and other lunatics. And for precisely the same reason.

16. IN DEFENSE OF THE REDNECK

Oh I got plenty of money
And money's plenty for me . . .
　　　　　—M. Proust

There's a town in Arizona called Glob. Named for a nugget. It's a mining town, specializing formerly in gold and silver, now devoted to copper. The smog produced daily by the local smelter poisons the air for fifty miles downwind. The smell is like that of a decomposing jellyfish. Nobody here seems to mind. The Glob businessmen have built their golf course and country club at the foot of the 500-foot-high tailings dump. They are proud of the dump. When the wind blows, the air is filled with fine white powder. The golfers inhale the powder and the gases and swell with pleasure. Mention pollution and they say, "Son, that smells like money to me."

Of course they're right. I like Glob myself. You get used to the stink. I drop in there every other week to pick up my mail, buy some groceries, and have a drink or two before heading back to my job in the mountains. For instance:

I had a late lunch at the U-Et-Yet Café, then parked my '68 VW Fastback in front of the Broad Street Social Club. Closed. The only hippie bar in town—closed. Probably because of my friend Greenspan, who played here last week. Bob Greenspan and the Monkey Wrench Gang. His new song, "Big Tits, Braces and Zits," a ballad of adolescent passion, had been a hit. But as usual he overdosed on ego and bourbon and insulted first the management, then the audience, then the Glob law enforcement people. Not a wise thing to do. Now, I suppose, he was back in Boulder.

I drove on up the street, following the parade of gleaming new welfare-financed pickup trucks. Every Chicano, Navajo, and redneck Anglo in the state drives a pickup. They can't afford condoms, diaphragms, or birth control pills—but they all seem to find the financing for a $10,000 Ford Ranger or Chev Apache or Dodge Power Wagon. Wish I could do it. My poor old Nazi folk's wagon is burning oil, has a slipping clutch, no shocks, squealing brakes, the floor corroded by battery acid, and a sprung hood that I have to latch with a length of rope.

The bumper sticker in front of me read: Ass, Gas, or Grass— Nobody Rides for Free. I liked that sentiment better than what I saw when I pulled into a slot close to the Ruins Bar. The sticker on the rear of a tractorlike pickup truck—gun rack in the cab—said: Did the Coyotes Get Your Deer? Being an old-time coyote lover, I resented the bigotry and yokel ignorance of that remark. There was a broad-tipped marking pen in my car. With heavy strokes of indelible black ink, I wrote across the windshield of the truck: Did the Rednecks Get Your Coyote? Like Nietzsche says, Live Dangerous. Ho was a mountain man too.

I straightened the yellow nylon carnation on the hood of my VW (every sporty car should wear a boutonniere) and felt my way into the bar. Out of the dazzling desert sun into the darkness of the cave. I ordered a tall double gin screwdriver with lots of orange juice. A healthy drink. A man should take care of himself. The body is the temple of the soul. I braced my foot on the rail, steadied my right hand with my left, and drank. Feeling better, I ordered a second and smiled at the half dozen gloomy, mean, hostile, ravaged faces ranged around the bar, staring at me. "Why do they call this place the Ruins?" I said.

Nobody answered. None of them even laughed. I'm not going to get out of here alive, I thought. Unless I crawl out on my hands and knees, feeling along the wall for the door. Maybe not then. Silently, the bartender served me another screwdriver, took my money, leaned back with folded arms. A baseball bat stood in the corner. Ignoring me now, the regulars resumed their mumbling conversation. Two hardhats, two cowboy hats, and two crew cuts. The bartender was bald—a tough egg. He smoked an economical cigar, which had at least this virtue: It neutralized the all-pervasive stench of the copper smelter. But not the smell of hatred. I rubbed my hairy jaws, then sidled off to the jukebox to check out the musical values of this here metallurgical community.

As I'd suspected, there was no Gustav Mahler available. No Purcell. No Palestrina. Not even filthy Mozart. Nothing but the standard country-western stuff from a big city in the East called Nashville. Music to hammer out fenders by at the Shade Tree Body Shop. Music to vomit by after a shift in the copper pits. Take this job and shove it. I picked out a couple of Johnny Paycheck numbers and retired for a minute to the men's pissoir. I read the writing on the wall. The voice of the people:

> Will trade three blind crabs
> For two with no teeth

Suggests the political situation in these southwestern states. But what about this one?:

> If you ain't a cowboy
> You ain't shit

Food for thought there. I looked at myself—quickly—in the cracked fragment of mirror screwed to the wall. Found consolation in the fact that I still didn't look as bad as I felt. Or feel as bad as I looked. I returned to my friends at the bar. None of them spoke or looked at me. I studied the placards tacked to the wall above the ranks of bottles:

This is a high-class place
Act respectable

Helen Waite is our credit manager
If you want credit go to Helen Waite

Finishing my second health drink, it occurred to me that more and more we communicate with one another as indirectly as possible. Through wall placards. Through graffiti. Through bumper stickers, headgear, lapel buttons, T-shirts . . . anything but face-to-face exchange. Perhaps this has been obvious to everyone else for a long time. Perhaps I've been living too long in the mountains. Perhaps I should rejoin what they call civilization. If there is one. I'm willing to listen to reason. If I hear any.

Direct communication. I turned to the morose face on my right, a new arrival. He was wearing a baseball cap with the legend BEEF stitched on the forepeak. His mate's cap said CAT. Mr. Beef and Mr. Cat.

"Where you fellas from?" I asked politely.

Mr. Beef stared at me for a while. "Flat Rock," he finally said.

"Where's that?"

The long stare. "East of here."

"Why do they call it Flat Rock?" Careful, I thought; you're not getting out of here alive if you're not careful. Receiving no immediate answer, I repeated the question. "Why Flat Rock?" Live dangerous.

Mr. Beef exchanged a glance with his taciturn friend. Mr. Cat nodded. Mr. Beef said, "Because of the rain."

"Because of the *rain?*" I paused for a moment. "What do you mean, because of the rain?" I pushed my empty glass toward the bartender.

"The way it comes down."

"The way it comes down?"

"Yeah." Mr. Beef toyed with his can of Coors, scowling at his thumbs. "Like a cow."

The bartender brought me my third drink. The turning of the screw. I had a momentary feeling of vertigo. But I plunged recklessly ahead. "The rain comes down like a cow?"

"That's right." Mr. Cat raised his head. The two men stared at me solemnly. "Like a cow pissing on a flat rock," Mr. Beef said.

I paid for the next round and recorded the story, for posterity, in my cerebral files. What do I have against rednecks? Nothing. I am here to defend them. My father has been a sidehill farmer, a logger, a schoolbus driver most of his life. My little brother is a construction worker and truck driver. Another is now a cop in L.A. I am a redneck myself, born and bred on a submarginal farm in Appalachia, descended from an endless line of dark-complected, lug-eared, beetle-browed, insolent barbarian peasants, a line reaching back to the dark forests of central Europe and the alpine caves of my Neanderthal primogenitors. Like my neighbor Marvin Bundy says (he lives on the other side of Wolf Hole Mountain), like Marvin says, "Us poor folks got to stick together."

A few words about my neighbor. Marvin Bundy is a poet and female liberationist. "Wummin?" says Marvin. "I liberate a wummin ever' chanct I git. Wummin's place is in mah arms. The destiny of her anatomy is in mah hands." True enough, Marvin; us nature mystics got to stick together. However, it is with Mr. Bundy's poetry that I am here primarily concerned. The other day he came over the gap and asked me to read his "latest masterpiece."

"Well, Marvin," I said, "I have yet to see your first."

"Read this," he said, "and I don't need no smart-aleck criticism."

Did the coyotes git your deer?
40,000 shitkickers caint be wrong,
Did the screwworms git your cow?
Yeah! thass mah song.

Them goldam Sahara Clubbers
Them candy-ass Defenders of Fur Bearers
Them sombitchin' FOES of the Earth
I say shoot 'em all full of arrers.

Googly-eyed bleeding hearts
Cryptic Communist pointy-heads
Little ole ladies in inner tubes
All need brain retreads.

Mining is Ever' Body's Future.
Sahara Go Home. Exxon Come Along.
Save Oil, Burn Conservationists.
Thass mah song.

Now entering Utah. (Set watches back 50 years.)
Golden goddam Beehive State.
Full of busy buzzin' bees.
Latter Day Shitheads. Cottonwood trees. Jaycees.

95,000 us deerslayers. 95 deer.
Got 92 last year.
There's one left on Blue Mountain,
One down in Slickhorn Gulch,
And the other one's a queer.

Don't care what them Bambi-lovers say;
Like I tell my wife,
Ever' time you shoot a deer
You're savin' some cow's life.

Outa work? Hungry?
Eat a environmentalist.
They taste like jungle boots
But sure wont be missed.

Puttin' on weight and losin' mah hair
But gotta new boat.
Gotta new pickup so I don't care
And them as caint swim better learn to float.

Got mah CB radio.
Got mah *Hook & Bullet News,*
Got mah old wummin and eleventeen kids,
And they never wear shoes.

So long.
Thass mah song.

Marvin is a special case, a coy and crafty fellow, not a stand-ardized rustic. More common, perhaps, is a young fellow I once worked with in the Coronado National Forest, down along the Mexican border in Arizona. I'll call him Calvin. We patrolled the woods and collected garbage from the public campgrounds. Dumping our load one afternoon at the forest landfill site, we saw a large chulu, or coatimundí, picking its way across a mound of garbage looking for something to eat. The chulu is a rare animal on the American side of the border; it looks like a hybrid mix of bear, anteater, and raccoon. A strange and interesting creature. Calvin's immediate reaction, when we spotted the animal, was, "Gee, I wish I had my gun."

I argued with him, but it was a waste of time. Like most rednecks, rural or urban, he could see nothing of interest in the world of nature unless he was trying to shoot it or set a hook in its throat or trap it and skin it. Same with humans. After work that evening, I suggested to Calvin that we go into Nogales and pick up a couple of women. Calvin shrugged. "Ah haint too interested in girls," he mumbled. Then he gave me a shy, sly, sidelong look: "But you oughta see mah gun collection."

Not that I'm against guns. As I've said elsewhere, I keep a few myself. The freeborn American's right to own and bear firearms is and must remain inviolate. Nor am I against hunting and fishing, when the prey is abundant and the primary object of the pursuit is to put meat on the table—or in the skillet. I do think we should take it easy, out here in the West, on our dwindling deer population: The mountain lions need those deer more than we do.

This thought leads me to that contemporary phenomenon, the instant redneck. The natural redneck comes from the country, from small towns, and is generally too dumb or too stubborn to leave. The instant redneck comes from the city or the affluent suburbs, where his father has made a lot of money. Cushioned by a nice trust fund or comfortable inheritance, the instant redneck migrates west, buys himself a little hobby ranch, a pair of tight jeans, a snap-button shirt, one of those funny hats with the rolled brim like the male models wear in Marlboro ads, and a ninety-dollar pair of tooled leather boots with pointy toes (for kicking snakes in the ass) like those you'll see on the feet of the pretty young men walking their poodles in Greenwich Village.

Now in full cowboy costume, he buys his first pickup truck, a huge lumbering four-by-four tractorlike gas hog of a *deus machina* loaded with roll bars, mag rims, lug tires, KC road lights, gun rack, spotlight, AM-FM cassette player, Kleenex dispenser, gyroscopic beer can holder, CB (Cretin Broadcasting) radio, and Tampax slot. He buys a gun for the gun rack, pops the top from his first can of Coors (a sweet, green provincial brew mass-produced from reprocessed sewage water near Denver), and roars off in all directions to tear up the back country and blast away at the wildlife. The instant redneck. A real man at last.

But not interesting. Much too familiar a type. More problematic were those chaps surrounding me (on all sides) at the Ruins Bar in Glob, Arizona, on a hot summer afternoon in 1978. Two more cowboys had come in, accompanied by their heifers. All wearing the funny hats, the tight pants, and flowered shirts. You could tell the cowboys from the cowgirls by the wider hips. On the cowboys. The girls looked like they couldn't calve a salamander.

And then a cool young woman, elegant as a sylph, golden-haired, walked in and sat down at the bar one stool away from me. She wore oversize black sunglasses, opaque, inscrutable, and a T-shirt printed with the image of a life-size owl. Two great protruding eyes confronted me. Like an oaf, I stared; the lady gave me a slight smile.

I was about to move onto her adjoining stool when a burly fellow came between us, taking the seat, putting an arm about the girl and a large hairy elbow on the bar in front of my face. The bartender was silent as he poured my fourth double-shot screwdriver. I was getting tired of the orange juice, but figured I'd best stick to the regimen. Strict self-discipline, that's the secret of a full, healthy, productive life. I stared at the blonde, aware of the owl.

"You like my girl?" the large fellow said. He was a Mexican, a Chicano, with round, brown, solemn face, dark eyes, the shoulders of a fullback.

"Now, Primo . . ." the woman began.

"You like her, eh?" The dark eyes were aimed at me—not at the wall, not at the mirror, not at the other guy.

I knew he probably carried a knife, a switchblade. All *cholos* carry switchblades, everybody knows that. The trouble was he was so big, and ugly, and mean, he wouldn't need a knife. My sole weapon was my superior intelligence. Which only functions, however, in retrospection. "I'm never getting out of here alive," I said, to myself but aloud.

Primo smiled, laughed, gripped my shoulder in his enormous paw, and said, "You're right, man. You're not. Better buy us a drink."

Under the volcano. I was glad to buy time by buying Primo and his Blondie each a drink. Bar buddies. He called me Grizzly Adams; I called him Pachuco. We discussed his occupation. He was an operating engineer, he said with pride—a Cat-skinner, a bulldozer driver. I asked him the best way to disable a D-9. "You mad at the company?" he asked. "That's right," I said. Primo recommended pure shellac, about two quarts, in the fuel tank, and a few handfuls of fine sand in the crankcase. But don't touch *my* machine, he added with a slow, smiling flash of teeth, gripping my shoulder again. I could hear the gristle squeak.

We spoke of my trade. Fire-tower lookout. Lightning on the tin roof. The sound of trees breathing. Ten days of solitaire, two days of Glob. "That'd drive me crazy," Primo said. "What you do for love? Screw chipmunks? You must be crazy as a bedbug, Griz." To the bartender, he said, "Bring old Grizzly here another double OJ. Before I have to cut him up."

"Why not?" I said. Never argue with the man who's buying the drinks. Growing more reckless, foolish, even suicidal, I kept leering at his woman. "Take off them big shades, honey," I said. "Lemme see the light of your eyes. *La luz de mi vida.*"

She smiled, but shook her head. Probably had a black eye, thanks to her pet gorilla here. Maybe two. He looked like the type that would do it. She looked like the type that had it coming. The idea excited my sadistic fantasies. "I like your owl," I said "Both of them." I was seeing double. Better get out of here. Fairly soon. For the first time I noticed the four young thugs in a nearby booth, watching me. *Compadres.* But not *my* compadres. *La raza,* here and everywhere. *"Viva la causa!"* I heard myself shouting. Not a friendly face anywhere—except Primo himself, my Primero, sitting here beside me.

He whacked me on the back. "What cause you talkin' about, Griz?" His eyes were glowing now, reflecting perhaps the blood in my own; his grin looked bigger, more fierce than a scowl.

His slap made me spill part of my drink. I muttered three Spanish words, five little syllables that one should never utter, aloud, in the border states, unless one is prepared to die. I could see the words floating on the smoke before us.

The chatter came to a stop. The cowboys looked at me with pity. But not much pity. Drunken hippie, they were thinking. A dog's death. Kicked to pieces in a dusty ditch. And I was thinking (I think), well, what the hell. This is it. Never apologize, never explain.

Primo turned his glass in his big hands, looking solemn and serious. "Griz," he said, "we better go outside for a few minutes."

"Right," I agreed. Really. The happy hour. I got up and looked for the front door.

"No," he said, "this way." One arm around my shoulders, he guided me out the back door. Into a sun-bleached alley, among the crumpled garbage cans.

Blinking and swaying, I turned to face him. The sunlight dazzled my eyes. Primo looked for a moment like my brother Howard, the dark one, the truck driver, the high steel man.

"Griz," he said, "you know what you said in there?" I said nothing. "You must be crazy." I was silent. Primo said, "I'm not going to kill you, Griz. You're too drunk and ugly and stupid. But don't come back in there. If I was you I'd go out in the desert for a while and crawl under a bush and get some sleep. But before you pass out, try to think about some things. If you got any brains left." He watched me; I watched the hard edge of a silver cloud move above the skyline of the backside of the Dominion Hotel.

A door slammed. "Primo," I said—or meant to say. But he was gone. Never apologize. Never explain. I stepped carefully down the alley, leaned around the corner, and felt my way brick by brick back to my car. Some son of a bitch had snatched the flower off the hood. I got in and drove out of town, through the shining miasma of my drunkenness, turned off the highway, and went up a steep dirt road that led to a pass between a pair of cactus-studded hills. I stopped there and shut off the motor.

I could hear the insane singing of the cicada in the desert heat. About 102 degrees in the shade. But there was no shade.

Not a mesquite tree in sight. I thought of Hemingway—Lieutenant Henry—walking through the rain. Catherine has just died in childbirth. Much to the hero's relief—no, that's not it. It's the screaming of the locusts defying the sun, which sounds in a way like rain.

Towering clouds hung on the far horizon, shot with a flickering incandescence, twenty miles to the east. Thunder. God growling at me again. I don't care. I ain't afeard of Him. Not with that big .357 magnum in the glove compartment. Under the gloves. Ain't gettin' outa here alive? Ain't none of us agettin' outa here alive. That's the way it is, boys, and that's the way it's meant to be. It's hard but it's fair. Is that gun loaded? Of course it's loaded. What good is a gun that ain't loaded? Guns don't kill people; people kill people. Of course, people with guns kill *more* people. But that's only natural. It's hard. But it's fair. My God, but this car is hot.

I stumbled out, opened the flowerless hood. The engine was gone. Damned Nazi automobile. I took out my canvas cot, unfolded it, set it up on the shady side of the car. Why sleep on the ground if you don't have to? Only an idiot sleeps on the ground from choice. Little bugs crawl in your ears. A panicked pissant, scrambling over your eardrum, sounds like a horse marching through cornflakes. Horrible, undesirable, unnecessary sensation.

Miles below, the tough little town of Glob wavered under heat waves. Went to the town library once, asked the librarian for a book—*The Philosophy of William James*. The librarian, a middle-aged lady with mustache, began rummaging through her card index under the letter *F*.

I lay down on the cot, placing my hat over my eyes. Who built this old road? Why? Who knows? Who cares? Who found that big nugget down there? Forgotten now. I thought of my brother. I thought of Mr. Bundy, hunting his cactus-fed cows along the Utah line. Seventy years in the sun. Forgotten. Fear no more. Primo? Somewhere in Missouri a truck driver named Hinton pulls into an all-night truck stop. Kidneys aching. Forget him. I thought of my father at seventy-eight, still going out to the woods every day to cut locust posts for the coal mines. Pit props for the miners, down there in the dark. Forget them too. I thought of those who do the world's work, and are never paid enough, and never will be, and rise, and are beaten down, and always lose in the end.

The clouds grumbled on the east. God crept closer, mumbling. I raised the right fist, shook it at the old Bastard, and passed out.

To wake in the dark, hours later. There were no stars. A soft and misty rain was falling on my face.

17. DEATH VALLEY JUNK

Friday afternoon, at 1611 hours, Terry and I jumped out of the airplane. Death Valley, like a dream, revolved below us in a web of alkali and phosphorescent chemicals. Years ago.

Unwrapping the small packet of tinfoil, Terry gave me a single capsule containing a bluish powder in a base of white cornstarch. "Three hundred and fifty micrograms," he said, grinning. He removed one for himself. We broke the capsules open for quicker action and gulped them down with a slug of beer. Except for the beer, our stomachs were empty.

Smoking some California weed, we drove far out on the valley floor, ten miles beyond the end of the pavement, deep into the desert. We found a spot we liked and built a fire of arrowwood and mesquite. We sat down on the sand to wait. Terry leafed through a newspaper—the *LA Times*. I did nothing, feeling nervous, irritable, uncomfortable. The setting sun seemed very hot, the light a painful glare. Nothing was happening.

Except for this cold grip, this icy hand on the back of my neck. Nobody there, of course; I felt to make sure, reaching back with

170

an arm that seemed fourteen feet long. That first sensation passed, but as the sun went down behind Telescope Peak and the Panamints, I began to feel surprisingly cold. Clumsily, groggily—each movement seemed to require special attention—I dragged myself closer to the fire. I noticed then an extreme sensitivity in my sense of touch. Sitting on the ground, my rear end felt like a cluster of ice-cold needles. My bones squeaked as if made of glass.

Our bones are constructed of calcium, I told myself. They could turn to powder at any moment. This experiment, I decided, is not necessary. I swear I'll never touch another drop. Never drop another touch.

Terry sat on the opposite side of the fire, cross-legged, grinning like an idiot Buddha, staring at nothing I could see. But he was aware of my discomfort. Maybe that's why he was grinning. He was an old hand at this business, a master of the occult arts, lysergic acid, meditation.

The flies annoyed me; they buzzed around my face as if I were already dead. Nor did I much care for the praying mantis or whatever crawling up my backbone.

Something stirred in my hair.

I raised a slow-moving hand to my head, touched my hair. A huge, glittering butterfly shimmered off into the brush. *Butterfly,* I thought, startled but silent.

"What butterfly?" Terry said.

"There was a butterfly on my head."

"No. There wasn't any butterfly."

Why you liar, I thought.

Lightly, I touched my left eyelid. I don't know why; maybe it itched a bit. Suddenly there was a flash of golden lightning through the radiant pink and silent emptiness of Death Valley. A flash of lightning under a cloudless sky. I waited for the sound of thunder. Waited and waited, and after a while, forgot about it. I was having other problems.

I kept shifting my position on the cool sand, trying to get comfortable. But it's hard to get comfortable when you're sitting on a glass ass and your joints clank at every move with a metallic snapping noise like the bending of a beer can.

The solemn slowness of the time. I never knew a sundown so lingering. The fire burned steadily but did not consume the wood. I never saw such clear, such leisurely, such passionate flames.

The ground is breathing.

Let's pretend we don't notice that. Let's read this here newspaper lying on the sand. I could read all right, though the print tended to swim before my eyes and the words to leak out and run down the margins of the page. After a minute—thirty minutes?—I gave it up. Nothing could have seemed more trivial, less interesting, than the "news."

The ground *is* breathing.

The ground, the sandy desert earth between my legs, was palpitating slowly up and down, up and down, like the lungs of a sleeping animal.

Well, all right. I can accept that. And the writhing dance of the mesquite trees, I'll accept that too, though I don't like it, though plainly there is not the faintest breath of a breeze moving through the hot evening air.

The mountains across the valley, glowing in the sunset light, looked glorious, vividly palpable and tangible—as indeed they are—but don't always appear. Called the Funeral Range, as a matter of fact. The Fun-for-All Mountains. They, too, were breathing. And they no longer looked like mountains; they looked like raw lungs, a mile-high mass of pink lungs, alive and well, breathing at me for chrissake.

My sense of time and duration fell apart. There was no duration. I was trapped in limbo between two worlds—a place too queasy and queer to be the waking world, too bright and definite and three-dimensional to be the world of dreams. I didn't know where I was, except that I didn't much like it. Jelled in this static medium, where nothing happened but the clatter of my tin joints when I essayed to move, I felt paralyzed. An infantile paralysis.

I played old songs on my harmonica. *"Red River Valley."* *"Down in the Valley."* *"Lonesome Valley."* The secondary theme from the third movement of Beethoven's Fourteenth String Quartet. Oh, I've never heard such sweet and poignant tunes, such vibrant tones. I wanted to weep for the tragic beauty, the lovely sorrow of our lonely, floating, lonesome world. And I did.

Looking down at my legs I was amused to see how absurdly

long, misshapen, and remote they appeared. The legs of a deformed giant, seen from the shelter of a two-holed cave, far away.

The stars began to move.

They moved in a kind of viscous dance, as if caught in a web. As if trapped and tangled in a quivering spiderweb with moony spokes of light radiating from the hidden center. I felt sorry for the stars. God is the Great Night Spider.

Cassiopeia was a silver blue firefly snared alive in the quilted folds of the cobweb sky. The stars were points of light shining through pinholes in that rumpled mass. (Oh ho, I thought, so the ancients were right all along. Thales, Anaximander, Anaxagoras, those boys.)

I didn't like this jellyfish world. Worth visiting once, maybe, but I don't want to live here. An intellectual nausea rose in my soul. When do we get out of here? How do we get out of here? Panic gripped me for a moment. It passed.

Taking great care, I got to my feet and cautiously walked away from the fire, the bones in my pelvis grinding on one another like splintered glass. My body was a foreign object, a gigantic robot; I was the tiny pilot behind the eyesockets high in the bridge of the skull.

I noted the extravagant, excessive clarity of everything about me and within me, as if I were wandering through a grade B 3-D movie. What am I doing here?

What I meant to do, feeling my way around in the Valley of Death, was take an ordinary bourgeois piss. But when I started taking that weird thing out of the fly of my jeans—shall I describe that? that way it kept unreeling, like a firehose?—I discovered I couldn't. Because I knew, knew with absolute conviction, that if I urinated I would be urinating blood. So I stuffed it back inside, carefully, which took about an hour.

Terry still sat by the fire, motionless, the beatific grin on his saintly, silly, obnoxious face, enjoying his metaphysical picnic. His brains turning soft as Camembert in the acid bath. Well, he had the proper set, the correct predisposition. The power of faith. Miracles come to those who need them. I envied and hated him.

"Look at that swine," I said loudly, addressing the Great Spider in the Sky. "Look at him sitting there grinning at me like

a diabolical Fu Manchu, like a sinister Svengali son of a bitch."
The firelight gleamed on his prescription spectacles; all I could
see of his nearsighted eyes were two opaque, mirrorlike disks.
His balding dome. His groovy mustache.

"Say something," I roared. No reply. I roared again.

Nothing moved him. He merely sat there staring at me, smiling.

I knew by now that nothing more was going to happen. The
peak had passed. Whatever might happen to others, it was not
going to happen in me. And I didn't care; I was happy, pleased
with what I considered my power and strength. By God, no
lousy little 350 mikes of LSD was going to blow *my* brains to
the moon. My sense of self was too strong to be dissolved in
mere chemicals.

Once I decided I had whipped the acid god, I was able to take
pleasure in this miserable, strictured mode of intoxication. The
mesquite flames rising serene from their bed of incandescent
coals seemed more than beautiful. They were enchanted
flames, magical, holy, mystical. The writhing trees, the palpitating mountains of fresh liver and raw lung, the breathing earth,
the stars struggling in the cobweb sky, all struck me now as no
longer strange and fearful but simply as the way things are—
amusing, charming, delightful.

But there was no sense of joy or exultation in the floating
opera of my nervous system. Sometime late in the dead shank
of the night, with our firewood gone and the fire down to a few
smoldering rubies—but oh the intensity of those glowing coals;
they watched me like radiant red eyes—we put our beer-can
bones and crystal limbs in gear and shambled toward my old
pickup truck. Terry drifted onto the passenger's side of the seat.
Out of habit I slammed his door shut behind him—that door was
always hard to latch—then turned back to the remains of the
fire to get something I'd forgotten: a shoe, a sausage, I forget
what, maybe a shovel.

"Ed!" he screamed, "don't go!"

I stopped, returned, hugged him to me, did my best to comfort him for several minutes. Several hours? He was in a bad
state, trembling, sweating, terrified. The slamming door, my
turning away, had shattered his bliss.

We rattled home to Furnace Creek. Although I had driven

the acid clean out of my head and felt—up there—clear and triumphant as a winning warrior, my bones and flesh remained hypersensitive for hours. On the dirt road each pebble, each grain of sand beneath the wheels, set my teeth on edge. All the same it was good to know I was free from the glassy paralysis and coming home, coming back to earth. Nothing had ever seemed better. I had escaped, or so I thought, that dreadful web in which the stars are trapped, that galactic spider out yonder in the dark attic of space.

Later though, for weeks following my abortive flight, I suffered from a shade of disappointment and loss. Some ancient way remembered but not found. The trail not taken. For me at least, it now seemed clear—there was not going to be any magic shortcut into wisdom, understanding, peace. There would be no easy way.

18. FIRE LOOKOUT

Men go mad in this line of work. Read a book called *The Dharma Bums* by Jack Kerouac and you'll see what I mean. He spent a summer as fire lookout in a shack on Sourdough Mountain in the Cascades, a lookout haunted by the spirit of Gary "Japhy Ryder" Snyder who had also worked there. Kerouac never recovered. A few years later the Forest Service offered me the same job at the same place. Trying to maintain their literary reputation. Prudently I turned it down.

Women too go mad in the solitary confinement of a mountain peak, though not so readily as men, being stronger, more stable creatures, with a lower center of gravity. Perhaps the severest test of a marriage is to assign a man and wife to a fire lookout; any couple who survive three or four months with no human company but each other are destined for a long, permanent relationship. They deserve it.

My career as a fire lookout began by chance. Having injured my knee during the Vietnam War (skiing in Colorado), I was unable to resume my usual summer job as patrol ranger in a

176

certain notorious Southwestern national park. I requested a desk job. The Chief Ranger thought I lacked the competence to handle government paper work. He offered me instead the only job in the Park which required less brains, he said, than janitor, garbage collector or Park Superintendent. He made me fire lookout on what is called the North Rim, a post so remote that there was little likelihood I'd either see or be seen by the traveling American public. An important consideration, he felt.

The lookout tower on North Rim was sixty feet tall, surmounted by a little tin box six feet by six by seven. One entered through a trapdoor in the bottom. Inside was the fire finder—an azimuth and sighting device—fixed to a cabinet bolted to the floor. There was a high swivel chair with glass insulators, like those on a telephone line, mounted on the lower tips of the chair's four legs. In case of lightning. It was known as the electric chair. The actual operations of a fire lookout, quite simple, I have described elsewhere.

My home after working hours was an old cabin near the foot of the tower. The cabin was equipped with a double bed and a couple of folding steel cots, a wood-burning stove, table, shelves, cupboard, two chairs. It made a pleasant home, there under the pines and aspen, deep in the forest, serenaded by distant coyote cries, by poor wills, and sometimes by the song of the hermit thrush, loveliest of bird calls in the American West.

My father came to visit one day and stayed for the season. He was given the job of relief lookout on my days off. In the evenings after supper we played horseshoes. Whenever I hear the jangle of horseshoes now I think of North Rim, of that forest, that cabin, that summer. My father has powerful hands, hard, gnarled, a logger's hands, very large. In his hand a playing horseshoe looks like a quoit; a horse's shoe can hardly be seen at all. His pitch is low and accurate, the shoe—open end forward —sliding with a soft *chunk* full upon the upright, rigid peg. A firm connection. Top that ringer, son, he'd say. We walked the Grand Canyon from rim to rim that summer, and once again a few years ago. The second time he was seventy-two years old.

The first sensible thing I did at North Rim, before my father appeared, was fall in love with the ranger. Not the Chief Ranger but the one who manned the park entrance station a few miles down the road. Park Ranger Hendrickson (GS-4) was one of those golden Californians from the San Diego area. She wore her sea-bleached hair in a heavy ponytail that fell below her clavicles. Like most girl swimmers she had a well-developed pair of lungs, much admired by the boys. Pretty as a Winesap in September, she looked especially fetching in her ranger suit: broad-brimmed straw hat, white blouse with Park Service pin, the snug skirt of forest green twill that ended, as was the fashion then, a good six inches above her knees. Like most sexual perverts I've always suffered from a fatal weakness for women in uniform—for cheerleaders, majorettes, waitresses, meter maids, prison matrons, etc. On my first meeting with Bonnie Hendrickson (as we shall here name the young woman) I said to her, frankly, "You know—I've always wanted to lift a ranger's skirt."

"You'll need a hiking permit," she replied. A quick-witted girl —with a B.A. in French. We soon became good friends. On my days off I sometimes helped her get through the tedious hours at the entrance station. While she leaned out her little window collecting entrance fees from the tourists, answering questions, chatting about Smokey the Bore and the fire danger, I was kneeling at her feet, unseen from outside, gently rolling down the ranger's pantyhose. We played various such experiments in self control. I experimented, she displayed the self control. An innocent game, like horseshoes, with similar principles. Top that ringer . . .

On her days off she would visit me in the lookout tower, assisting me in *my* duties. As I'd be reporting a fire over the Park Service radio system she was unbuttoning my Levi's. "Fire Dispatch," I said into the microphone, "this is North Rim Lookout."

"Yeah?" The Fire Dispatcher had the weary, cynical voice of a police desk sergeant. "What's your problem now, Abbey?"

"Reporting a smoke, sir."

"Yeah? And where do you think this one is, Abbey?"

"Well sir, I've got a reading of zero-four-two degrees and thirty—oooh, watch those fingernails!—thirty minutes. Near Fredonia."

"Yeah . . ." A long pause. Then the weary voice. "I hate to tell you this, Abbey, but that's the same fire you reported last week.

Like I told you then, that's the Fredonia sawmill and it's been smoking away in that same spot for fifty years. Ten four?"

"Yes sir, ten four. Oh Christ . . . oh *yes . . .!*"

"No swearing on the airwaves. These here transmissions are monitored by the Federal Communications Commission."

One cold rainy afternoon Bonnie and I were down in the cabin on the bed, a fire crackling in the stove, when our experiments were interrupted by a banging on the door. Bonnie ducked beneath the covers, I yanked on my pants and cracked the door open. Two Park Service fire fighters stood there grinning at me through the drizzle, their truck snuggled against the plump round rear of Bonnie's little car. "Hey Ed," says one, "we got a report of a hot fire in this area."

"Get out of here." I slammed and barred the door.

But I don't want to give the impression that a fire lookout's life is all work. There was time for play. One night a week we'd drive to the village on the Canyon rim and visit the bar. My Hopi friend would be there, old Sam Banyaca the shaman, and the veteran mule wrangler known only as Walapai, a leathery runt of an Indian cowboy who always squatted on top of his barstool, having never learned to sit anything but a horse. Behind the bar was Robert the intellectual bartender, smug smirk on his fat face, about to recite a new limerick. He claimed to be the only living composer of original limericks in America. I still remember two of them. I wish I could forget.

> A modest young fellow named Morgan
> Had an awesome sexual organ;
> It resembled a log
> Dredged up from a bog,
> With a head on it fierce as a Gorgon.

And the other:

> An old Mormon bishop named Bundy
> Used to wed a new wife every Sunday;
> But his multiple matehood
> Was ruined by statehood—
> *Sic transit gloria* Monday.

"Mundi!"

"Monday!"

"It's Tuesday, f'crush sake," says old Walapai, turning his bleary eyes toward us and swaying on his stool. "You honkies drunk already?" He crashed to the floor.

I spent four sweet summers on that sublime North Rim, not always alone in my tower. During the third summer a thing happened which caused me the deepest grief of my life. So far. The pain of my loss seemed unendurable. I called an old friend, Ann Woodin of Tucson, for comfort. She came to my part of the forest bearing apples, a flagon, black caviar and a magnum of Mumm's. We sat on a log under the trees at evening, by a fire, and listened to the birds, and talked, and ate the caviar and drank the champagne and talked some more. She helped me very much. A lady with class, that Ann. A lady *of* class. The same who once rescued me, at two in the morning, from the Phoenix City Jail down in Goldwater country, where the police had locked me up for what they called "negligent driving." Joseph Wood Krutch, another Tucsonan, dedicated one of his books to Ann Woodin. She is, he wrote, "an ever-present help in time of trouble."

Four summers. Sweet and bitter, bittersweet hilarious seasons in the forest of ponderosa and spruce and fir and trembling aspen trees. The clang of horseshoes in the twilight. The smell of woodsmoke from the cabin. Deep in the darkling pines the flutesong of a hermit thrush. Lightning, distant thunder, and clouds that towered into evening. Rain on the roof in the night.

One day somebody in Park headquarters, down on the South Rim of the Canyon, the bad rim, said to somebody else, "Do we really need a fire lookout on North Rim?"

And the other man said, "I didn't know we had one."

The lookout was closed at the end of my fourth season and has never been used since. My father had long before returned to his own woods in Pennsylvania where he still lives and works. He is now seventy-eight. And Ranger Hendrickson—sweet witty lovely daring Bonnie—she had gone back to California where, I've heard, she married well, to a man with a steady job, property, money, prospects, a head on his shoulders. Not a fire lookout. Not by a long shot.

19. THE SORROWS OF TRAVEL

When I think of travel, I think of certain women I have known. So many of my own journeys have been made in pursuit of love. In pursuit of pain. And in flight from both.

Landscape and women. Whenever I discover a natural scene that pleases me, that I find beautiful, my first thought is: What a place to bring a girl! And our world is so rich in both—beautiful places, lovely women. We should all be as happy as birds. How clever of the inventor of this scheme to create from such abundant, glorious materials so tangled a web of confusion and misery. The medieval Schoolmen in proving God's existence overlooked this potent variation on the argument from design: The world's disorder, cruelty, and desperation could not possibly have resulted from chance alone.

Scene One: On the northbound bus from Fort McClellan, Alabama. During the war. My first furlough after completing basic training. In the fertile darkness of the crowded bus I find myself seated beside a young woman, a stranger, a southerner. I am eighteen, a virgin, shy as a doe; she is perhaps five years older, married, lonely. Her husband, she tells me, is in Italy, has survived Sicily, the disastrous landing at Anzio, the battle of Monte Cassino. She prays for his safety and longs for his return. As she tells me about him, her hand comes to rest on mine; she takes my hand and places it on her silken knee. She asks me to tell her about myself.

What have I to tell her? My life is nothing. All I know is my own homesickness. I am sick for home. I think of the hills of Appalachia—the red-dog dirt road that winds beside the crooked creek, under the massed transpiring greenness of the trees, toward a gray farmhouse where a kerosene lamp glows behind the curtains of the windows that face the road. But I cannot tell her what that scene means to me. She leans close and kisses me and lifts that inert, ignorant hand of mine to her breasts. Kiss me back, she whispers. Touch me. Touch me! And we fumble at each other's bodies in the constrained plush gloom of the rumbling bus, make love with our hands, in a fashion, through the awkward obstacles of buttons, snaps, garters (this was long ago).

The bus enters the outskirts of a city. Clasping my left hand between her thighs, trapping it where she wants it, she whispers in my ear: "Stay with me tonight. I have a place here." And when I make no reply, she repeats: "Please. Stay with me. Just tonight."

That was some time ago. Writing these funny sentences, I pause now and then to perform other duties. I get up from this small table, step out the door, and pace the catwalk that forms a complete balcony around the four glass walls of my one-room house. My house stands fifty feet above the ground on a skeletal tower of steel, and it belongs to the United States Forest Service. Unlike most writers, I work for my living. I watch for forest fires, and when I see one I do something about it.

This tower is 8,000 feet above sea level, and the view is good. When the air is clear, I can see the San Francisco Peaks near Flagstaff and the desert ranges south to the border of Mexico. There are many black bear in the wilderness that surrounds me; also whitetail deer, coyotes, a few mountain lions, vultures, hawks, falcons, and odd creatures like the javelina and black rattlesnakes with yellow lateral bands. Right now the blackberries are ripe; the clownish bears shamble through the forest with stains of red juice streaking their muzzles, paws, summer fur. A bear does not pick berries with a little tin pail; instead, the bear grasps an entire blackberry branch between its paws, bends it down and into the mouth, and strips it clean of berries, thorns, leaves, bugs, spiders, everything. The bear rolls this mix around for a while in its mouth, looking thoughtful, like a wine lover sampling a new wine, makes distinctions, spits out the leaves and thorns, and grabs another branch.

And the woman on the bus? I did a cruel thing. As cruel as it was stupid. I declined the lady's invitation. I let her leave that bus, in that midnight southern city, without me. I rode on into the cold North alone, simple and single-minded, bound for home. For that sin I shall pay, all my life, in the cheap coin of regret. It has not escaped my reflections on the incident that the young woman may have been a prostitute, or part-time prostitute, conning a country boy—an easy trick. I don't think she was; I believed in her then and I believe in her now. What she wanted, I imagine, was to hold me while thinking of her husband. It makes no difference. My rejection of her remains, in my eyes, unforgivable.

At present I am alone here. In the evening I descend from my tower and walk through the forest. Nearby is an escarpment of sandstone, a kind of natural promontory projecting above the canyons, nearly flat but tilted slightly, like the deck of a listing ship. A few yellow pines have taken root in the fissures of the stone, and some stunted, twisted Arizona white oaks, and a few mescal or century plants—that odd member of the amaryllis family that resembles a rosette of bowie knives planted hilt-first in the ground. Like a girl, the mescal blossoms splendidly, but only once, and much more briefly, in its lifetime.

On the rim of the scarp sits a weathered figure of rock, semihuman in form; you might think some Druid priest had seated himself there, 5,000 years ago, resolving never to move again, and allowed himself to petrify, cell by cell, through the centuries. Each time I approach this sacred grove with its white rock and quiet, listening trees, I am reminded of the Mediterranean. I think of Delphi and half expect that stone figure to rise

at last and confront me, prepared—after appropriate sacrifice
—to answer the question I have been seeking, all my life, to
learn how to ask.

But the figure does not stir. Not yet. I gaze across its shoulders, through the trees, at the vast sea beyond. Not the blue sea
of the Mediterranean but the rust red sea, the lilac purple sea,
the wave-wrinkled but static sea of the desert. On that motionless immensity ride enchanted ships: Table Mountain, Four
Peaks, Haystack Butte, Aztec Peak, Battle Mountain, Helio-
graph Peak, the Superstition Mountains. And others, many others, floating on waves of haze, at distances we measure but do
not comprehend. Contemplating this picture (but picture of
what?), I feel again the vague but poignant urge to grasp it,
embrace it, *know* it, all at once and all in all; but the harder I
strive for such a consummation, the more elusive and mysterious that *it* becomes, slipping like a dream through my arms.
Can this desire be satisfied only in death? Something in our
human consciousness seems to make us forever spectators of
the world we live in. Maybe some of my crackpot, occultist
friends are right; maybe we really are aliens here on earth, our
spirits born on some other, simpler, more human planet. But
why then were we sent here? What is our mission, comrades,
and when do we get paid?

A writer's epitaph: He fell in love with the planet earth, but
the affair was never consummated.

Edinburgh. The Firth of Forth. The dank, dark, medieval
walls of the university, inside the old quad. In midwinter I
escape the miasmal shades of Hume, Reid, Boswell, Scott, Burns
by fleeing to the Arlberg, Saint Anton in the Tyrol, Austria. In
a company of British students—ruddy young folk, but very
proper—I take a room in a pension or hostel, here in this fairy-
tale village high in the magic mountains. I don't waste much
time in the pension, among those severe Scots and stern *Anglais;* the Austrians seem livelier and the Germans more romantic, in their usual sinister but comic way—stock villains
from a Nazi melodrama. One of them, a sturdy young fellow
named Kurt or Wolfgang or Helmut, I forget which, becomes
my daily skiing companion. We like each other; or at least we
interest each other. Like me, he is a university student, a would-

be intellectual, and very competitive. We ski all day; he is the better skier; we eat and play chess in the cafés in the evening —he always wins—and drink together and dance with the girls until closing time. We talk about the war, of course, and agree that it was a most regrettable affair; like me, he was too young to have taken any direct part in it. But the war is not over, never over, when two young males discover the same likely female.

Her name was Penelope Duval-Holmes; she came not from England, however, but from South Africa, a smart, witty, liberal South African of the Alan Paton variety (one could talk with her). She was traveling Europe alone and she was very beautiful. *Very* beautiful? Well, a bit short in the leg—her tragic flaw —but beautiful all the same. Long, soft, light brown hair; great violet eyes with coal black lashes; breasts like two fawn at play in a garden of roses; a superior assembly of delectable parts. Wolfgang and I spotted her our third day together and bore down like twin schussboomers grooved for collision.

She seemed to like us both. Too wise and too amused to accept one and cast off the other, Penelope kept the three of us playing together. We skied as a threesome, picnicked together high on the snowfields under the alpine crags, dined and talked and drank and danced together every evening. Wolfgang proved each time, in his droll Continental manner, that he could out-ski me, out-drink me, was the better dancer, knew more songs and sang better, knew more languages, had read more books, and knew more about music than I ever would. Defeated, all I could do was make surly jokes about Ludwig van B. and His Viennese Jug Band, Amadeus and the Wolfgang, Tony Bruckner and The Tyroleans.

Getting nowhere. Each night Penelope said goodnight to the two of us, but her eyes seemed always to linger last on my charming rival; I knew that I was losing and that one night soon she was going to invite Wolfgang—not me—to her hotel room. That room on the second floor, with balcony, above the frozen snowbanks of a narrow sidestreet. Yes, I knew well enough where her room was; I'd spent several chilly interludes between closing time at the bar and my cold bed at the pension standing in the street watching Penelope's light go on, the blinds come down, the light, after a time, go out again. My futile and hungry love.

A week passed in concealed but intense competition for the favor of a girl—an aristocrat—much too good for either of us. In another week I would have to return to Edinburgh. I made overtures to other women, even to one of those clean, bright, prim English girls in the tour group, but my heart was not with it. I thought of cutting my vacation short; back to the bloody books, the charcoal fire in my cold tiny digs on Prince's Street, bloodsausages for breakfast, scones and cakes at teatime.

One night I prepared to give up. Sitting at a little table in the bar of Penelope's hotel, sipping my fifth or sixth double schnapps, I watched Wolfgang and my sweetheart embraced in dance, some lush slow romantic Viennese number, the last dance—as the bandleader had announced—of the night. Wolfgang whispered in her ear; she was smiling. She nodded in assent to his obvious question. One possible gesture remained; a graceful surrender on my part. I slipped out before the dance was over, so drunk I could hardly see; or was I weeping? Or both?

Once in the street, however, I was overcome by the agony of jealousy. I could not suppress the self-torturing need to watch my defeat made plain before my eyes. I leaned on a corner wall below her room and waited and watched. I was freezing, no doubt, and drunk, but despair kept me warm.

Finally her light went on. I could see, through gauzy curtains, Penelope enter her room. My heart jumped. She was alone. She closed and locked her door, began to undress. Then remembered to lower the blinds. As she came to the French windows of her balcony, peering, it seemed to me, down into the street, I shrank back into the shadows. She lowered the blinds. A moment later the light went out.

I stared at the darkened room. The balcony. The high-piled bank of hardened snow, reaching to within two or three feet of the balcony's supporting members. Yes. Why not? Remember —Siegfried! I scrambled up the frozen snow, found a hold on the balcony supports, pulled myself up, got a leg over the railing, fell inside, scrabbled on my knees to the French windows, tried the handles—locked. "Penny," I groaned.

"Who is it?"

"It's me, me."

She opened the doors. "Edward, what are you *doing* out

there? *Idiot.* Get in here before you freeze." I staggered into the warm room, into her even warmer arms—she was wearing, I remember, some kind of slippery little nightie. She guided me to the billowy luxury of an Austrian feather bed, tucked me under the quilt, crawled in beside me. I reached for her—and passed out.

But all turned out well next morning. "My God, Penny," I said, "I've been wanting to do this—since the first moment I saw you. For a week!"

She replied, "Why didn't you ask?"

Later I said, "Did Wolfgang . . . did he ask?"

"Oh yes, the very first night. And every night since. He's been very persistent. Of course, he is a gentleman and so sweet about it, but—oh dear, he is so *very* persistent. So awfully—*tenacious.* Let's go to Vienna."

"And you turned him down?"

"Of course. Shall we go to Vienna?"

I could not refrain from probing further. Savoring my little victory. "But why?"

"Why go to Vienna?"

"Why did you turn him down?"

"I don't like Nazis."

"Nazi! Wolfgang? But he's a Christian Democrat—whatever that is. And a gentleman. You said so yourself."

"He would have been a Nazi."

I thought that over. A Nazi and a gentleman? Both? After a moment I said, "Guess I'm lucky."

"Yes," she said, "you are. But you deserve it."

"Maybe I'd rather be a goddamned gentleman."

She laughed. "Dear Edward, that you'll never be. And besides—we've seen so *many* of *those.*"

1400 hours (forest time) on the lookout tower. 2 P.M. I sit here chuffing on a cheap cigar, watching the cumulo-nimbi gather above. Rumbles of discontent—shattered molecules of air—sound from overhead. Penelope Duval-Holmes, where are you now? I was a happy man that week. We went to Vienna, where I fell asleep during a performance of the Saint Matthew Passion. We said goodby in Paris. I never saw her again. Oh lovely and patient Penelope, how are you now? Back in Johannesburg, no doubt. Married, I suppose, with two or three babies. What is your husband like? Does he keep a shotgun in the bedroom? What will become of your children when the Zulus and Bantus overrun your beloved country? *Whose* beloved country? Dear Penelope, how are you now?

A rattle of hail on the tin roof. A jagged bolt of lightning plunges into the forest below, where I have counted eleven different shades of green. A puff of pine dust and a twist of blue smoke rise in the air and drift away. I disconnect the short-wave radio. Incommunicado now. Through a mist of rain to the north, less than a mile away, I see pink lightning vibrate, an illuminated nerve, between cloud and mountain. Five seconds later comes the crash, the sound like toppling masonry. I shut the windows, close the door—lightning follows air currents.

The storm clouds hover close above me, dark as death ships. From the steel legs and struts of this tower rises a curious singing, the thin, high, metallic tremolo of billions of agitated electrons. I sit inside a little cabin mounted on the negative pole of a high-voltage open circuit; at any moment, unpredictable but certain, a gigantic spark—lightning—is going to leap the gap. As long as I stay inside, I'm safe; the tower is completely grounded, with a resistance, say the electrical engineers, of ten ohms. It doesn't sound sufficient, but it is.

This tower has been struck several times with me inside it, and so far as I can tell I'm no crazier now than before taking up this lonely trade. In any case, there is no escape; I can only wait while the screaming of electrons in distress builds gradually in intensity toward the unendurable climax. Another bolt strikes below, through the rain, a fireball dangling at its tip. My turn. Here. Now. The *crack!* of a whip above my head, the flash of blue light, a smell of ozone followed by waves of thunder reverberating outward—the noise suggests the sound of something rugged, immense, and rigid being ripped apart by hands of unimaginable force. A huge limb wrenched from a giant oak.

After the storm, in the twilight of a misty rain, work day over, I walk again through the forest. A pint of Foster's Aussie lager in my gut. A buzz in my brain. Out on the prow of my listing sandstone ship, beyond the sacred grove, the stone priest still sits in contemplation, rain dripping from his weathered head and eroded shoulders. No sign. I walk down the trail deep into the woods, under the ponderosa pine, the spruce, the white fir, the Douglas fir, the aspen, and smell the fragrance of wet weeds, pine needles, rotting logs, the soaked and respirating earth. Glowworms shine in the rich corruption. Like foxfire in Appalachia.

Other girls, other places. Sandy and Death Valley, our camp at Texas Springs—she betrayed me by running off with a cheap movie actor. Bonnie Claire and our idyll on the rim of the Grand Canyon—*she* betrayed me by running off with her husband. And Ingrid in Berlin. Rita and Provincetown. Judy in New York, her little room in the hospital—Mount Sinai!—and the two of us listening to Mozart on the radio while firecrackers sputtered like frying grease in the streets below; my God, it was the Fourth of July; and I betrayed her by letting her die. By letting it happen. By finding no way—no way—to stop the thing that was destroying her. I loved and still love all of them.

I stumble over a rock in the trail. Sun down and gone, not a star in the clouded sky. The woods are deep, and very dark, and not lovely. I stop and stare at the dim silhouettes of the trees against the fainter dark of the sky. Sound of crickets down below; it must be August one more time. An autumnal month here in the mountains. And I'm alone again. Once more I ask myself the simple, obvious question: Why not die? Why keep hanging around, stumbling over rocks, bending boor cans, hurting people with your stupidity, losing your children here and there? What are you waiting for, you drunken clown?

But I'm grinning in the dark, not about to give up yet. I find it comfortable here in the cool damp womb of the forest, alone in the velvet night. I think I could stand here all night long and if it doesn't rain too hard, be content. Even happy. Me and the crickets and the oafish bears (they'll never make it as gentle men), snuffling about through the brush, grubbing for something good to eat. At this moment I think: If he'd let me I'd get down on all-fours and shuffle along side by side with Cousin Bear, rooting for slugs, smearing my hairy face with crushed blackberries, tearing at roots.

Aliens on this planet? Us? Who said so? Not me. And if I did, that was yesterday. Tonight I know better. We are not foreigners; we were born and we belong here. We are not aliens, but rather like children, barely beginning here and now in the childhood of the race to discover the marvel, the magic, the mystery of this gracious planet that is our inheritance.

Fools talk of leaving the earth, launching themselves by space shuttle and revolving cannisters of aluminum into permanent orbit somewhere between here and the moon. God speed them. While others plan the transformation of the earth through technology into a global food factory, fusion-powered, computer-controlled, supporting a close-packed semihuman population of 8 billion—twice the number already stifling themselves in the mushroom cities of today. R. Buckminster Fuller thinks it can be done. Herman Kahn thinks it can be done. Their counterparts in Europe, Brazil, Russia, China, Japan, Uganda, everywhere, think it can be done. And if it *can* be done, therefore, by their logic it *must* be done. But Kahn and Fuller and their look-alikes are in for many a surprise before that Golden Age of Technocracy encloses us. (It never will.) As with all fools, their lives shall consist of a constant succession of surprises, mostly unpleasant, as surprises tend to be. The Devil take them.

The Devil *take* them!

Brimming with malice and glee, I trudge up the trail, up the ridge, back to the tower. Only one thing is lacking to complete my happiness. I want to wake at dawn with a woman in my arms. I want to share the day's beginning with her, while woodpeckers drum on hollow snags of yellow pine and the sun rises into the crimson clouds of morning. I want to share an orange, a pot of black cowboy coffee, the calm and commonsense of breakfast talk, the smiles, the touch of fingertips, the yearning of the flesh, the comradeship of man and woman, of one uncertain human for another.

No need for doubt. She will appear. She has always come before and she will come again. At least once more.

CODA:
CAPE SOLITUDE

There comes a day when a man must hide. Must slip away from the human world and its clutching, insane, insatiable demands.

For nearly a month I'd been in the air and on the road. Doing the college lecture bit from Pennsylvania to Wisconsin, from Arizona to Alaska to the Wabash. (Why do I do it? Not for the money—those insincere paper checks from boards of regents. For the ego massage, that's what for. To spread the message. To meet the audience face to face. To meet those lovely girls. "My name's Sharon," she says. Or Susan. Or Kathy. Or Pamela. Or Tammy. And, "Oh Mister Abbey, I've been wanting to meet you for years!" "That's funny," I reply, "I've been wanting to meet you too; how about a drink as soon as we can sneak away from this mob?" "Oh, I'd *love* to," she says, "and"—she tugs at the arm of a shy, pimply, long-haired, very tall and thin young lady standing a bit to her rear—"and this is my boy friend George." Jack. Henry. Willy. "He wants to meet you too.") And going to hearings, reading prepared statements before bored bureaucrats in business suits. Wearisome interviews. Writing letters to hostile congressmen, editors, tycoons. Trying to save the world, that's all. A piece of the West at least. Something. Useless stuff.

Tales of the Western lecture circuit. Marge Piercy, feminist novelist, doing her best for women's liberation in a sophomore seminar at the University of Colorado. "But *I like* being a girl," says one of those mountain coeds, wiggling on her seat. The decadent West. Amazing Grace Lichtenstein, Denver-based reporter for the *New York Times,* accused me—when I told her this story—of being thirty years behind the times. "Thirty years?" I said, insulted. "I'm a hundred years behind the times."

Weary, discouraged, still smelling of nervous sweat, I pointed the old Dodge carryall south by east, heading for a place I know. Call it—Cape Solitude. I like the name. A fictitious name, of course, but the place is real. Or a real name for an impossible place. A high, open, uncrowded point on the rim of the canyon, on the edge of the world, fifty miles by wagon trail from the nearest paved road, twenty miles from the last Navajo hogan, sixty from the nearest white man's house. I was going there alone—alone!—and I was going to stay there, hardly moving, until I felt ready to return to human society. Whether it took twenty-four hours or forty days. Or longer. I had plenty of dried beans and green chili and canned corn in the truck, and enough water for a while—if the rains failed and the potholes were dry.

We came down through the valley, me and the truck, across the river, up past the Echo Cliffs, down to the Little Colorado, west on the highway to the turnoff. Two hundred miles. I opened a wire gate in the fence, drove through, closed the gate, locking it shut with a Gordian knot of rusty barbed wire. This route is seldom used. Now it'll be used less. I took a broom and swept away my tire tracks, then drove north on the dirt road until I was beyond sight and sound of the highway, stopped, shut off the throbbing engine, sat up front on the hood with a bottle of wine and listened to the silence. Each time I come here, I wonder why I ever go back. Every time I go anywhere out in the desert or mountains, I wonder why I should return. Someday I won't.

Nerves, nerves. I held my right hand straight out, palm down. The hand trembled. I brought it back to the bottle where it closed at once—the sensitive plant—around the cool smooth glass. Hold on to something steady, solid, secure. You can count on us, say the Christian Brothers. We'll not fail you, old buddy, says Gallo's Hearty Burgundy. I'll stick by you to the end, says Almadén. No doubt. The day he stopped drinking was the day that Mulligan died.

The high plateau stands on my left, a forest of jackpine on the horizon. Ahead lies a rolling, sandy plain and a scatter of juniper and scrubby little piñon pine stretching toward infinity. On the east, below, the Painted Desert shimmers in the afternoon sun —lavender hills, burnt cliffs, rosy pinnacles of mud and clay.

> *Oh that the desert were my dwelling place,*
> *With one fair Spirit for my minister,*
> *That I might all forget the human race,*
> *And, hating no one, love but only her.*

I don't even want her right now. Right now I want no one, least of all myself. All my life a loner, an outsider, a barbarian from the steppes, the wolf on the snow-covered hill looking down at the lights of the village, I think I've never been accepted by my fellow men, fellow women, never been a bona fide member of the club. And looking back at the human race, feeling I never belonged, my first thought, right now, is—thank God. Or Whatever.

The wine sings in my blood. Blood and wine, wine and bread, bread and love and music. The full circle. Back to the flesh. Getting nowhere. Going home. The sky hangs over me, that delirious dome of burning blue, where white, woolly, quiet clouds drift slowly eastward like a herd of grazing sheep. Who or what is the herdsman of that flock? The sun? But the sun is going the other way.

I discover, to my surprise, that the bottle is nearly empty. I finish it off, take a hearty burgundy piss on the sand, crank up the engine, and drive on. The truck bumps over the stones, thrashes in low through a stretch of soft sand, brushes over the sage and prickly pear and spiny yucca growing in the high center of the road. I shift down into compound low, climbing the sandstone ledges up and around a hill. The rear wheels spin, I have to stop and pile rocks in the back to gain sufficient traction. We go on, passing an empty hogan of cedar logs chinked with mud. The blank, black, open doorway, facing the east as a proper hogan doorway should, has a long-abandoned look.

I stop to contemplate. The wooden bed of a buckboard wagon, *sans* wheels, rests half-buried in the sand; the tongue of the wagon rests in the crotch of a juniper. No sign of recent occupancy. The few tin cans strewn about are well rusted, the old tokay bottles blue from sunlight. No plastic, paper, or aluminum anywhere in sight. Somebody died here long ago, but the ghost still lingers; that is why, according to Navajo theology, the place cannot be used. I'm not afraid of ghosts, being chiefly a ghost myself, and for a moment I'm tempted to pause here, stay a few days before going on to the cape. I decide against it; the attraction of the abyss is too strong.

We drive on.

The going is good, gets better all the time, rougher and rockier, more brush, more sand, more cactus. The parallel tracks meander like snakes toward the unimaginable goal. I follow with caution, nursing the motor to keep it cool, babying the old, loose transmission (this truck was born in 1962), watching for oil-pan-ripping stones in the high center.

One mile short of my destination I turn off the trail and hide the truck under, or rather within, the sheltering branches of the biggest juniper nearby. It is possible to drive a motor vehicle to the very rim of Cape Solitude, but that seems disrespectful. And unnecessary. I load my backpack and walk the final distance.

The land tilts upward, stony and harsh. The long shadows of the yucca, the cliff rose, the squawbush, the scrubby juniper stretch across basins of sand, the humps and hollows of monolithic sandstone—golden in the evening sun. I sense an emptiness ahead.

I come to the edge. The verge of the abyss. Three thousand feet below and little more than a mile away, as a hang glider might descend, is the river. The Grand River, as it once was known. Not far, but inaccessible from here. On my right is the dark, narrow, snaky gorge of the Little Colorado, the bottom of it out of sight, concealed in depth and shadow.

On this point I halt. One step further would take me into another world, the next world, the ultimate world. The longest journey begins with a single step. But I pause, hesitate, defer that step, as always. Not out of fear—I'm afraid of dying but not of death—but again, from respect. Respect for my obligations to others, respect for the work I still hope to do, respect for myself. The despair that haunts the background of our lives, sometimes obtruding itself into consciousness, can still be modulated, as I know from experience, into a comfortable melancholia and from there to defiance, delight, a roaring affirmation of self-existence. Even, at times, into a quiet and blessedly self-forgetful peace, a modest joy.

We are more than 6,000 feet above sea level, but the warm air rising from the canyon, flowing over the rimrock, supports desert plants like cactus and cliff rose that flourish here a thousand feet above their usual habitat. Standing in the balmy, blessed flow, I drop the pack, shed my clothes, even hat and boots, kneel down naked on the stone and build a little fire of juniper twigs. I want incense and ceremony and there is no incense finer, no ceremony more fitting—for my soul and this place—than the cedarlike aroma and smokeless flame of burning juniper.

I add larger sticks to the fire, take my flute from the pack, stand, and play a little desert music. Improvised music: a song for any coyotes that may be listening, a song for the river and the great canyon, a song for the sky, a song for the setting sun. Doing only what is proper and necessary. I stop; we listen to the echoes floating back. I write "we" because, in the company of other nearby living things—lizards, ravens, snakes, bushes, grass, weeds—I do not feel myself to be alone.

The desert world accepts my homage with its customary silence. The grand indifference. As any man of sense would want it. If a voice from the clouds suddenly addressed me, speaking my name in trombone tones, or some angel in an aura of blue flame came floating toward me along the canyon rim, I think I would be more embarrassed than frightened—embarrassed by the vulgarity of such display. That is what depresses in the mysticism of Carlos Castaneda and his like: their poverty of imagination. As any honest magician knows, true magic inheres in the ordinary, the commonplace, the everyday, the mystery of the obvious. Only petty minds and trivial souls yearn for supernatural events, incapable of perceiving that everything— everything!—within and around them is pure miracle.

Or so I say. So I have always thought. But I am willing to see my whole world splintered by a sword of light, if such can happen. What choice would I have? Let it come down. Let God speak, here and now, plain and honest and once and for all, or forever hold His peace. Enough of this muttering in the distance, that awkward blundering behind the scenes. Come on out, whatever You are, show me Your face, kiss me, embrace me, enslave me in bliss. Or else shut up.

The silent desert makes no reply. I put the flute aside and urinate on Mother Earth, respectfully, as always, taking care to avoid the little living things, the sand verbena, the phacelia, the dry, tawny bunches of grass. Letting the fire die to a bed of coals, I sit on the edge of the rock, my feet dangling over a 1,500-foot drop-off, and try not to think about what I know I am going to think about.

(I enjoy the feel of the stone on my bare skin; I find pleasure in the rock's abrasiveness, its staunch solidity, its purchase on the cliff's rim—which might, who knows, give way at any moment.)

I came here to forget some things, at least for a while, but in order to forget I must first remember what I wish to forget, the confused scene presented by my country, the only one I've got, in this summer of the year. Which year? It makes little difference.

My country? *Our* country? The U.S. of A.? Whose country, indeed? Everywhere I went in my little tour of the American campus I found majority support for the idea that we must bring the growth machine to a halt; that we must change our collective way of life; that we must conserve, not waste, energy and other resources; save, not destroy, the family farm, the small enterprise and independent business—that we must preserve, not obliterate, what still remains of the American wilderness, the American hope, the American adventure.

Overwhelming support—for if anyone objected to the thesis I was promoting in my slapstick, slapdash, sex-crazed manner, they failed to speak up. Indeed, the only objections I had to deal with were accusations that I myself was exploiting the land, the wild, the agrarian life by writing about it. A charge to which I pled guilty; for it's true, I've made a stack of easy money praising country life and attacking the greedheads (as Hunter

Thompson calls them) who own and operate America. Nothing easier.

My defense, as I pointed out, consists solely in this, that I give a tenth of my income (as a good Mormon should) to the conservation cause. While the other ninety percent goes to support my family, myself, and the useless federal government.

Some of us are beginning to catch on to something. Government does not exist to ease, facilitate, moderate, and preside over necessary social change. On the contrary, the purpose of government is to prevent change. At all costs. By any means. That is why government reserves to itself the monopoly of coercion, of organized, large-scale violence.

Take this job and shove it.

Too much, too much. Too much is enough. I get up from the cold rimrock, pull on my pants, a shirt, a vest. Sun long down and the air is chilling fast. Let somebody else save the world for a while; I'm tired of even thinking about it. Not that I seriously imagine myself a thinker. I am a feeler, not a thinker, and proud of it. An extremist? Yes. And a revolutionist? Naturally. Do I advocate another revolution? What do you mean, *another?* We have yet to see the first. But it's coming.

Take a look in your local disco this coming Saturday night. Observe that jampacked multitude of solitary dancers, the critical mass, the unquiet desperation. Hear the urgency, feel the murderous beat, of that deafening, tremendous, overpowering sound. (Not music—*sound.*) Some day that energy is going to discover its secret meaning, find the hidden door, burst out into the night, go blazing up the avenue toward those dark towers of glass and aluminum that dominate our lives—and shatter them to bits.

Take this job . . . and shove it!

There is a little town in Arizona called Why. (Why is a good name for any town.) But in the America of my dreams there is a city called Why Not.

I restoke the fire, warm hands and kneecaps, scratch my itchy shanks, and think of supper. But we're fasting tonight. I open another bottle from my Christian Brothers. Vintage '77, California Red. Seventy-seven—double good luck. Here's to you, my brothers, my sisters. To us, the green elves. We are everywhere. Nothing is more subversive than grass. Joy, shipmates, joy.

But as I was saying, let others save the world for the time being. Tonight and tomorrow and for the next few days I am going to walk the rim of Cape Solitude, along the palisades of the desert, and save myself. Without half trying.

When the dawn comes I'll crawl from my sack, naked as the snake in my hand, face the east, kneel on the bare rock, and make an offering for Mother. Then stand and face my god, that savage and merciless deity, brazen with fire, as he rises from beyond Shinumo Altar, the Painted Desert, the Echo Cliffs. Shall I pray for justice? Mercy? Eternal life? I think not. For what then? For nothing. There is nothing to pray for. Let us pray.

> Black sun
> Heart's sun
> Black raging sun of my heart
> Burn me pure as the flame
> Burn me and take me
> And let me sleep
> Down by a river I know
> In the land of stone and sky
> Until we wake again
> In a new and bolder dawn.